Gary Mic[...]

Time

As told by Rob Flemming and Anne Barclay

To my parents, Joy, Alison and Helena: without your support it would never have been. Thank you all x

Table of Contents

Chapter 1 – Araminta

Morgan was nowhere to be found, the radio receiver as silent and lifeless as the brick it resembled. Cold rain seeped from a slate grey sky that made me cold, wet and disconsolate. Morgan had simply disappeared over the treetops in hot pursuit of a parliament of crows without a backward glance.

"Blasted bird, where the hell are you? And you're not being any bloody use either," I snarled at the yagi.

Nor did she put in an appearance at any time during the following day. However, I simply thought of the magical third day, so called in falconry speak because one invariably finds errant falcons on the third day. So I was up with the lark and full of beans.

'Yeah, she'll turn up today,' I thought positively.

Once again, the weather was foul. I searched all day, staring through a veil of constant heavy drizzle that turned everything grey, and buffeted by intermittent but icy winds. Not a sign of Morgan. By the time that dusk was falling I was sodden, frozen and a bit down in the mouth, to say it politely. I returned home totally exhausted.

"What did I get involved in this game for?" I muttered, trying desperately to get some warmth back in my feet. "It's a mug's game." Then the phone rang.

"Hallo," I snarled as I picked it up.

" Good evening, I understand that you've lost a falcon. Correct?"

"Yep," I grumped, "who am I talking to?"

"My name is Araminta."

Nobody has a name like Araminta, surely! Rather well spoken, the lady had a voice that was unique in a way that is almost impossible to describe. Soft but forceful, she talked as though she was playing a flute across its whole tonal range.

"I'm a medium and not far away. I will find your falcon and reunite you with her once again."

And I'll be flying pigs next year! Massaging my temples with my free hand, I closed my eyes. I was cold, wet, hungry, fed up and I was talking to a fruitcake who was

1

probably trying to tell me that we'd find Morgan by travelling across some astral plane. I felt like slamming the phone down.

"My dear, birds of prey are my spiritual guides and they will lead me to your falcon. If you would like to meet me in the morning, together we will go to find your bird."

I sighed. What had I got to lose?

"Thank you very much. I'll call you in the morning. Can you give me the number? Oh, and your address please."

After taking down the details, I put the phone down thinking: 'What a load of bullshit'.

One never sleeps well when you've lost a bird because you know she's out there and it's horrible. I'm sure I spent half the night staring into the darkness thinking and the other half, lost in those horrible dreams where things just get worse and worse.

Dismissing any thought of Araminta, I continued the search at first light but to no avail. Desperate and fatigued, I finally capitulated and rang.

"Could you come round and pick me up, please. I don't have a car, I'm afraid. Then we will go to find your beautiful falcon."

On my arrival, the door opened to reveal a most extraordinary looking woman. An almost elfin face with dark flinty eyes looked out from under a bird's nest of black hair. And she was tiny. She couldn't have been taller than four feet but was plumply rounded.

"There you are, dear boy. Let's go and find that falcon of yours. Shall we?"

This time her twittering voice reminded me of one of my heroes, the late Patrick Moore. The female version. Pulling her somewhat incongruous duffle coat around an array of colourful flowing clothes, she slipped past me and into the car.

'What in the name of God am I doing?' I thought.

"Right. Just hang on for a tick, will you?"

Pausing for a moment, she inhaled deeply and closed her eyes. For a couple of minutes she barely breathed at all and seemed to go into a meditative trance-like state. Then the eyes snapped open and she exhaled loudly.

"Right. You need to drive out along Greet Road."

By this time the rain was torrential and the windscreen wipers were on overdrive. The visibility was appalling and Greet Road was awash. Forced to drive at a snail's pace, I hunched over the steering wheel, cursing myself, Morgan, Araminta and the Gods for letting this all happen.

"Stop!"

The barked command frightened the life out of me.

"Jesus!"

I slammed on the brakes.

"Not quite the deity I was thinking of," she said wryly. "Those woods up there, on the hill, do you see them? That's where she is."

"Right."

A little further along the road, we came to a muddy lane bearing off to the left that clearly led towards the woods. Brown water streamed past us as the car lurched from slick boulder to bone-crunching pothole. After slowly climbing for what seemed like hours, I stopped the car as close to the woods as I thought we could get.

"Your falcon's here."

"Where?"

"In those woods."

It defied my knowledge, experience, sense and logic.

'Falcons do not inhabit woods,' my brain screamed. 'Falcons are not woodland birds. They don't live in woods, fly in woods or bloody hunt in woods! If Morgan was a sparrowhawk, a goshawk or even an owl – then yes, she could be here. But she's a flaming falcon!'

"Whereabouts?" I asked with forced calm.

"Right in the centre."

'No, no, no! Please no,' I silently screamed.

"Go out and do whatever you have to do and she'll come to you."

I trudged grindingly through the lashing rain and mud, stopping at various points to swing my wretchedly sodden lure. My calls were muffled by the rain hammering through the branches or torn away by jagged winds. By the time I returned to the car some minutes later, I was drenched and shivering.

"No luck then?"

"No, no luck."

"Well she is in those woods, I can assure you. I know. She's talking to me and I can hear her."

I shook my head in despair.

"Look, I've really got to forge on and see if I find other avenues to explore."

"Please, my darling, please try once more. Go a bit further into the woods. She's there, waiting."

"OK, one more time. But only one more."

Once more into the breach. I dragged myself through the trees, several hundred yards further than before, until I found a small glade. Blinking the water from my eyes, I swung the soggy mess that used to be a lure with little hope.

"Bugger me!"

Suddenly I heard the jangle of bells and Morgan came swooping down through the branches. I could not believe my eyes. I could not bloody believe it! Grabbing the falcon, I quickly hooded her and yomped my way back to the car, shaking my head with amazement. I shoved her on the cadge at the back, climbed into the driver's seat and stared at Araminta. She just stared back at me without saying a word.

"How on earth did you know?"

"I told you, birds of prey are my spirit guides and they talk to me. Your falcon talked to me. She told me she was waiting for you and where she was. And then I told you."

The elation of having Morgan back banished freezing cold, the ghastly feel of waterlogged clothes and pangs of hunger. My stress and concern had evaporated, transporting me to that wonderful Cloud Nine! Driving back to Winchcombe was wonderful. Marquis House, Number Two, North Street, Winchcombe, home to a most amazing clairvoyant. I managed to pull up a few yards from her door.

"How on earth can I repay you?"

"Well, you can do two things. The first thing, my dear, is to come for a reading. I charge five pounds."

'That will be the best fiver I'll ever spend,' I thought fervently.

"The second thing is," she continued, "would be to notify the newspapers. I think that they might be interested in the story. Don't you think so?"

"I don't know, maybe. But I'll do that for you and come round for a reading."

And I did. A week or so later I returned to Marquis House for my reading and happily paid the modest sum of a fiver. It was quite poignant at the time and there were things that she said would happen that did happen. There's more to heaven and earth than we know. The world may be full of charlatans but she can't be one of them.

To this day I have no idea how she did it but whatever the truth of the matter, she came up with goods and led me to Morgan. I had failed, even with telemetry I'd failed. (Ironically, I discovered later that the receiver had malfunctioned, probably because it had become waterlogged.) Without technology, knowledge or experience she'd found my bird. Did she hear Morgan calling her through the wind and the rain? I will leave you to decide.

'Medium finds lost Sudeley falcon in woods.' It made quite a nice little piece in the Gloucestershire Echo. I hope that it brought her some business of the psychic kind and perhaps earned her a few more fivers. And I think that she's still there, in Marquis House. Who knows whether she could delve into the past or have really foreseen what the future might hold.

Chapter 2 – Graveyard beginnings

It all started with slowworms in a graveyard. I used to keep the legless lizards in my school desk. No books, just slowworms; for which I got into terrible trouble, but that's another tale. But what else was a boy to do, growing up by the River Severn in rural Worcestershire? In those halcyon days before Game Boys and PS2s fried the brain, we made our own entertainment and I spent much of my time in the countryside. The river was there to be languidly fished, there were waifs and strays to bring home, orphan tawny owls to rescue and I even had a pet hare. And there were slowworms.

One lazy summer's evening, as the dappled sunlight warmed the churchyard, I was hunting for slowworms among the old gravestones. I scanned the golden pools of light for those that might be basking and the shadows that could hide the more timid. Apart from the murmuring breeze and the trill of birdsong, it was all very peaceful. Until that peace was unceremoniously shattered by a terrible racket coming from the church tower.

Looking up for the source of the noise, I was just in time to spot a pair of falcons landing simultaneously on a ledge. Clearly they had nested up there and had brought back food for their chicks. All thoughts of slowworms disappeared as I watched the little heads stretch upwards for their meal. Enthralled, I propped myself up against a gravestone, watching the falcons to the sound of the shrill kee-kee-kee calls. Every evening, for the next few weeks, I gazed in rapt attention at the family in the tower. Every day there was something new, something special to see. I watched the chicks grow and mature, saw them flex their wings in anticipation of flight. But eventually, the youngsters fledged the nest and my heart sank with disappointment as I mourned their absence.

Whether it was luck, coincidence or simply fate, only three or four weeks later I was sitting in front of the TV at home, absorbed in my favourite programme – Animal Magic. And there was Johnny Morris in his favourite zookeeper's uniform, with Phillip Glasier standing calmly at his side with a falcon on his fist.

" … so I opened the Falconry Centre in 1967 with just 12 birds, with the idea of running falconry courses for beginners. Didn't really expect that there would be too many but here we are and we're still going. I've always believed that it's easier to be taught falconry by someone who knows what they're doing rather than try to learn from books."

"You learned falconry from an expert, Captain Charles Knight?"

"Absolutely. My uncle was a very experienced and successful falconer, and I was very lucky to have him teach me. Anyway, let's see the lady fly," said Glasier as he turned on his heel and strode down the path.

Riveted, I stared at the screen as Glasier gently nudged the bird into the air. The camera erratically tracked her as she climbed effortlessly upwards and away. She banked hard, levelled out and flew over their heads, circling and waiting. Back to ground level as Glasier threw the lure out onto the ground to one side. Without hesitation, she stooped, speeding downwards towards the lure. Which was then whisked away from her grasp and she flew through, onwards and upwards for another attempt.

"Wow! This is amazing," I said out loud.

Again and again Glasier swept the lure away until finally, he threw it high above his head allowing the falcon to catch it mid-air. It was truly mesmerising.

As the credits finally rolled up the screen, I thought: 'I've got to go there'.

Grabbing pencil and paper, I wrote – Falconry Centre, Nueent - (I never was much good at spelling!). And off I rushed off to find my parents.

"Mum, Dad, can we go to the Falconry Centre at Nue-ent? Puleese! I just saw it on Animal Magic and it was fantastic. Can we go?"

They smiled.

"Sure."

This was the late Sixties and in those days they used to dust off the car on a Sunday and go for an afternoon drive.

Newent was as good a place to go as anywhere else and 'the boy seemed keen'.

Not everyone can pinpoint the moment that they fall in love but I can: one glorious July afternoon in Gloucestershire. A golden sun shone in an azure sky as I walked into that Falconry Centre and I was transported to heaven. I gazed adoringly at the hawks on their bows and the falcons on blocks. For the first time in my life, I saw a live demonstration of falconry, watched a falcon fly and return to the fist. And I knew, with absolute certainty, knew that this was going to be something that would stay with me for the rest of my life.

"Mum, Dad? Can we go to the Falconry Centre? Can we? Puleese!"

That was the following Sunday and the request became a mantra that was repeated on many subsequent Sundays. God bless them, they would always agree, to the point that actual visits became boring for them.

"Would you mind terribly if we dropped Gary off and you keep an eye on him for us?" my father asked. "We'll pick him up in a couple of hours, if that's all right? … It is? Wonderful! Thank you so much. Back in two hours then."

And that's what happened. They would drive me to the Falconry Centre and leave me in Phillip Glasier's tender care. At the end of the day, it was pretty obvious that I was fairly keen. As a little boy, I did have a lot of friends but essentially I was a loner. Mum and Dad were always trying to get me to join the Cubs, then the Scouts or anything similar that occurred to them but I never showed the slightest iota of interest - until then.

"Can I go on one of the courses at the Falconry Centre - puleese Mum, Dad?"

They knew it was genuine. And agreed. I had the most wonderful parents although they were chalk and cheese in many ways. My mother was loving and caring but not clever academically while my father was, and of a slightly sterner mould. But I was never frightened of my parents in the way that I was of Phillip Glasier. He had something of a military air about him, a reflection of Captain Knight or a Regimental Sergeant Major; slightly gruff, commanding and, seemingly, unrelenting. In other words, he was so alien that he scared the crap out of me from the outset.

Nevertheless, I attended the two week course with Glasier and he taught me the essentials and basic husbandry. Most of the people on the course seemed so big and grown up; there no kids and aged 13, I was by far and away the youngest. At the beginning, I trooped along with my notebook to take, well notes, as instructed, feeling more than a little trepidation. For someone who didn't mix that much, I was out of my comfort zone but I just knew that I had to do this course.

All seemed to go well until one afternoon, around the halfway mark. We had been given kestrels to handle; they had to be weighed each day, fed and the other things that went with the programme. On this particular afternoon we were to attempt to 'train' our birds, even though they had probably been trained a million times before on previous courses. (Not that the thought would have entered the head of a young boy.) And we would have an audience. Naturally people were constantly coming to the Falconry Centre to watch a flying display and the instructors had decided to put the beginners on show.

A young gentleman called Martin Jones, who had been instrumental in setting up the Falconry Centre, was usually the instructor in the afternoons and was co-ordinating the order of the display. My cup positively overflowed with joy to have kestrel on my gloved hand as I stood waiting for my turn to fly. A mix of excitement and nervousness bubbled silently in my head as I watched a fellow trainee walk back towards our group. Relief and delight had put a grin on his face that stretched from ear to ear.

"Go on Gary, your turn," said Martin quietly.

Nodding once, I walked out across the flying ground, eased the kestrel onto a post and then retreated some eight feet, the thin line of the creance unspooling in my wake. Taking a morsel of food from my hawking bag, I put it between my gloved thumb and forefinger, raised my arm and called the kestrel in for her reward. And the world exploded with harsh noise.

"Hee-yaw, hee-yaw, hee-yaw …"

I hadn't noticed the nearby donkey beforehand but now he was suddenly a highly visible bad dream. And it was going terribly wrong.

"Hee-yaw, hee-yaw …"

While the donkey brayed and kicked out like a demented banshee, the kestrel launched herself into the air and flew away from the ghastly noise. And in the wrong direction. Despite being on a creance (my fingers were only little) the force of her flight was enough to pull the line from my hand. She flew off into the middle distance dragging the creance behind her. Frozen, immobile with horror, I stared after her as the audience's laughter rippled around me, replacing the braying of the now silent donkey. That broke the ice and I ran in the direction she'd flown.

"Gary! Don't run after the bloody bird!"

I stopped and looked back.

"If you run, you'll just scare her," Martin said as he caught up with me.

We walked slowly down through the meadow and spotted the kestrel in a tree, the creance looped tightly around several branches. Telling me to wait, Martin walked to the base of the tree and wove his magic; I have no idea as to how he did it but somehow he managed to make all the frightening tangles disappear.

"Go back a bit and then call her down."

Somewhat nervously I followed Martin's instructions and, somewhat miraculously, the kestrel followed mine. As soon as I called, she dropped from her perch, the creance snaking liquidly through the branches behind her, to land lightly on my outstretched gloved hand. After the fleeting surge of relief, I didn't know whether to applaud or dig a hole in the ground and bury myself. As neither seemed quite appropriate or practical, I simply cursed myself and the donkey for what I saw as a catastrophic mess.

At the end of every afternoon we would all troop in to the wonderful dining room in the big house for a 'how we had all done on the day' discussion, chaired by Glasier. As I trailed back behind Martin, my mind was tumbling down a path to hell. I was dreading facing the Sergeant Major, the inevitable tongue-lashing and the shame of failure.

10

Bumbling through what little remained of the afternoon, I walked disconsolately into the dining room after my fellows and took my place at the long table. Glasier was sitting in his normal place at the head, gimlet eyes taking in the assembled company through black-rimmed glasses as he stroked his small goatee beard.

"Good show, but ..."

I barely listened to the analysis of the day and the varied comments as I sat there feeling ashamed. Petal, the inappropriately named Great Dane, shook her large head in despair before sinking to the floor. Stags' heads glared down from the walls; I felt their disapproval and condemnation.

"Useless. Idiot. Failure," they muttered.

Words cluttered the air.

"You completely screwed up today didn't you? Committed the cardinal sin. Not only did the kestrel fly off, but you let it fly off with the bloody creance, ending up with the poor bird tangled up in a tree. And in front of the crowd!"

Petrified, I was trembling with fear as I awaited my fate. Glasier left me to the very last. Dismissing the rest, he called me to his side and looked down at me for a moment without saying a word.

"We all make mistakes," he said softly. "Don't let it stop you. Carry on, well done."

If at that moment he'd come down on me, that might have been the end of the story. Because I might have just shrugged, walked away demoralised and left my shattered dreams on the floor. But he was brilliant and I felt reprieved from my terrible sins. I was very fortunate because he was an excellent falconer, one of Europe's greatest and he gave me that new beginning.

Having successfully completed the course with no further mishaps, the first and most important question in my mind was: where and how do I get a bird? That was the thing. It was a huge problem as there was little or no captive breeding. I'd done the course, got the pass slip of paper in my hand but where did I go from there? Am I coming to a dead end? I asked myself. You could only get a hawk or a falcon by getting a licence from the Home Office to take one from the wild or possibly importing a bird. In the late 60s and early 70s you could count the number of British falconers on three hands and I had very few contacts. I applied to the Home Office for a licence to take a kestrel from the wild. When the rejection arrived, I was heartbroken: I was too young. My father phoned Glasier.

"You know Gary applied to the Home Office for a licence. Well he's been refused because of his age, so we wondered whether you might be in a position to sell one of the Centre's kestrels?"

"I'm afraid that's not possible. Our breeding programme is in its infancy and we really don't deal with the sale of birds. It's not …"

"So where does Gary go from here?" my father interjected.

"As I was about to say, I think that I might know someone who might be able to sell your son a kestrel. Chap named Henry Santa. Lives in Leicestershire. Henry's actually pioneering breeding kestrels in captivity. Not sure what the situation is at the moment, I haven't been in touch for a while, but it's definitely worth a call. Have you got a pen and paper there?"

After giving my father the telephone number he added: "Give him a ring, tell him I gave you his number and see what happens. Oh, and tell him I've recommended the boy."

When I heard the news, I could barely wipe the grin off my face. Glasier had come to the rescue and hopefully Santa would be my Santa Claus. We phoned Santa.

"Well, it is at the experimental stage at the moment, breeding domestic bred kestrels. But all the signs are hopeful. I'll be in touch."

He was as good as his expectations and his word. The breeding programme had gone well and he agreed to put one aside for me, to be picked up around my 14th birthday. My parents paid £13 for my avian birthday present. My father was good with his hands on the carpentry front and constructed a mews from scratch. Built in our back garden,

12

it incorporated a wooden shed attached to an enclosed weathering and flight. I bought all of the equipment I needed from the Falconry Centre with my pocket money, apart from the glove and the falconry bag. My older brother's redundant motorcycle gauntlet supplied the glove, my old school satchel would serve as my hawking bag. Everything was ready.

The drive up to Santa's place in Wigston was like a dream and when we arrived, there she was, sitting on her block, a real kestrel. I picked her up carefully and gazed with wonder at this marvellous bird sitting calmly on my glove. Santa had obviously handled her a little as she had been manned to a certain extent. Overwhelmed with excitement and joy, I sat with her in the back of the car on the drive back home.

"Penny," I whispered as I introduced her to her new home. "I think you're definitely a Penny because you're copper coloured. What do you think? Penny?"

The sun had barely peered through the veil of clouds at 6.30 the following morning but I was already washed, dressed and sparking. I do not get up at 6.30 am, as everyone who knows me is well aware. But my excitement had banished all sleep; the prospect ahead was positively thrilling. Creeping out to the garden, I wondered what my parents were saying; perhaps they had heard me or were even watching from the bedroom window.

"The boy's already up. What's going on here?"

"It's the bird that's got him up. How sweet."

"Sweet? Extraordinary I'd say!"

The first part of training a bird being manning, the task in hand was to get her on the glove, acclimatise her to her new environment, and me. And that's what I did. Bird and boy, we meandered along the bank of the River Severn to the tune of the songbirds and the lapping water. Technically her manning had begun but I just glowed with the delight of having Penny on my fist. It was a lovely walk, and one that was often repeated, but there was more to her surroundings than the riverbank.

When I wasn't at school, she was rarely off my fist and our various routes did not exclude walking along the streets. And a boy carrying a falcon in the 1970s was a remarkable and unusual sight. It elicited two distinct opposing reactions which, in their different ways, were both slightly intimidating. A lot of people would actually cross the road to avoid confrontation but their eyes kept us clearly in focus. I could almost hear the whispers.

"That's dangerous isn't it?"

"Wouldn't like to get too close to him. Bird looks vicious."

"Where'd he get it?"

"Dunno, but a young boy like shouldn't be out on the streets with something like that."

A few of the brave would make a beeline for us, sometimes to challenge but usually out of curiosity.

"What you got there then?"

"Where d'you keep him?"

"Does it catch rabbits?"

"That's a strange kind of pet you've got there son. Is it tame?"

I felt like some kind of alien as people took to you or not but there were always the looks and the comments. My responses were usually fairly basic and kept as short as possible.

"Yeah, this is my kestrel and I'm training her."

This was my main line but inside, there was a maelstrom of words.

"I'm not an expert but I've just completed a falconry course with Phillip Glasier at the Falconry Centre in Newent and this is my first bird which is a kestrel and I'm training her and I'm chuffed as nuts to have her on my glove, so I'm thinking that I'm the bee's knees because this is definitely everything that I want in life so I'm glad you're interested but I'm not sure that I really want to answer any more questions because, as I said, I'm not an expert but I'm learning."

Phew!

Training began in earnest in huge nearby field. My dear father who, with hindsight, wasn't vaguely interested – came out with me every evening to watch our progress. Little by little, I extended the length of the creance until

14

Penny was flying to the fist some 50 yards with confidence. However, I was not quite as confident, procrastinating over the next step for several days. But that step had to be taken.

My heart was in my mouth as I walked away from her post without the security of jesses or creance. Nothing was there to stop her flying off into the distance as I raised my arm and called to her with the traditional cry.

"Ho!"

Swift as an arrow, without hesitation, she flew directly to me, alighted on the glove and began to pluck at her reward. My smile was as big as the field itself and I saw my father silently clapping in applause. Considering I was a beginner, we trained her very quickly; it had taken only about five weeks before she was flying loose. From then on she flew consistently well and was a truly wonderful bird. Until she was about 12 months old, when it all went terribly wrong.

One grey and dismal morning, I went out to the mews to check on her before going to school. She seemed to be breathing quite heavily and her eyes looked dull. Winter was closing his cold fist on the world and I knew she needed warmth. Setting up a large cardboard box in my bedroom next to the radiator, I settled her on a block in the box and unhappily left for school.

Throughout the long school day, my thoughts were of Penny rather than tedious studies. When the bell rang at 3.45, I raced back home, hoping that she was alive but fearing the worst. To be honest, it hadn't looked good when I'd left but I was panicking. When I walked into the bedroom, before I'd even opened the box, I just knew she was dead. Very slowly and very quietly, I peered over the cardboard leaves of the box and there she was, cold as stone with sightless eyes open wide. Kneeling on the carpet beside her, I wept a fountain as my shoulders heaved. I just wept a fountain.

While I was lost in the shadows of grief, it fell to my father to phone Henry Santa for advice.

"Can you get a post mortem done?" asked Santa.

"I'm sure I can. But where? Are there any vets that deal with birds of prey?"

"Not really. Best thing to do is take the bird to the Ministry of Agriculture and they'll carry out the PM. We should find out what killed her anyway but it's also important for me to find out from a breeding point of view. Whether it might be genetic, you know. Captive breeding is such a new science. Sorry to be blunt."

Coincidentally the Ministry had a big place in Worcester and my dear Mum took my beloved kestrel there in a shoebox. The report revealed that Penny had died from a form of aspergillosis. It wasn't my fault but in a way that was entirely irrelevant; I was devastated and felt that my world had ended. While I was lost in the black fog of despair, my stalwart father called Santa. As he read him the results of the post mortem over the phone, I stared through the rain-splashed window, seeing and hearing nothing.

"What's the boy going to do? Is he going to carry on?" asked Santa.

"I don't know, to be honest. At the moment he's feeling like giving it all up. He's totally distraught."

"Put him on the phone."

I felt my father's hand, soft on my shoulder.

"Gary, it's Henry Santa. He wants to talk to you," said my father, holding out the phone.

"Mr Santa?"

"Gary, I'm sorry. I've heard the results of the post mortem and it was nothing to do with you. It wasn't your fault. Just one of those things." He paused for a moment, then said: "You need to have another bird".

'How do I replace Penny?' I thought, 'How can I replace her?'

"I'm bringing some goshawks in from Finland," he continued, "and I have a friend who's bringing in some lugger falcons from Pakistan. You need to move on."

"I want another kestrel," I said slowly, my voice almost pleading.

"No, time to move on. You've done your apprenticeship with the kestrel. You want to be a falconer? We both know you do, so you have to move on now. It's either a goshawk or a falcon. Let me know."

And that's how he left me.

16

Chapter 3 – And her slacks fell down

As much as I mourned the loss of my beloved kestrel, Santa's words echoed loud in my ears.

"We both know you want to be a falconer …you've got to move on … a falcon or a goshawk … a falcon or a goshawk."

The thought of a Finnish passage goshawk with glaring eyes and probably weighing over two pounds scared me witless. It might arrive as a youngster in immature plumage but would quickly become a vicious, cantankerous and mature killing machine. And I was merely a kid.

"Mr Santa?"

"Gary. So, have you made a decision?"

"Yes Sir, I think I'd like to have a falcon."

"You think?"

"Well, I was thinking that it would be nice to have another kestrel but …"

"Falcon or goshawk," he interrupted. The statement left no further margin of choice.

"Falcon," I replied, suddenly knowing that it was the right choice.

"Good. A policeman friend of mine, Mr Wood, is bringing some lugger falcons over from Pakistan shortly. I've already spoken to him, just in case, and he'd be happy to sell you one when they arrive."

"When will that be? How much will it cost? Is it a lot of money? Where does Mr Wood live?"

Once I'd decided, the questions all came tumbling out over the phone. But almost a year elapsed before Wood called to invite me up to see the newly arrived birds. In the meantime, school continued and more decisions were looming on the horizon.

"Have you thought about what you want to do when you leave school?" asked Mr Dewar, teacher and quasi careers master.

For a moment, I gazed at the trees through the window, vaguely considering what the question really meant. The white goalposts in the field caught my eye and, since I was a football fanatic, an option occurred.

"A footballer, Sir?"

"Don't be ridiculous, Cope. Try to be serious for a moment."

I looked back at the trees and the clouds scudding through the sky.

"Actually, I'd really like to be a professional falconer, Sir."

"A what?"

"A professional falconer, Sir. You know, fly birds of prey for a living. That's what I'd really like to do."

"I told you to be serious, Cope! That's not a proper job. In fact, I'm not even sure that it's a job at all. And even if it were, it's not very likely that you could make a go of something like that, is it boy? You need to consider something that will give you the skills that will lead to gainful employment. An apprenticeship. That's what you need to think about."

Thus an apprenticeship in carpentry followed when I left school at the tender age of sixteen. Those were the days of Ted Heath's three day week and power cuts. Properly signed indentures would have made arbitrary redundancies illegal but few put pen to paper. I was no exception and when I was finally turfed out onto the street, I was still living at home with no real prospects.

When Wood's call finally came, Mum and Dad drove me up to his house in the former mining town of Coalville, Leicestershire.

"Do come in. Good drive up? Excellent. Let me show you around."

In the early 1980s the ubiquitous Harris hawk, beloved of 21st century falconers, had yet to take flight in British airspace. Everyone was into goshawks and Wood was no exception. He led us past two monstrous specimens who stared at us malevolently with great orange eyes that burned pure hatred.

"Wonderful birds, aren't they?" he said, smiling fondly at the murderous pair.

"Absolutely," my father agreed politely.

'Thank God I didn't choose one of those,' I thought silently.

18

Eventually, we were escorted into a garage dominated by a long screen perch on one side. Seven or eight falcons were standing in a line along the perch, settled and almost motionless in their hoods.

"I'm afraid they've been a little battered by their journey. They've only just come in recently from Pakistan where they were trapped in the wild," Wood explained. "And then, of course, they were shipped over. Naturally a few broken feathers but they'll moult out in due course. Other than that they're all fine birds. Now, that one, that one and that one are already spoken for," he continued, indicating each bird with a pointed finger, "but you can choose any one of the others."

Slowly walking down the line, one falcon just seemed to stand out. A little less ragged than the rest, her breast feathers shone especially white and she looked good.

"Can I have a look at that one please?"

"Of course."

Taking the bird onto his glove, Wood opened the braces with his teeth and fingers of his free hand and removed the hood. She stood there without baiting, looking intensely at me with big piercing eyes that glowed darkly in the low light. After a few moments he popped the hood back with an expertise born of experience and looked at me questioningly.

"Yes, I'll have that one please."

With a young mind dreaming of being a falconer, I decided to call her Lundy, named after the eponymous island's famous peregrines. Lundy the lugger (an awful name if I'm honest) cost me the grand total of £32, which included the airfreight. A haggard falcon, Lundy was at least three or four years old by the time she arrived at the Cope household in Worcestershire. She had spent most of those years hunting prey in the wilds of Pakistan and consequently was by far and away the more experienced of the two of us: she was to teach me a lot more about falconry than I was to teach her.

Once she was installed in her new English home, I quickly noticed that Lundy was heavily in moult and many of her feathers were in blood. But it was a state that I simply noted, rather than realising its import, in my keenness to get her flying.

"You're not a bloody falconer, boy, until you've caught something."

Glasier's words were ringing in my ears and all my thoughts were bent on getting Lundy flying as soon as possible.

"I'm not a falconer until I've caught something with my bird."

The sentence replayed over and over in my head, pushing me on to get her trained as fast as possible. Until I found her standing on her block one morning, bleeding profusely. A feather in blood had broken and was haemorrhaging badly. Despite the fact that it looked far worse than it actually was, the incident put the fear of God into me and stopped me in my tracks.

"Perhaps I'll let her moult out, let the new feathers get hard penned and then I'll start her training," I thought to myself.

And that's what I did. She was duly manned until reasonably compliant, allowed to moult out and once she was fully suited in shiny new feathers, training began in earnest. It no time at all she was confidently flying to the lure, then flying free and happily exercising to the thrum of a swinging lure. At which point she decided to chase things without any input or instruction from me: she was teaching me the gentle art of entering rather than the other way around.

Not that she actually caught anything. She may have been named after the famous strain of grouse hawks on Lundy but failed to emulate their excellence. I suspect that the crows in Pakistan were a lot smaller than their English cousins. Nevertheless, she would stoop courageously into a murder of crows but baulked at the last minute, pulling out of her blood, guts and glory dive. The English carrion crow is a big black nasty bird with a hatchet for a beak and you could almost hear her thinking:

'Bloody hell, these have grown a bit since I saw them last!'

Not that that deterred her from harassing the local crow population. While she had fun chasing crows in the sky, I had as much fun chasing her at ground level and, fortunately getting her back on the fist – until the day that she decided to disappear. The last thing I saw was Lundy stooping beautifully at a pair of crows over nearby woodland, only to pull out, pump upwards again and fly off over the treetops. No matter of running around through trees and across fields brought her into sight. I was mortified and not a little worried.

Leaden grey clouds and a bitter wind reflected my mood at dawn the following morning as I set out again in search. Standing in a field, forlornly swinging the lure in the hope of finding the bird was a fruitless exercise. Now officially a working apprentice, wood and chisels demanded my attention until lunchtime. At which point I returned home with the intention of continuing the search, only to find Lundy calmly sitting on her block and preening in a locked mews. Unbelievable.

"Well, welcome home madam!" I breathed a sigh of relief. "So would you explain to me exactly how you managed to fly back into your mews and lock the door behind you?"

Her only response was to give me a brief sideways look before glancing over her shoulder. I swear there was the hint of a smirk somewhere.

"Never mind, at least you're back."

On closer inspection, my prized lugger falcon was clearly unhurt and behaving as though nothing had happened. Apart from the obvious conundrum, the only other curious aspect was the way that the leash had been tied; certainly, this was no falconer's knot. I returned to work none the wiser, not to be enlightened until the early evening.

"Is she all right Gary?"

Auntie Avril's cheerful face appeared around the door which eclipsed the rest of her body.

"Hallo Auntie. Is who all right?" I asked, dimly missing the obvious but unlikely link.

"The bird. I tied her up as best I could and she looked all right but I just wanted to check."

"You put her back in the mews?" I asked in amazement. "You found her and brought her back!"

Leaping up, I gave her a huge hug now that she was fully in the room.

"I love you. But how? What happened? Tell me?"

"Well ..."

And so Auntie Avril told her tale. With a few errands to do, she had been walking past the shops along Pinkett Street, not far from our house, when she'd seen a small crowd gathered in the road. Even at a hundred yards or more, she could hear the buzz of voices, see the upturned faces and the pointing arms. Curiosity being a strong attraction, she quickly moved in to see the object of their attention for herself.

"What you all looking at then?" she'd asked one of the onlookers at the fringe of the group.

"It's up there, innit. Bloody great bird on the roof an' it's got bells on its legs. Hear 'em?"

"So I looked up and there she was, on the roof of one of the houses there," Auntie Avril recounted. "I was sure it was your bird Gary, immediately. Didn't know what she was doing up there but I knew you weren't anywhere about."

"Of course not. I had to be at work and was worried sick. Go on."

"Anyway, there's your bird up there and me down here thinking, what on earth am I going to do because I'm not a falconer. Course, I've seen you messing around with the bird but I don't know what to do. And then I thought – what would Gary do?"

God bless her, she'd run down the road to our house and straight into the mews. Grabbing the old motorcycle gauntlet and a couple of chicks, she dashed back to the High Street, stopped well short of the crowd. Standing in the road where she was sure that Lundy could see her, she raised her glove with a chick in place.

"So I called her just like you do Gary. You know – Ho! Ho! Well, she just bobbed her head a couple of times and then dropped down and landed on the glove as sweet as pie. Then while she was tucking in, I managed to get those leather things, jesses I think you call them, and pull them down. I knew enough to do that much. She'd finished eating and I was standing there clutching the jesses, thinking – now I need to get her home. The funny thing was that the crowd was all laughing and clapping and going: 'well done Avril, well done'. I suppose it wasn't bad for an old know-nothing."

"Not bad Auntie," I exclaimed, "it was bloody marvellous!"

But that was not the end of the tale. Auntie Avril happened to be wearing a pair of slacks that were secured at the waist by two pieces of fabric tied in a bow. Which, as she left for home, decided to untie. As she walked along the pavement, her dignity was disappearing in conjunction with the slow descent of her slacks down her legs. Unlike a falconer, Avril had not threaded the jesses through her fingers but simply clutched them tentatively in her gloved fist. And there she is, in the middle of the street, with her slacks now around her ankles while hanging on to the gradually sliding jesses for dear life.

"So what happened?"

"Well, I stopped walking for a moment. They were all laughing at me then. I suppose it was a pretty funny sight, not that I thought it was funny at the time. Funny the things you think of isn't it? I thought: 'thank God I put clean knickers on this morning'. Anyway, there wasn't much else I could do but start to waddle my way back to your place. Fortunately, Gwynn was there. My neighbour from two doors down? God bless him, he came up and asked whether he could help. It was a bit embarrassing but that's as maybe. He pulled my slacks back up again, retied the bow and we were on our way. We got back here and I tied her up as best I could and locked the door. So is she all right?"

"Auntie Avril, she is absolutely fine. And you are an absolute angel!"

Thanks to Auntie Avril, flying recommenced and continued happily along for some time. But the incident did not stop Lundy from chasing crows. She just loved chasing the brutes even though she never actually touched the black feathers. Carrion crows are very territorial and, since they were always in the same place, neither of us was ever short of sport. Eventually, however, the inevitable happened and I lost her forever. The last time I saw her, she was stooping with great grace and beauty until she decided that she'd had enough for the day. Powering upwards after one final stoop, she flew straight across the woods towards the horizon and out of my life. As before, I searched high and low but without telemetry (as yet undreamed of electronic wizardry) I was doomed to failure. Lundy had vanished and I never saw her again.

On a more prosaic level, the world of carpentry also left me in the lurch, not that that was a great loss. Once again time moved on and I took a desk job with the Civil Service, by which time I was flying sparrowhawks. One of the great things about the Civil Service was that it operated a system of flexitime.

In essence, one simply had to put in a specific number of working hours each week but it was up to the individual as to how his or her schedule was organised. It was the perfect scenario: it gave me the opportunity, especially during the winter months, to take time out during daylight hours to fly the birds. Which enabled me to fly the sparrowhawks pretty much at will and it got to the point where I was doing the absolutely bare minimum in the office. It all fitted in rather nicely.

Notwithstanding my somewhat dubious working schedules, the powers-that-be seemed to think that I was actually doing rather well. If one believed the rumours whispered in the shadows, I was being groomed for greater things. The message from Mr Sheldon, the Higher Executive Officer to 'pop round to my office at 10 o'clock for a chat' gave me the idea that there might be some substance to the rumours. At the appropriate time, I knocked lightly on the polished teak door.

"Come," said the muffled voice from the room beyond.

When I stepped into the spacious room, he immediately arose from his leather- bound chair and smiled benevolently.

24

"Good morning Cope. Glad you could make it. Do have a seat old chap."

Once we were seated on either side of his huge leather-lined desk, he leaned forward, resting his elbows on the mahogany trim with one hand clasping the other. I glanced up at dark portraits of Civil Service mandarins on the wall above his head. Sheldon's voice drew my eyes back to level view.

"I suppose you're wondering why you're here? Well we'll come to that shortly. First of all, how do you think you're getting on?"

Leaning back in his chair once more, he tugged briefly at his moustache before fixing me with an inquisitive stare. Ex military? RAF? No, army, I thought.

"Fine I think, Mr Sheldon. At least, I haven't had any complaints."

"Fine eh? Well we think that you're doing rather better than that. In fact," he said glancing down at the slim file on the desk, "we think that you're actually doing rather well. Showing great potential, young man, great potential. So, it's been decided that we'd like to groom you up for use in the Diplomatic Corps. What do think about that?"

"It sounds wonderful," I replied, wondering simultaneously what joining the Diplomatic Corps would mean.

"Excellent opportunity for you, Cope. We're thinking of sending you to Hong Kong. It truly is a wonderful place, full of buzz and challenges. I'm sure you'll love it out there. Fit in very well. Of course, there'll be a bit of work to do beforehand, shaping you up and getting oriented in service ways."

"Thank you, Mr Sheldon."

"Good luck," he said, waving one hand in dismissal.

Hong Kong, I thought as I walked down the corridor, what's in Hong Kong? It's a fading British colony near China, isn't it? Thousands of bloody miles away from England's green and pleasant land! In the absence of modern internet services, my modicum of research had to be carried out at the local library.

Five million people crowded in a sprawling city that covered less space than Inner London which was home to just over half as many people. It seemed to be filled with skyscrapers, packed dirty markets, streets crushed with people, cars and trams. Where the city ended, the water began; little countryside within reach and no gentle woodland at all. The only birds of prey in the skies were the black kites that circled the mists wreathing the Peak and they were absolutely useless for falconry purposes.

'No, I can't fly falcons there,' I thought, 'so why even consider the idea?'

It was a quite an important moment really, thinking back. I suddenly realised that I was simply playing at earning a living in an office environment and using the system. What I wanted to do was be a professional falconer, to have a career flying falcons. My 'working' life was already geared to enable me to fly birds - the Civil Service simply provided a financial crutch. Hong Kong was obviously not an option and I even felt vaguely guilty about messing all these people around, using them for my own ends. Decision made: I had to find a way of earning my daily crust by working and flying birds of prey.

"Dad, I've left the Civil Service."

"You've what?"

"I've resigned, left the Civil Service."

"You blithering idiot! So now you've got no job and no money. What's your brilliant plan for the future? You stand there and tell me you've thrown away a promising career, for what may I ask?"

"I'm going to be a professional falconer."

"Don't be so bloody ridiculous!"

And there was an element of the ridiculous in my aspirations. There were no falconry centres and no jobs connected with falconry apart from one: working with bird control on airbases. Glasier had done it up in Lossiemouth at some time around the 60s, so why couldn't I do the same? That was it, my target for the future: I would set up a company dealing with bird control. There was only one small fly in the ointment - a total lack of money.

The simplest way forward was to take industrial work and build up some capital. A string of unsavoury, foul and dirty jobs followed. Most of it was factory work, operating presses through the night as we worked continental shifts. There were three shifts running from six am to two pm, two to ten pm and the worst, 10 pm to six in the morning. Physically testing, I hated it but the pay was good. However, it wasn't long before boredom set in and I contacted a bird control company that I'd discovered called Longwings. I applied for a job with a cunning plan in mind: industrial espionage. Since I really had no idea as to how a bird control company operated, I thought that by working with Longwings I'd get the necessary experience and then glean the knowledge needed to set up my own company.

Since they weren't paying me, I had absolutely no qualms in plundering intellectual property, practices and contacts. I worked there for three or four months before handing in my notice. Then I phoned Martin Jones.

"How do you fancy going into business together doing bird control on airbases?"

"Why not? But have you got any contacts?"

"I know the contracts and I've got the contacts."

"Excellent. Got a name?"

"I thought Avian Clearance could work."

"Sounds good to me."

Done deal. Our target market was bird control on American airbases in the UK with the potential of RAF bases to follow. It all seemed so simple especially since the USAF had bases close by at Upper Heyford and Fairford. Contacts made, Martin, another chap and I, were invited to a meeting to tender for our first contract.

A vast boardroom table took up most of the space, edged by uniforms and a trio of representatives from Longwings. If looks could have killed, I'd have been dead on the floor. Their animosity was palpable but they needn't have worried. Avian Clearance's tender for bird control was rejected; Longwings' tender accepted. And it was just the same at subsequent meetings. Essentially, Longwings had a monopoly on bird control, winning contracts with such low budgets that made it impossible for us to compete. The result? No contracts were awarded whatsoever to Avian Clearance in its short trading history. We were flogging a dead seagull.

I needed to change tack, but how? The ancient sport of falconry … practised by kings and princes … a goshawk for a yeoman and a kestrel for a knave. History. History was the key. The Falconry Centre at Newent was pretty much the only centre of its kind and they weren't marketing an historical link. Nobody was doing anything with falconry against an historical backdrop, at all. Innovation being a minor talent and necessity being the mother of invention, I thought:

'Why on earth not? The ancient art of falconry demonstrated and practised against ancient battlements. And nobody's had the idea let alone doing something about it, so I will!'

At which point I started writing letters to all the stately homes and castles in England and beyond.

"Dear Lord and Lady/Your Highness/Duke/Earl/Sir/Madam (please delete as applicable)

"I'm a professional falconer who has been involved in the ancient art and practice for blah-blah-blah. I'd like to bring this display to your visitors at XXX, flying a falcon and giving a talk about the history and the art of falconry. For that is what it is – an art. I am sure that you will be interested in the benefits that it will bring …"

And got just three replies: from Warwick Castle, Leeds Castle and Sudeley Castle. I would hazard a guess that most of the recipients, not having clue what I was talking about, consigned my carefully penned letters to the bin. But three was better than none.

Leeds was rejected as being too far south but I arranged meetings with both of the others. Warwick Castle was truly fabulous and the people were delightful but there just that something that wasn't quite right. But Sudeley was a perfect fit. As I walked towards those old, old walls past trees that had been there for hundreds of years, I felt at home. Every fibre of my being said: 'Gary Cope, falconer, this is your style'.

"Welcome to Sudeley Castle, Mr Cope. I'm Tony, Tony Tilley, the manager here. Let me give you the quick tour of the grounds."

As we wandered through manicured hedges, past magnificent trees and glorious vistas, he told me more about Sudeley and its history while I expanded on my plans.

"Sudeley gets around 120,000 visitors every year."

"Impressive."

"Summer is always fairly busy but on Bank Holidays we're positively seething with people," he said as we turned the corner of the Dungeon Tower. "So how would you like to do a display for us this coming Bank Holiday Monday? It would really add colour to the proceedings."

"Yeah. That's fine. Great, let's do it."

Stunned and delighted, I walked back to the car with a very big smile on my face. And then it dawned on me that I only had one bird! How was I going to put on a falconry display with only one bird? Contacts. By now I'd built up a few friends in falconry and I hoped they'd be my salvation.

"Listen, I've got a falconry gig at Sudeley Castle on Bank Holiday Monday and I could do with some help?"

"No worries, what do you need?"

"You, a falcon and a few more besides. Contact your contacts and let's get everyone turning up at Sudeley for a fabulous falconry fun day. And everyone needs to bring birds!"

"You got it, Gary. And where is it again?"

"Sudeley Castle. It's near Winchcombe, in Gloucestershire."

Driving down the M5 that Monday, falconers were overtaking me in cars, Land Rovers, vans and even one bike. A veritable army of falconers rocked up that day at Sudeley and every one with a bird. While I flew a lanner to the lure and exercised another, between 25 and 30 falconers were there with birds on their gloved fists, to walk and talk with the people. The public were enthralled and I will forever be in debt to all those wonderful guys. And when the final bird was hooded and taken home, I saw Tony approaching across the grass.

"Gary, that was absolutely fantastic. What can I say but – Wow!"

Then a few days later, he phoned.

"You know, Monday was a fantastic success and the crowds really loved it. Can we talk?"

"Yes, sure we can," and smiled broadly as I put down the phone.

Chapter 4 – Sudeley Castle

"Two display days per week it is then. Settled," said Tilley in conclusion.

Home was a cottage in Cifton-upon-Teme on the Worcester/Shropshire border at the time and the drive to Sudeley took about an hour and three quarters in my knackered-out Vauxhall Chevette Estate. On each of the allotted days, I'd pile in all the birds and equipment to rattle my way down to the Castle, only to repeat the process in reverse once I'd finished. That was the way of things for most of the first season and, towards the end, travelling was becoming a serious bore. But then, it was only two days a week. Some time after I'd started, Tilley called me into his office for a 'Progress Meeting'.

"Your displays have become really quite successful. The public love them and the footfall has increased. We're thinking of increasing the number of displays but obviously that would also increase your travel costs. I believe you own the cottage in Clifton-upon-Teme. That right?"

"Yes."

"I thought so. How would feel about moving to Winchcombe? Perhaps you could let your place and make a bit of money that way. And we can offer you one of the estate cottages, not far from the castle. Rent free, of course, so you'd save time and make some money to boot. Would make it easier for all concerned."

"That sounds absolutely marvellous," I replied with a large grin.

"Excellent. Why not come down next, um …" He flicked the pages of his diary and then pinned one with a decisive digit. "Next Tuesday? We can show you a few then."

It goes without saying that the offer was hugely attractive. The only question mark in my mind concerned the availability and nature of the garden. There had to be a garden. Whenever I go to see a prospective house, the first thing I look at is the garden, to ensure that there's somewhere to park the birds. The house itself invariably takes second place in importance in the eyes of a falconer. I needn't have worried. After being shown several cottages which I mentally deleted, there was 13 Vineyard Street.

Hardly a cottage, number 13 was a three-storey house built of light amber Cotswold stone with a warm and welcoming atmosphere. And, to my delight, in the grounds I discovered a matching stone barn that would make an ideal mews. Some decisions require little thought.

"This seems just perfect," I said happily.

So I moved to Winchcombe, quickly settled in and installed screen perches for the birds in the barn as I'd planned. My stay there was a truly happy one and I loved it from the start. There was just one thing that was slightly unnerving. When I put the birds in the mews for the night, there was always a slight chill in the air that raised the hairs on my arms. Impossible to quantify or explain, it was just an odd, strange feeling. It made no sense since this was the place where my beloved birds were safely kept for the night.

The only explanation for the phenomena wasn't revealed until some years later. Since I also have an interest in history, I carried out some research on the property only to find that the mews had been built on the site of the town's ancient mortuary. Perhaps the barn was still the haunt of old spirits who suddenly found that they were sharing their space with a flight of falcons. Whether they took umbrage or were content with the new arrangement is open to conjecture. But whatever the truth of the matter, there was certainly something distinctly odd about the place come nightfall.

As Tilley had indicated when suggesting the move to Winchcombe, Sudeley raised the ante and I found myself doing three or four flying displays every week. The public eagerly responded and the crowds of onlookers got bigger and bigger. Sudeley Castle was pulling serious numbers of visitors and I had to meet the challenge. Not that you'd notice, but I was quite shy and had to combat bouts of nerves as well as honing my skills. It's one thing to fly a falcon for yourself with only trees and crows for company. It's a whole different ballgame flying a falcon under the gaze of an amphitheatre of hungry eyes. Practically,

32

emotionally and every other way that one might think of, it presented a seriously steep learning curve. Of course I made mistakes but I slowly developed my style to the point where I started to enjoy my part in the play. Nevertheless, before a show there was always that malicious dark imp digging claws into my shoulder, whispering malevolently into my ear.

"You're not good enough Cope. You'll screw the whole thing up and make a fool of yourself. Wouldn't be the first time would it? Walk away while you can. They'll laugh at you and jeer. Get real, you're a fraud, a joke! No good and can't cut the mustard."

At the beginning of every show I was sick to my very core as my nerves cramped the muscles in my stomach and turned my legs to lead.

"Ladies and Gentlemen, Welcome to Sudeley Castle. My name is Gary Cope and I'm the resident falconer. This afternoon, I would like to fly a falcon for you ..."

Meanwhile the imp is whispering: "You're not flying! The falcon's the one that'll do the flying and then it'll bugger off. Or maybe you'll find another way to foul it up. Prat!"

Slowly but surely, I worked through my fears, becoming more efficient and more proficient until I finally managed to silence the imp for good.

Away from the madding crowd, I was trying to build up the mews and acquired a couple of lanner cross lugger hybrids from Martin Jones. Living at The Lodge in Huntley, there were numerous practical things to be done about the place for which he had neither the time nor inclination. Since I was pretty handy with hammers, nails and wheelbarrows, I carried out the odd chore and maintenance job. In return for my skivvying, rather than pay me in filthy lucre, he would pass on a couple of falcons which I was then able to add to my growing mews.

And one little bird that came my way was a three year old lanneret called Cid. To be honest, he was a horrible avian brat, totally unmanageable and it took a huge effort on my part to get him trained. But in many ways, that bird put me solidly on the falconry map. (Over the years I have been extremely lucky that certain birds have come into my life and made it all possible. It's a thread that weaves a path through the whole of this tale. But for now, back to Cid.)

Once trained and compliant, the once ghastly little bird morphed into the most stunning flyer that I have ever seen. And I've not seen his like since then! When exercised to the lure, most falcons will fly in predictable figures of eight which is perfectly fine, if a little boring. What made Cid so special was that he did not accept any limitations or comply with the norm. Cid was a born performer and the crowds were in awe.

Instead of stooping to the lure as soon as he'd been cast off, Cid would mount up and up until he reached around 500 feet or more. Banking elegantly above the upturned faces of the onlookers far below, he would calmly cruise until I produced the lure. Reacting immediately, he would drop like a stone in a fast corkscrew, sweep down over the people's heads and through, climbing once again with rapid beats of his wings.

"Wow!"

The collective sighs of admiration lent an audio track to his flight as Cid repeated the process three or four times. Then he would move on to his second manoeuvre. As he stooped vertically downwards, I would pull the lure through, a hair's breadth from his beak and he would power up again on another vertical. Reaching his preferred apex, he would then perform a full barrel roll, flip onto his back and power through a complete vertical circle. And would keep the momentum going for several more loops. It was quite unbelievable; an extraordinary and wonderful thing to watch.

After one particular flying display had been successfully completed and the crowds had dispersed, one man stood alone, quietly watching me sort out the birds and equipment.

"That's quite a falcon you have there," he said, nodding towards Cid on his block.

"Thank you I'm glad you enjoyed the show."

"Absolutely amazing. I've never seen a bird fly like that How does he do it?"

34

"What do you mean?"

"The Gs it's pulling. G-force. The amount of Gs that bird must be pulling when he flies like that are going to be massive! I'm a pilot, fly fighters with the RAF and I know what that means. Quite extraordinary."

No question, I really made my name with Cid and fan mail flowed in from all over the world. Sudeley attracted a lot of foreign visitors (which it still does, of course) and letters would arrive from Hong Kong, Canada, the United States, Kenya et al. They came from pretty much anywhere on the global map. More often than not, a photograph would be enclosed that had been taken during a display with little notes in accompaniment.

"Thank you so much for Cid."

"How's Cid doing?"

"Cid velly gooood burd. We like velly much."

"I am seeing many birds as Cid in wild but none is so stupendous as his good self."

Cid was the undisputed star of the show. From being a wild, unmanageable, bad mannered git, he'd been transformed into the most extraordinarily tame falcon I've ever had. Unlike his colleagues, he lived untied in the kitchen and free to roam. At one point I even flew him at tame hack and, like a homing pigeon, he never failed to return. Which also meant that he was incredibly fit.

By this time, not only did I have Cid for company, I also had a wife. (I'd married her on my 21st birthday which might be romantic, somewhat clichéd or possibly, just sad. You, my dear reader may choose!) Whatever. Number 13 being a fairly spacious abode, Joy and I used to throw the occasional party. Totally unfazed, Cid would sit there on his perch in the kitchen with one leg hauled up, fluffed out and definitely chilled. Apart from one night when it appeared that he'd inadvertently participated in the evening's jollities.

Taking a moment to check how young Cid was getting on with the assembled company in the kitchen, I found him noticeably swaying on his perch. In addition, I smelled the distinct scent of an illegal substance drifting in the air.

"Are you all right, Cid?" I asked somewhat pointlessly.

Looking wildly around the room, I spotted the guilty party trying desperately to stub out the still smoking joint.

"What are you doing to my falcon, for God's sake? He's bloody stoned out of his head! Out, everybody out. Now!"

Everybody fled while I rushed around, flinging open windows and flapping a tea towel to accelerate the dispersal of marijuana fumes. Fortunately no harm was done although he might have been a bit bleary-eyed the following morning. But perhaps that was my imagination.

Cid had a high Arabic-style perch in the kitchen and every morning he habitually performed a wonderful little routine. As a rule, the first person down to the kitchen would put the kettle on to make that vital early morning brew. It was one of those tall electric kettles with a broad handle. Cid would calmly wait until it had cooled down a little, fly off his block and perch on the handle. I swear that he liked the warmth on his toes.

It was during this time that I first met Lord Ashcombe, at the end of one sunny Sunday afternoon. The displays were held in a paddock to the side of the Castle, beyond the tree line. As the visitors made their way back to their cars, a short, wiry gentleman in tweeds walked towards me, his image flickering in the late rays of the sun filtering through the leaves.

"You must be my falconer," he said without any introduction.

"Lord Ashcombe," I acknowledged.

"Bloody good show!"

He beamed with a most engaging smile and talked for a moment or two about the shows and falconry, clearly having a sound knowledge about the sport himself. And slipped into a little nostalgia.

"Heard of Kim Muir?" he asked. "Used to live at Postlip Hall, not far from Winchcombe near Cleeve Hill. Barn of a place it was, dating back to the 15th century or earlier if I'm not mistaken. Kim was a great chap and a bloody good falconer as well. You might have seen Lodge's painting 'Black Jess'? It's a wonderful painting of Kim's intermewed eyass peregrine, hooded and standing on the glove. He trained and flew her before the Second World

War. Poor chap was in the 10th Royal Hussars and bought it at Dunkirk - bloody shame.

"Anyway, I knew him long before we came to Sudeley. In those days, we were living at Denbies House, (great pile of a place with almost 100 rooms) and I'd travel up from Surrey to see Kim and fly goshawks. I remember we'd drive off in a red shooting brake with the birds in the dickey and we'd have great times flying the hawks at rabbits on the wolds. Caught a lot as well. Watching you flying brings it all back."

We seemed to talk for ages. Lord Ashcombe and I had a lot in common, with the love of falconry and birds being the key component. A strong friendship was forged that day in the paddock and it wasn't long before he was coming round every Saturday and Sunday morning. We'd sit there for hours retelling anecdotes, discussing the merits of different birds and talking about falconry and other field sports. A big shooting man, Lord Ashcombe ran one of the best pheasant shoots in Europe, at Helmsley in Yorkshire. He also smoked liked the proverbial chimney, one Marlboro after another, so our conversations were held in a grey fog, lubricated by numerous cups of dark rich coffee. Those were wonderful days and our friendship grew ever stronger. Little did I realise then how it would affect my life or how important his support and patronage was to become. From little acorns do great oak trees grow.

Charismatic, well bred and a true gentleman maybe, but Lord Ashcombe did have some strange habits. For instance, he'd never knock on the door, preferring to peer through the window and occasionally at the most inopportune moments. He continued to do that for 20 years and I can still see him there, in my mind's eye, appearing like a sprite at the window.

"Whoops, Lord Ashcombe's here. Better go and let him in!"

In the meantime, the displays progressed and I became ever more competent. Mum and Dad often came to see the shows and the first time that they turned up was surprisingly emotional. Her pride at seeing her son's accomplishments was not unusual; I could never do anything wrong in her eyes. If I'd mugged an old lady and nicked her handbag, Mum would still have made excuses to the police, God bless her.

Never one for handing out praise, Dad's approbation was unlooked for and therefore much more powerful. In my early days of football mania, I was actually quite good at the game and a few clubs, including West Bromwich Albion, showed an interest. But he never said 'Well done, lad', it was always, 'Forget it, lad, you've got to be realistic'. He almost took those last two words as his personal motto. Ironically, before World War II he had himself been a proficient player and had been due to sign for Bristol City when war broke out. Bristol City was a good team in those days but the war shattered his dreams and that was the end of his career in football before it had even started. Not wanting his son to share his disillusion and disappointment, instead he shared his motto. And every time that he'd tell me to be realistic, Mum would take me to one side.

"Your father means well," she'd say, "but you should always reach for the stars."

And I always have done. But on that day when Dad first saw my display, his eyes mirrored stars and his smile was broad with reflected glory.

I'd seen them standing at the back and smiled with pleasure but focussed on falcons and flying. And as the crowd left the field, they were on their own and walking towards me across the grass.

"Oh my boy, my boy," Mum said in her gushing way. "Isn't he wonderful, Harry? Isn't he absolutely wonderful?"

Dad just looked at me for a moment, those steely blue eyes brimming with emotion. Then put one hand on my shoulder.

"I am so proud of you, son - so very, very proud. Well done."

Even now, when I think of him and his words, I can feel the lump in my throat. I knew that he was always proud of me at heart but he very rarely displayed his emotions. For me, that was a very real mark in time and I knew that I was on the right road.

Not long after that, a ghost from the past appeared at the rear to watch the noon display. Schools used to take their pupils out for day trips during the summer in those days and if Sudeley was on the itinerary, they always turned up for the 12 o'clock show rather than those later in the day. The coaches would line up along the drive, disgorging hordes of screaming unruly kids - and I hated those school jollies! But on day of the ghost's appearance, there seemed to be something familiar about this particular group of loathsome brats.

'Bloody hell,' I thought, 'they're from Bishop Perowne!"

The dark blue ties with the diagonal stripes were my first clue. Seeing the blazon of Worcester's three pears on jacket pockets were the second, confirming the first.

'My old school's turned up to watch!'

And there at the back was an only too recognisable face.

"Good old Dewar!" I exclaimed out loud. "So he's still there, pushing kids around. Probably still telling them that their dreams are bullshit."

My humiliation in front of the whole class still rankled. Dewar's damning phrases echoed cruelly in my mind: 'not a proper job' and 'even if it was, it's not very likely that you could make a go of something like that, is it boy?'

"Watch this then!"

Naturally enough, not all of the displays ran smoothly but, fortunately, this one went really well. After the last bird had been flown, I watched him make his way through the melee of blazers and impromptu scuffles. It was tempting to give him the finger but one didn't do that type of thing to schoolteachers. I gave him a smug smile.

"You did it, Cope!"

"Yes, I did, Sir." (Old habits die hard.)

"You did. And very well too," he enthused. "Well done. I have to admit, you were right and I was wrong."

'Yeah, and what if I'd listened to you mate?' the little voice in my head whispered.

But his praise was obviously genuine and he meant well, I suppose. Either way, it did no harm to my ego and gave another small boost to my confidence.

But not all displays were flawless or quite so satisfying. An acquired lanner falcon called Zulu served up a cautionary reminder that things don't always go as planned. A social imprint, Zulu was incredibly tame on the fist and she could fly. Quite often she would simply speck out on a cloudless sky, wander high above the roofs of Winchcombe and disappear. I wish I could get a grouse hawk to climb as high as Zulu. Once she'd learned the ropes, she flew quite well but on her own terms.

It was one of those glorious summer days when the sun shone hotly down from a cloudless, deep blue sky. A large crowd had gathered for the two o'clock session, listening attentively as I confidently gave my spiel. Casting Zulu off the fist, we all watched as she climbed ever upwards until she was a mere dot in the heavens. Then the dot blinked out, disappearing from the radar of human sight. We waited. Nothing. Nowhere. Feeling like a complete idiot, I dashed over to the weathering on the edge of the paddock, picked up Zulu's understudy and flew her in 'Houdini's' absence.

By around quarter to six when it was time to pack up and go home, there was still no sign of the little blighter. There was simply no point in staring at the sky. Birds in the mews and equipment stashed, I walked into to house to sound of the phone ringing.

"Is that Mr Cope?"

"Yes it is. Who's calling?"

"The RSPCA," said the disembodied voice. "Have you lost a falcon by any chance?"

"Yes, I have. You've found her?"

"Well, we've picked it up from the chap who found her. We tracked you down from the bird's closed ring number."

"Marvellous. How did he find her?"

"Apparently, she perched on his roof. Since he'd recently been to a falconry show, he recognised the bells and put two and two together. He said he rushed back into

40

the house, attacked the fridge and found a pork chop which he tied to a piece of string."

"A pork chop? You have to be joking."

"Not according to him. Anyway the idea worked. Chap dashed back into the garden and chucked the chop on the front lawn. Luckily for you, the bird came down and grabbed it. She was probably pretty hungry after her long flight. Actually, seriously hungry would be my guess. So, while she's hacking at the chop, the chap threw a jumper over her, shoved her into a cardboard box, phoned us and here she is, safe and sound."

"Incredible. But that's absolutely brilliant. Can I come and pick her up?"

"Yes, of course you can."

"Excellent. Where are you?" I asked, assuming that it was only a matter of a few miles.

"Southampton."

"Southampton! Thank God she stopped there, otherwise she'd have been across the Channel and exploring France."

Given that Zulu left Sudeley at two o'clock, I estimated that she should have arrived in Southampton at around about five. Then I estimated that the round trip to Southampton, including collection and brief grateful conversation would take up the best part of five hours. It was time to pull rank and be mean.

"Nick, I've got a little job for you. Jump in the car and collect Zulu from the RSPCA in Southampton."

Actually, it was horribly mean but I didn't want to drive all the way to Southampton and back. So I sent Nick, who went very willingly without a murmur of complaint. And here I should add a few further words about the young lad who became hugely important and stayed with through much of my career.

His parents were lovely people, obviously cared about the future of their son and took his wishes into account. Nick's father was the vicar at Tewkesbury Abbey, moved upwards in the clerical hierarchy and ended up at Windsor as the Queen's own pastoral guide. To plagiarise William Cowper's hymn, the Lord moves in mysterious ways and so it was that the good reverend brought his gangly son to me under the aegis of the government's Youth Training Scheme. Or YTS, as it was best known. Nick's ambition was to become a professional falconer.

Many people derided YTS as a waste of time, saying that it was pure exploitation and a way to favourably squeeze youth unemployment figures. But it certainly worked for Nick and, I'm sure, for many others. I believe he's in charge of the bird section at Cotswold Wildlife Park near Burford these days. And that gives the lie to the doubters.

However, I digress. Nick happily returned with Zulu who was singularly unfazed by her adventure. But the whole episode did set me thinking and not just about birds popping over to Bayeux in honour of their forbears as depicted on the famous tapestry. Falconry was lifting off in a big way across the country and falconry centres were sprouting up like poisonous fungi. The competition was proliferating at the speed of a falcon's wing beats and, to my absolute horror, people were even running displays at the back of garden centres. Sacrilege! It was time to raise the bar a few notches.

Chapter 5 – Dog, hawks and burglars, oh my!

To my mind, there was only one way to stay in the game and remain competitive: keep one step ahead of the pack. And that would require a touch of courageous innovation. Having settled the mews for the night, I looked at the birds in dusk's fading light and pondered. One of the falcons raised a foot to energetically scratch her hooded head as though sharing my thoughts. The sound of her shaken bell rang through the quiet evening air, disturbing her neighbour who snapped her head in the direction of the irksome noise.

"Two falcons! That's it!" I exclaimed. "Nobody's flying two falcons to the lure at the same time."

I'd never seen anyone fly two birds to the lure simultaneously, nor had I attempted the feat myself. Suffice it to say that it's extremely difficult. The first step was to train and condition the birds so they worked as a team. That was a bit of a challenge but one that I achieved without too much difficulty. Flying the pair to the lure was just a touch harder. Suddenly, I found that my lure work required the skills and dexterity of a Shaolin warrior monk weaving complex aerial patterns with a Chinese flail. The only differences being that I had to avoid contact and the falcons were meant to be on my side.

They, on the other hand, are working as a team with the sole and joint intention of nailing the lure. The first would sweep down to make a pass at the lure which I'd pull through and away. A nanosecond later, her teammate was on it and not always from the same direction. The words hammer and anvil spring to mind which, on consideration, might be excellent names for a cast of falcons. The flights were certainly crowd pleasers but the potential for mistakes and mishaps was too close for comfort. I did do it quite a few times, mainly when I felt like showing off; never on a regular basis. As Falstaff said, 'The better part of valour is discretion' and I didn't keep it up for too long.

Perhaps with Zulu's marathon and discretion in mind, I also acquired a new set of telemetry. The yagi antenna was much the same as they are today but the receiver was the size and weight of a house brick. Nevertheless, I felt it provided me with a good safety net when the inevitable bird-goes-awol happened.

However, on the whole everything was pretty much on track and the falconry centre was well established at Sudeley. The friendship with Lord Ashcombe was growing and I got on well with Lady Ashcombe and her children. They were all among the constant stream of visitors that frequented 13 Vineyard Street. All that was missing was a dog and I decided that I needed a pointer. Bracken seemed ideal for the position and came to stay.

As there was no grouse hawking locally, I had started to go up to Caithness in the north of Scotland with a friend. The only time we could afford to go up there was in October when it was almost at its bleakest and we had to rough it a bit. It was a lot of fun but a dog was definitely required. Since Glasier had a wonderful German shorthaired pointer called Trudi, it seemed only sensible to follow in his footsteps.

I acquired Bracken from a highly respected and extremely good falconer, Nigel Warrington, who lives down in Wiltshire. Professionally, he's a bird control falconer for the Royal Air Force. On the drive back to Winchcombe after picking up our newest bundle of fun, Bracken was nicely settled in Joy's lap. And proceeded to pee copiously all over said lap! It was clear from the outset that he was going to be trouble. Even when he got old and grey he remained an unrepentant rogue. A supreme escape artist, he had a terrible habit of just bogging off and disappearing. It was a trait for which he became infamous among the good citizens of Winchcombe.

He regularly practised his vanishing act when let out of the house at night for a pee. The woods behind Number 13 that backed down to the River Isbourne were his favourite haunt and, because he was predominantly chocolate-coloured, he believed that he was perfectly camouflaged. On hearing searching footsteps he would stand perfectly still, trying to blend in with his surroundings. He'd go into stealth mode, slink off down to the Isbourne and stay out

44

for an hour or more. What really scared the hell out of me was when he'd disappear for 12 hours at a time.

An occasional visit to a local farm was not unusual. The Scudamores were big tenant farmers on the Sudeley estate and they were not amused by Bracken's attention. At least one sheepdog was invariably on heat and, I suspect, he went up there with the aim of sowing his seed. Whatever the case, a phone call from one of the Scudamores always meant trouble.

"Your bloody dog's up here again," Mrs Scudamore bellowed down the phone line. "Do you want to know what he's done this time? Well, I'll tell you. He's only dragged a dead sheep out of the farmyard and now, he's disembowelling it on my lawn!"

"I am terribly sorry, Mrs Scudamore. I'll be right over."

When Bracken saw me drive up in the truck, he knew he was in trouble. The truck meant I was annoyed, he'd refuse to get in and run hell for leather down the lane. I would then drive right up his arse to teach him a lesson. But I wasn't annoyed, I was downright furious. I never hit dogs – or children, women, blokes or anybody – but I was livid. Grabbing Bracken by the scruff off his neck, I gave him a couple of sound clips on the backside.

"What are you doing? How dare you hit that poor dog? It's not as if he's doing any harm!"

A quick reality check was in order. Wasn't this the same woman who'd been screaming at me because Bracken was disembowelling a sheep on her lawn? She ripped into me as though I'd been chewing on her sheep's liver and Bracken had been an innocent bystander.

"Poor thing," she said, stroking Bracken's head. "Pity you have to live with such a horrid man." Then looking at me: "You take him off home and do not, do not hit him again. Get off with you."

You can't win, can you? But Bracken did as Bracken fancied. All in all, Bracken was an absolute nightmare, albeit a lovely fellow, and he did turn out to be an excellent hunting dog. Which takes me back to Caithness.

I was still a young man learning his craft and so very fortunate to be able to go grouse hawking. We would rent a very basic croft, complete with burning peat fires when it was freezing cold. I had little money – we ate road-kills for food. We certainly couldn't rely on catching grouse to keep our stomachs full; Caithness was hardly overrun with the birds. Further south, in Yorkshire, they were everywhere and hunting only required you step outside the door. In Caithness, one expected to have to trek over five miles or so of freezing tundra before you caught a glimpse of grouse. I could imagine what their Yorkshire cousins would say if invited to move north from their comfortable nests.

"I'm not living up there for God's sake. Too bleak, too bloody cold and not enough food. Bugger that!"

Occasionally Martin Jones and Stephen Frank, an internationally renowned falconer, joined us for a little sport. And one early evening, we're all out there on the tundra. It was still hard for me to believe that I was actually out hawking with the great Stephen Frank. However, the day had not been very successful since we hadn't had a single point. Now we were lost, yomping way out on the tundra with no idea where the car was or even the way back to the road. Black clouds loomed ominously and cold rain started to fall as yomp turned to trudge.

Consensus held that the most sensible thing to do was try to backtrack rather than push forwards. This brief discussion and obvious decision took place on the banks of a burn.

"Enough is enough," we agreed sagely.

Then we heard the sound of a mighty splash.

"Salmon!"

Turning around as one, we found Stephen fishing around under the edge of the bank for slippery salmon. This wiry little man in his 60s was up to his waist in the fast flowing waters of a Caithness burn in sub-zero temperatures, searching for fish. He reminded me of a manic pixie. Finding nothing lurking below, he nimbly hopped back onto the bank, grinning happily even though he was now a drenched mobile iceberg. Eccentric and a total nutcase maybe, but Stephen had an incredible spirit and a wonderful appetite for all things wild. It was his

46

inspiration that led me to proper hawking, hunting game with a bird of prey.

Staying with him at his cottage was an experience in itself. During the shooting season, he used to hire out pointers to the guns as a way of making a living and had most of the dogs housed in a massive kennels. At night, however, he always had eight or nine in the tiny cottage, which meant there were pointers everywhere. It was truly like being a bit player in Disney's One Hundred and One Dalmatians but the dogs were pointers and definitely not cartoons. The place was far more chaotic and messy than 13 Vineyard Street but that didn't matter. Stephen was a wonderful host, a larger than life character.

"I'll show you your bedroom," he said as he started up the stairs. "There you go. All yours."

I looked around the room in awe: the walls were covered with superb paintings of game birds, hawks and falcons. This wasn't a bedroom, it was an art gallery.

"Stephen, are these all by George Lodge?"

"Mmm-hmm."

"And they're all originals?"

"Yes. I sort of stuffed them all in here since I didn't know what to do with them really. No space downstairs. They're jolly good though, don't you think?"

"I certainly do," I said, thinking, 'this lot must be worth a mint!'

Here was a man who lived a basic life, existing on a never-ending stew that bubbled in the background like a witch's cauldron. Whenever the level got a bit low, he would simply chuck in anything that happened to be to hand, maintaining the perpetual diabolic pot-au-feu. How he never got food poisoning is beyond me but, to be fair, it was very tasty. But while frugality was the norm downstairs, the room upstairs held a displaced fortune in paintings!

We were due to leave at around six o'clock the following morning to travel back south and by four-thirty Stephen was lighting the stove to get the place warm. And there we all sat, eating this marvellous full Scottish breakfast which he had prepared in his wonderful cottage on the moors. Living up there on his own in the middle of nowhere, I think he put a high value on visitors and enjoyed their company.

But Sudeley called and I was soon back in harness, flying displays at the Castle in a slightly more temperate climate. The hunt for elusive grouse was replaced by the less interesting but dependable and ever present lure. And life puttered comfortably on, although I did sometimes wonder what twists and turns fate would take next.

One evening I decided to visit my local hostelry for a relaxing pint or two, and perhaps a few amusing discussions. The mews were secured, Bracken was locked safely in the kitchen and the door to the washroom, which was temporarily housing a couple of Harris hawks, firmly shut. A chap called John Anderson, who lived in Riyadh, had persuaded me to take the pair on loan for a while.

"Would you mind looking after them?" he'd asked. "They're pretty wild I'm afraid but I'm sure that a man of your calibre can handle them."

How could I refuse a freebie brace of Harris hawks to play with? Since the washroom at the back of the house was quite spacious, it seemed to be the best place to put them. They were duly installed on a screen perch that I'd erected at one end but there was a draught coming from the window at the other. Drawing on my ancient carpentry skills, I tacked a piece of hardboard over the broken pane and they were snug as bugs in a rug.

Having taken drink, I returned to the house in a pleasantly mellow frame of mind and was pleased to find that Bracken had not made too much of a mess. I stretched out on the sofa, enjoying the comparative silence after the bustle of the pub. But half an hour later, the rap of knuckles on the front door abruptly intruded. To my surprise, I found myself confronted by two uniformed policemen illuminated by the flashing blue light of the car behind.

"Good evening, Sir," said one. "Are you the owner of this property?"

"Well, no, not really, I'm renting it from the Sudeley Estate."

"I see. And do you happen to keep eagles?"

48

"I haven't got any eagles, no. I do keep hawks and falcons but no eagles."

"Can we come in, Sir?"

"Of course," I said, starting to panic, thinking: 'what on earth is going on? I didn't drive to the pub.'

Removing their caps, constables Coates and Johnson passed me through the doorway.

"Have you been out this evening?"

"Yeah, I went to the pub for a couple of pints. Why?"

"Are you aware that the house was broken into while you were out?"

"Someone broke into the house?"

"Not one, Sir, two. It appears that two men broke into the house through a window at the rear."
"You're joking?"

"I'm afraid not. We happened to be passing when we spotted two guys climbing over the wall at the end of the garden behind your property. Naturally, we wondered what they were doing and thought we'd better have a little chat."

"They were burglars?"

"Let's put it this way, Sir, it appears that's what they'd planned. Have you noticed anything missing?"

"Um, no, at least nothing obvious. I haven't looked properly but then I had no idea. Not a clue. What did they say?"

"Bit difficult to say at the beginning since they were gibbering wrecks." Pulling a notebook from his pocket, Coates flicked the pages. "Here we are – Thomas and Darren. They said that they'd noticed a broken window a couple of days ago, saw that it was only lightly boarded up and thought that it would be easy to get in. Um, they said they thought that there should be a good few things to nick since it was a nice house."

It wasn't too difficult to reconstruct the scene of the crime. Tom and Darren had been lurking in the shadows, watching and waiting. When they saw me lock the door and wander off up the road, they seized the moment.

"He's gone, get over there."

"Yeah, and we'd better be quick. Don't know how long he's going to be."

Once in the garden, the pair made a beeline for the broken window. The hardboard came off easily with the help of a screwdriver and Tom reached through the broken glass to release the latch. The window opened slowly of its own accord and they peered into the blackness.

"Can't see nuthin, black as pitch in there."

"Shine your torch down the wall. How far is it to the ground?" hissed Darren.

"S'easy. 'Bout four foot to the floor."

"OK. Go."

One after the other, they'd slipped through the opening and dropped down to the floor; the sound of shuffling and dull bell-like noises were accompanied by stiff staccato breezes that blew across the room. And it was all coming from inside!

"What the fuck's all that?"

"Dunno."

When the pair flashed their torches around the room, all hell broke loose.

"Eyarghh, yarghh, yarghh."

The harsh screams of the hawks would have been loud enough at the best of times, but in the confines of the washroom the noise was deafening. Hooked beaks hacked viciously and extended talons clawed the air as the pair bated off the screen perch towards the intruders. Arched wings flexed and beat in the torchlight, throwing menacing shadows across the walls. No longer mere hawks, these were surely kin to Gwaihir, Landroval and Meneldor, the mighty eagles who bore the Ringbearers from Mordor.

"Jesus!"

"Bloody 'ell."

"Get out the way!"

"Bugger off!"

Tom and Darren practically trampled each other to death in their haste to climb back through the window. Racing across the grass, they scrabbled their way over the wall and collapsed in two heaps on the pavement.

"Which is where we found them," said Coates. "One hurt his shoulder and the other was bleeding like a stuck pig. Seems he cut his arm on the broken glass."

50

"Quite a gash he's got," added Johnson, "I reckon he'll need a few stitches for that. They were both totally freaked."

Coates consulted his notebook again.

"D said that they had been confronted by 'two bloody great vicious eagles' which had tried to 'tear us apart'. T agreed - said that they were 'lucky to escape with our lives'. In fact, both of them said that you ought to be put away yourself for having dangerous birds in the house!"

"Are they dangerous, Sir?"

"No, officer. I suppose Harris hawks do look a bit like eagles but they're not dangerous. But naturally enough, if people jump through their window and wave flashlights around, they're bound to get spooked."

As soon as the policemen had gone, I went to the washroom to check on my two homeland security agents. Sitting quietly on the screen perch, they seemed none the worse for their encounter.

"Well done, ladies," I whispered as I closed the door.

I could just imagine completing an application for home insurance. Security: five lever mortice locks on outside doors, all windows lockable, one dog and two guard birds. Maybe birds of prey could be bred and trained for the purpose? But that would be silly. At least the idea of breeding was to prove prophetic.

Chapter 6 – Accommodating one and all

"Do you know anything about captive breeding? Of birds of prey, of course."

Lord Ashcombe and I were chatting away over coffee one morning and the question caught me slightly by surprise.

"Yes, I know a bit." (I had absolutely no idea whatsoever about captive breeding!) "Why do you ask?"

"When I was up in London the other week, I had dinner with a friend of mine, Prince Khalid. Khalid bin Abdullah al-Saud. He's a member of the Saudi royal family and breeds racehorses over here - won at Newmarket with his first one, Fine Edge. Anyway, we started talking about falconry and you obviously came up in conversation. And he wondered whether you knew anything about saker falcons and how to breed them."

"Yeah, enough. We can sort that out."

"Excellent. Give it some thought, Gary, and we'll talk again."

I did, vaguely.

"Have you thought about it?" Lord Ashcombe asked a week or two later.

"Yeah," I said cautiously.

"The point is, would you be interested in breeding some sakers for him?"

"What does he want them for?"

"Well, he doesn't spend a lot of time in Saudi Arabia, so what he'd like to do is breed some over here and send them over as gifts for his relatives. Is that possible?"

"Of course it is. But the problem is that there's not enough space to do it here. It's a lovely garden but no way is there room to put up proper breeding aviaries."

"I think that can be resolved. There are several properties on the estate that might be suitable. I'll arrange a meeting with Lady Ashcombe and she can take you around."

Accordingly, Lady Ashcombe and I drove off one sunny afternoon to inspect a few cottages and other possible locations. Picturesque, quaint or simply pretty, not one was

52

suitable as none of them had the necessary grounds. My enthusiasm was beginning to wane and the knot of disappointment growing.

"There is one more we can see, but I'm not sure that it'll be any good. It's the last one on the list but we might as well have a look."

After driving along Rushley Lane for a while, she turned left up a bumpy old track. Thick hedgerows squeezed the sides of the lane and the trees linked branches overhead. I felt a little like Alice following the white rabbit down a darkened tunnel. After lurching on for another 60 or 70 yards, we were suddenly bathed in sunlight. At the end of the tunnel was this wonderful island in the sea of trees. A large paddock stretched out before our eyes: riddled with brambles, alive with rabbits and encircled by a necklace of Victorian apple trees. And the centrepiece of this idyll was a derelict stone building, complete with grasses and weeds decorating the old mortar. It really was quite beautiful.

"Wow, what a place! It's fabulous," I exclaimed. "There's just something about it, don't you think? It's extraordinary."

We wandered slowly into the old ruin, disturbing a pair of jackdaws from their afternoon snooze. It was little more than two basic rooms with a loft space above.

"What is this place?"

"It hasn't been used for years but in Victorian times it was a slaughterhouse. Apparently, they killed pigs here and sent the carcasses up to the kitchens in the big house."

'A quaint turn of phrase from the Lady of Sudeley Castle,' I thought.

"This was the living accommodation, I believe," she said as we walked onwards. "Horrible. They called it a bothy."

Attached to this bothy was a wonderful 12-feet high red brick wall that stretched off for some distance.

"What's behind that?"

"I suppose you might call it the back garden."

"Can we have a look?"

The old gate was stiff and arthritic, the hinges grating in protest as I pushed it open. Ducking my head slightly, I went through the arch to find myself in a massive Victorian walled garden. The smell of wild honeysuckle blended aromatically with scents of mint and old lavender. An ancient wisteria spider-webbed its way across one wall while a Virginia creeper adorned another. The remnants of long forgotten greenhouses stood valiantly among panes of broken glass and fractured timbers. Fragments and short sections of piping were all that remained of the heating system that used to keep the frosts away from the vegetables and herbs that grew there. It was love at first sight.

From a falconer's point of view, the garden was absolutely perfect for breeding aviaries. Not only was it private, secure and wonderfully spacious, it was also a beautiful place. Everything about it gave out a good vibe. The only thing lacking was a place for me to live.

"So what do you think?"

"It's absolutely brilliant. Ideal."

"Good."

Leaving the garden, I followed Lady Ashcombe back into the bothy. She paused, and glanced around at the dirty crumbling walls, a slight smile playing on her lips.

"And what about the, um, living accommodation?"

"Not so good."

"Well, it could all be renovated. We could make this room into a kitchen and then turn the other one into a dining room. And then we'll add on a wing for the rest."

One of the pleasures of having plenty of money is to not have to consider the cost. A state in which 'add on a wing' is a decision rather than a calculation. Nevertheless, my pauper's mind just had to ask the question.

"That's not going to be cheap! And then there's the cost of clearing the garden, landscaping, building proper breeding chambers and aviaries. Do you have a budget for it all?"

"We'll worry about the finance. All you need to do is concentrate on designing the layout of the garden and everything you need for the breeding programme."

"Brilliant, let's go for it."

Immediately I thought of American-style breeding chambers with three feet deep footings and built with breezeblocks. One-way glass to be installed and not a bit of plywood! And they were going to renovate, design and build an additional wing? Unbelievably fabulous! This was all way out of my league but suddenly I was moving into the big time.

"Of course, it will all take a little time," Lady Ashcombe continued, oblivious of the thoughts racing through my mind. "So in the interim, I wonder if you would be interested in moving into the West Lodge?" (It wasn't really a question.) "I'm afraid that you'll have to move out of 13 Vineyard Street anyway. We need to let that out as a holiday cottage."

"That's fine."

Not that I was in a position to argue but the West Lodge bore no comparison to the spacious comfortable accommodation at Number Thirteen. The West Lodge was part of the aged, castellated archway that had once straddled the main entrance to Sudeley Castle. The drive now swept imperiously past lodge and tower, its original purpose sadly redundant. A similar principle had been applied to the interior. West Lodge was tiny, raw and invariably freezing. Nevertheless, there was something about living there for a short period that appealed. The inherent eccentricity was somehow attractive, bringing to mind the basic accommodation that T H White shared with his goshawk.

However, the similarities were limited. White only had one bird while I, on the other hand, had acquired more than a few. Added to which there was Bracken, my faithful Golden Retriever Saxon and a couple of ferrets. I brought all the furniture down from the cottage in Clifton-upon-Teme and crammed that in as well. Joy was unimpressed. A high-flyer in the business world, she was offered a job in Boston with luxurious accommodation included and saw that as a better option. As a temporary measure, Rob filled the slot and West Lodge became a typical joint bachelor pad.

A local chap, Rob had been coming to the Castle to watch the displays for some time and showed a keen interest in the birds. Quite the naturalist, he had an uncanny ability to see the detail in wildlife and just happened to be between places to live.

"Any chance of moving in with you?"

"Yeah, all right. Provided you're happy with the birds, dogs and ferrets."

"Not a problem," he said with a grin.

Finances, however, were always a bit of a problem. I had a little bit of money in the bank from letting Clifton-upon-Teme but was still not earning much from Sudeley and Rob's financial state was no better. In typical countrymen's style, therefore, we went out ferreting on a regular basis and usually dined on rabbit. On rare occasions, the odd pheasant or partridge would break the line of rabbits hanging in the archway beside the Lodge. Rabbit was the norm. The number of ways in which bunny can be cooked is fairly limited but it complemented the natural, organic lifestyle we had in our minimalistic accommodation. And it was fantastic. For some reason, I felt wonderfully free.

However, the levels of delight diminished in direct relation to the drop in temperature. When winter's chill fingers tightened their grip, the Lodge was bitterly cold. Going out for a pee in the middle of the night was sheer torture. Leaving the warmth of the bedclothes behind, one had to walk along the corridor over the archway and down the stairs. Then one had to go outside and stumble across the cobbles before re-entering on the other side to get to the bathroom. The cobbles were so cold that your feet almost welded to the stone. By the time you got back to your bed, you firmly believed that you felt the onset of frostbite.

In the absence of a shower, there was no option but to have a bath. And on at least one occasion, my appearance after bathing was a cause for embarrassment and not a little levity. Having enjoyed an enjoyable dip in a hot tub, I wrapped a towel around my waist and skipped quickly across the icy flags into the warmth of the kitchen. And, to my horror, joined a large group of unknown people. It

56

would be difficult to say which of us was more shocked. I looked at them with disbelief; their stares were a little more complex, ranging from curiosity through revulsion to amusement.

"Are yew Lord Aishcoomb? Y'all sure have a purty castle here. Downrite quaint, I'd call it."

I was terribly tempted to string them along and accept the laurel of nobility.

'Yes, absolutely, I am indeed Lord Ashcombe, Sir. Unfortunately I carelessly sided with the wrong army at the Battle of Tewkesbury and lost everything. Sadly, I lost almost all of my fortune and this pile of ancient stone is all that I have left. But, by the grace of God and Her Majesty, I am still here.'

A thin dripping man in a towel is really not in a position to act the part of a Lord, however impoverished. One definitely lacks the necessary gravitas and demeanour. Fortunately, I managed to maintain my grip on the towel.

"I'm afraid not. And this is the West Lodge. If you follow the driveway a little further, you will come to a slightly larger house. That's Sudeley Castle, home to Lord and Lady Ashcombe but you'll find your way in through the visitors' entrance."

At which point I scuttled out of the kitchen and up the stairs to safety. Under the misapprehension that the Lodge was the Castle, people wandering around the place was a regular occurrence. Thankfully, them finding me in an embarrassing state of déshabillé, was not.

Not surprisingly, my initial love of the Lodge quickly waned and life there was becoming a bind. Reminding myself that it was only a brief hiatus, almost every evening saw me dashing over to my island in the trees. What had been a crumbling bothy, was becoming a resplendent house which I named, with great originality, The Bothy. The broken two-trashed-rooms-with-gaping-loft was being transformed and the new wing taking shape. Cleared of decaying greenhouses and years of accumulated debris, my Victorian garden was showing signs of its former glory. But instead of new horticultural buildings, brand new aviaries and breeding enclosures were slowly taking pride of place. It was really, really exciting and kept me going through those long lean months at the Lodge.

The phone rang.

"Are you ready to move?"

"Am I ever?" I whispered fervently. "Yes, Lord Ashcombe. I'll start immediately."

The ravaged green Chesterfield, scarred oak table and my few other humble sticks of furniture were duly carted over to, and duly lost in, the lovely, spacious new abode. The architects and builders had done an incredible job; The Bothy truly exceeded my wildest dreams.

"Honestly, it's a palace, Joy."

"Compared to what?"

The line to Boston had a hollowness in which our voices echoed.

"Compared to … I don't know but it's seriously luxurious. They've spent a fortune on the place. The house alone must be worth at least four hundred and fifty grand. I wouldn't be able to afford a place like this in a million years. And that's just the house. There's this fabulous garden with breeding aviaries that Cornell would be proud of and the surroundings are stunning. The whole place is really beautiful. Come home."

"Gary, I have a good job out here and a nice place in Boston."

I sensed her resolve was weakening.

"So work from here. You've done it before. And I bet you haven't got apple trees in the garden and rabbits playing on the grass. Come home, Joy. I miss you and I promise you'll love the place. Let's give it another go, please?"

After 12 months in Boston, Joy flew back and moved in to The Bothy. Bringing her unique feminine touch into play, she kitted the place out beautifully as only she could do and made it a home. Once the initial excitement of the reunion had abated, we settled in to a comfortably warm relationship. We were sitting in front of the fire one night, watching the flames dance around the logs, when the icy chill of reality sent shards through my mind. A minor panic attack ensued.

58

"Christ! I've never bred budgerigars let alone falcons. I must be mad. The Ashcombes have given me aviaries that Cornell would die for and I haven't got a clue. I've never bred a bird in my life! Bloody mad."

As ever in a crisis, Joy came to the rescue.

"I know but look, first of all you've got the passion and that's a big thing. Secondly, if they can do it, so can you. Just run with it and you'll get there, I know you will. What have you got to lose?"

Her words set me back on track and I became single-minded in my search for information. It wasn't that easy since literature about captive breeding just didn't exist. What I did know was that in 1970, Professor Tom Cade of Cornell University had started a major programme to breed peregrines in captivity. Decimated by DDT, other contaminants and loss of habitat, peregrine numbers had dropped to danger levels. Cade and his team had been successfully breeding and releasing birds into the wild for over a decade. I wrote a long letter to Cornell University.

"The enclosed documents should provide you with all the necessary information and guidance. Please do not hesitate to get in touch again if you need further assistance. In the meantime, good luck and every success with your own captive breeding program. Do let me know how it all goes."

They were absolutely marvellous, sending over huge wads of paper and numerous files. Every imaginable aspect of captive breeding was covered in the vast number of documents. Of course, it all related to peregrine falcons but it gave me the information and knowledge that I so desperately needed. When it comes to breeding birds of prey in captivity, that I was talking sakers rather than peregrines was totally irrelevant. I read, studied, studied and read, absorbing everything that I could from Cornell's fount of experience. And gradually, I mentally built up a sound idea of what I was supposed to be doing.

"Of course, not every pair will breed even if they do seem to be getting on together. In that instance, we might consider artificial insemination. Cornell and McGill

University in Canada have had a lot of success using AI with birds of prey."

"Well, you certainly sound as though you know what you're doing," said Lord Ashcombe, looking pleased. "It also sounds as though you've done a bit of recent homework to boot. Excellent."

"The next problem, and it's a big one, is getting a few pairs of sakers. That's not going to be so easy."

"That might not be as difficult as you think, dear boy. Heard of a chap called Peter Whitehead? Made a lot of films in the late 60s about subcultures in New York and London. Did some promotional film clips with the Stones, Pink Floyd and Led Zeppelin. Extraordinary chap, he also says he's a mystic and has lived for thousands of years. Married Dido Goldsmith - pretty girl - she's the niece of Jimmy Goldsmith, the billionaire financier."

"The name Whitehead rings bells," I interrupted, "but I think you've lost me. Are you thinking that he might film here?"

"No, no," Lord Ashcombe said laughing. "The thing is, Peter spent the best part of a decade wandering around places like Afghanistan and Pakistan, trapping birds and breeding them. A couple of years or so ago, he started running a massive breeding programme for falcons under the patronage of Prince Khalid al-Faisal, King Faisal's son."

"Bloody hell! I think I'm getting the point."

"He might have some birds for sale. And, as it happens, he's a friend of Lady Ashcombe's. I'll ask her to get in touch."

A few days later, I was on my way to Pytchley in Northamptonshire. Over a cup of coffee, Whitehead regaled me with one or two hair-raising experiences from the past. Like the time in Baluchistan when he was hunting for falcons, caught black cholera and was saved by a local witchdoctor. He told me a little more about the Al-Faisal falconry centre, perched on Saudi's highest peak, Jabal al-Souda, the Black Mountain, And a little about courtship rituals in which he encouraged falcons to copulate with him. As part of the artificial insemination programme, he explained. It was over all too quickly.

"Anyway, I'm off again very shortly and most of the sakers and other stuff has to go. Take what you want."

I drove back to Winchcombe in a daze. From having nothing at all, I suddenly had some four pairs of saker falcons, loads of incubators, hatchers, candlers and a few other bits besides. Even a pair of snowy owls came to stay; Lady Ashcombe's idea.

The sakers were installed at The Bothy and were to be the foundation of our breeding programme. Best of all, they were not eyasses but two and three year old birds. Now all we had to do was wait for about 12 months and hope they produced some eggs.

In the meantime there were plenty of chores to be done, falcons to fly and displays to be flown. But nobody had told me that jobs like modelling and television work were included in my job description.

Chapter 7 – Fifteen minutes of fame

"Hi Gary. It's Julie at the Estate Office. How do you fancy getting involved in a photo shoot with Lord Lichfield?"

"Yeah, sure, why not? What do they need?"

"I've just been speaking to his producer who said they're doing the set to advertise Burberry's new autumn lines for women. And he said that it would be fabulous if they could have you with a falcon and two hunting dogs in some of the shots."

"Sounds great. When and where?"

"They said about eight o'clock - something to do with the light. They'll be on the lawn, in front of the Castle. It sounds as though there'll be quite a few of them so they should be pretty easy to find. And it's next Wednesday."

"Anything else?"

"Not really. Just don't forget the dogs and the bird."

Lord Lichfield's photographic circus was difficult to miss. The front lawn was littered with photographic lamps, silvered and white umbrellas on stands and a couple of big circular reflectors. People seemed to be everywhere. They were either scurrying around with clipboards and determined looks or in deep concentration as they fiddled with various arcane pieces of equipment. The two mobile trucks to the rear had obviously been totally stripped and evacuated. Leaving the dogs and bird in the car, I ambled across to join the melee.

I was quickly spotted. The short little chap was actually wearing a blue and white striped French sailor's shirt with a boat neck and a black beret.

'All that's missing is a string of onions,' I thought as he minced his way across the grass.

"You must be Gary, our falconer!" he exclaimed. "So pleased to meet you. I'm Gordon, Patrick's producer."

I shook the rather limp extended hand.

"We'll take you over and introduce you in just a sec but just to explain, you'll be standing in between the girls over there. The macho rough outdoors type with les belles filles en haute couture. Quite delicious! Oh, but where are the dogs? And the falcon?"

"Don't worry, they're in the car."

"Thank goodness you didn't leave them behind. Anyway, let's get you introduced."

"To Lord Lichfield …"

"Oh darling, don't ever address him as Lord Lichfield. He get's terribly upset if you call him that. It's always Patrick."

"Fine," I replied even though it seemed a bit strange.

Lord Ashcombe was a stickler about the way in which he was addressed. Naturally I'd never have dreamed of calling him Henry; it was always Lord Ashcombe. When I slipped up and mistakenly addressed him as 'Sir' on one occasion, he was clearly not too pleased.

As we reached the perimeter of the shooting circle, a tall elegant chap walked over and shook my hand with a much firmer grip than Gordon's.

"Glad you made it," he said, running his fingers through his perfectly coiffured thick grey hair. "We'll be ready for you in about 15 minutes. You have brought the falcon and the dogs, I assume?"

"Yes, Patrick. They're in the car."

"OK. Why don't you go back to the car and we'll give you a shout when we're ready. Thinking ahead, could we possibly have the dogs off the lead?"

"Yeah, no problem."

"They're obedient?"

"Oh yeah, bombproof."

"Good. We'll give you a call," he said and turned on his heel.

Forty-five minutes later, with typical creative delay, Gordon was tapping on the car windscreen.

"Right, we're ready for you."

Bird on fist and dogs in hand, I followed him back to the set where I was carefully positioned. As soon as I was poised, two absolutely stunning girls appeared to join me, one on either side. Suddenly I have a gorgeous model dressed to the nines in svelte Burberry fashion draped on either arm, a hooded falcon on my glove while Saxon and Bracken sit obediently at my feet. I grinned happily to myself as I imagined what our group looked like through the viewfinder.

The shoot crew was continuously on the move, changing the angle of a reflector, shifting a lamp or taming an errant lock of hair on a model's head. Everything had to be right, from the lighting to the drape of an arm. It was as though Patrick was directing the shoot by telepathy while overtly simply clicking the shutter.

"Gary, could you take the dogs off their leads?"

I'd been wondering why he hadn't asked earlier. Even a professional like Patrick Lichfield has to take a few test shots, I supposed.

"Yes, no problem."

For a moment, little changed apart from the fact that Saxon and Bracken were now without restraint. My beautiful new friends Sarah and Emily snuggled back on my arms, dogs and bird were nobly statuesque and I had to stop myself grinning.

And then I heard the sound of ducks quacking in the near distance. As though charged with electricity, all four canine ears pricked up instantaneously. The dogs' eyes refocused, locking on to a view over the pond with the koi carp, in the lee of the old tithe barn.

As the quacking increased, hunting instincts took precedence over photo shoots and Saxon exploded into action. I whistled frantically but was totally ignored. Bracken only paused for a millisecond before dashing after the older dog.

"Quack, quack, quack, quack …"

Ducks were flying everywhere to escape the fountains of splashing water as the pond erupted. The sounds of chaos clamoured in the morning air as Saxon and Bracken splashed in energetic chase. I was desperately whistling and bellowing, and wishing the ground would open up beneath my feet.

And suddenly, the canine charge that had been launched at the ducks took a fresh, new direction and the pair came hurtling back. They were as pleased as punch: they'd flushed game for Gary and done their job; and having had their fun with a flush of ducks, now there was a bunch of people who would sing their praises.

Like runaway trains, the two dogs were unstoppable and ran a wall of death around the set. Heavy lamps crashed to the ground, clipboards took flight and the girls fled for cover. A trail of muddy footprints tracked across the once pristine white surfaces of toppled reflectors. Bracken crashed headlong into the tea trolley sending coffee, tea, mugs, milk and sugar flying through the air. I was mortified.

After more whistling and bellowing, the two dogs eventually came back with tails wagging. I surveyed the scene with horror. The destruction was absolute and Gordon was not looking quite as amiable as he had at our first meeting. His face burned a fierce red under his black beret that was now askew.

"I'm terribly sorry," I blurted out, "I am so sorry. It was the ducks, you see? They saw the ducks and …"

"You told me that those dogs were controllable," he hissed loudly. "Well, we'll have to go and have a word with Patrick now, and see what he has to say."

'That's the end of my advertising career,' I thought as I trudged dismally behind the irate producer.

"I am really, really sorry Patrick. I mean, what can I say?"

I could have sworn that there was the hint of a grin on his face.

"These things happen, don't they? Why don't you go back to the car while we get everything set up again? And can you please dry off the dogs as well?"

"Yes Patrick, of course. I've got a towel in the car."

Cursing them both roundly, I took Saxon and Bracken back to the car and cleaned them up as best I could. An hour later, a somewhat calmer Gordon reappeared.

"We're ready for you now if you'd like to join us again."

Back on set, I regrouped with Sarah and Emily, feeling somewhat shamefaced.

"Would you like me to take the dogs of the lead?"

"I think we'll leave them on the lead this time," Patrick replied drily.

Fortunately, the rest of the shoot went smoothly and, amazingly, I even got paid for my time. It might not have a fortune but ninety quid wasn't bad for the mid-eighties.

No further mention was made of the dogs' rampage. Patrick Lichfield could have thrown the book at me but he was every bit the gentleman and incredibly understanding.

Some six months later, Joy and I happened to be wandering down Regent Street in London when I spotted the Burberry name.

"Come on, let's go in and see if they used any of the shots from Sudeley."

We walked among the manikins sporting Burberry's expensive clothes, stared at the blow-ups on the walls from which images of attractive models stared back. But there was no sign of a falconer with his falcon and his two hunting dogs.

So that was the end of my Burberry campaign. But it wasn't the end of my advertising career. Not long afterwards, I received another telephone call from the Estate Office at Sudeley.

"Hi Gary. Would you be interested in doing a TV advert for Scotch whisky?"

"Yes, sure."

"Great. Can we give your number to the company so they can contact you direct?"

Naturally I agreed. The phone rang again a few hours later. After a brief exchange of pleasantries, the wee man on the phone told me that the advert would only be broadcast in Scotland. And then the wee man got to the point in soft Scottish brogue.

"What we need is an eagle to fly down to camera. Have you got one that can do that?"

"I'm afraid I don't keep eagles. What I have got is a young Harris hawk which looks a bit eagle-ish and she's very obedient."

"That sounds good."

The following Thursday, I took Poacher up to the Castle as agreed and found a small camera crew milling around on the Mulberry Lawn, behind St Stephen's Tower. The massive camera on an equally large tripod seemed vaguely ludicrous and completely at odds with the surroundings. But those were the days when even mobile phones were the size of house bricks.

"Aye, she'll do nicely," the director said approvingly as he looked at Poacher from a safe distance. "What we want is for the bird to be right up there."

He pointed to the beautiful arched window, high up on the ruined walls of the old banqueting hall. Etched against a sapphire sky, the stone mullions glowed in the warmth of the afternoon sunshine, in that golden light beloved by photographers and cameramen alike.

"You mean you want her right in the middle?"

"Aye, it's got to be exactly there."

For a moment I wondered whether he thought that I was going to climb up there with Poacher and plonk her down in position.

"And then what?"

"We want you to tell your eagle, at the appropriate moment, to come swooping down and fly directly to camera. I want to catch the swoop and then fill the lens with eagle. Can you do that?"

I didn't bother to remind him that Poacher was a Harris.

"Yeah, we'll give it a go," I said cheerfully. Privately I was thinking, 'If this works, it'll be a bloody miracle!"

Casting Poacher off, I watched her fly gracefully up to the mullioned window and settle lightly on the transom. Dead centre and right on the mark, albeit facing in the wrong direction. But as soon as she heard my 'kikk, kikk', she obediently turned to face the camera.

"Right, ready to go."

"Excellent." Pause. "Quiet on set. Take one."

The clapperboard snapped down smartly and the assistant director did the three-two-one thing with his fingers.

"Roll sound, roll camera and, action."

Placing a choice titbit on my glove, I held it a hand's breadth over the cameraman's head. He ducked and started to look distinctly panicky.

"Keep still will you," I whispered, "and you'll be fine".

Dropping silently from between the mullions, Poacher came sweeping down and straight-lined the camera. She pulled out millimetres from the lens to land safely on the glove. 'Got it in one,' I thought and smiled proudly at the young Harris.

"Fabulous! OK, let's do it again."

"Again?" I asked, somewhat surprised. But then I'd never worked with television people before.

"Sure."

"Fine. Not a problem."

Poacher repeated her performance in superb fashion. Once again, she hit the sweet spot on the arch, turned and, on command, swooped down into frame - unbelievably perfect.

"Terrific! And again. Quiet on set. Take three." Snap went the clapperboard. "Roll sound, roll camera and, action."

Ten takes later and we're still rolling.

"Look, poor old Poacher's got a serious crop on her. Any moment now and she's going to say – 'I think not, I've had enough' – and go on strike. Surely you've got enough?"

"Yeah, that'll be fine. It's a wrap."

There were happy grins all round and they were clearly chuffed to bits. Once again I got paid for my trouble although I was somewhat disappointed not to receive even one bottle of the single malt we were advertising. And since Winchcombe is a little way outside Scottish broadcasting's coverage, sadly I never saw Poacher's magnificent flight on television.

Ah well, back to normality. And then phone rang. Sudeley's Estate Office was on the case as usual.

"Hi Gary, ITV are doing a programme on flight and they'd like you to be involved. You OK with that?"

"Sounds good to me. What does that entail?"

"All right. For the first part of the show they're planning to take you up in a hot air balloon," said Julie. "You know you're so lucky. I'd love to do that! Anyway, they're going to interview you while you're in the balloon."

"You do not like heights," my imp was whispering. "This is not a good idea. You know you don't like heights, so say no."

"Fine," I said.

"The second part is on the ground. You take them out, fly a couple of falcons for them and get interviewed again. I think you're meant to be talking about how falcons and hawks fly and flight in general."

"No problem. When this all happening?"

"Tuesday. You need to be here at 6.15 on the dot they said."

"No, no, no. That's a horrible time. I do not do early morning. Six-fifteen? Argh!"

"Prompt, Gary."

It was one of those glorious summer mornings when a golden sun shines down from a clear blue sky. As the dawn chorus sang its anthems, I rolled out of bed and looked at my watch.

"Bloody hell! It's six already."

Quickly dragging on some clothes, I stumbled out into a day that was already warming its face, jumped in the truck and screamed down Rushley Lane. Racing straight into Sudeley, I found the balloon inflated and people stomping around with irritated looks on their faces. I could almost hear them saying: "Where is he, where is he?"

Ripping the handbrake on, I hit the ground running and got to the balloon just as they were easing the tie ropes. I piled into the basket and flopped in a messy heap.

"Where the bloody hell have you been?" said a voice somewhere above my head.

The burners roared fiercely for a moment, heating the air in the cavernous envelope and drowning a few more expletives. An almost eerie silence followed.

"I'm really sorry. I got a bit delayed. Sorry."

I clambered to my feet. The pilot stared up into the envelope, the cameraman glowered and Sue Beardsmore, the presenter, smiled.

"Well, at least you're here now," she said kindly.

She paused as the burners roared again and I felt the balloon rise and gather speed.

"Stanway House is to the west, isn't it?" she asked the pilot.

"Yup. I'll take us up to around a thousand feet, level off and then push west. It might be a bit higher or lower, depends on where we pick up an easterly. But I'm guessing we'll find one at about a thousand."

"Fine." Beardsmore turned her attention back to me and continued. "You probably know Stanway House? Lord Neidpath's home? We'll do an interview with you on the way there, land in Lord Neidpath's garden and interview him as well. I don't know whether you've met him but he's a real character and Stanway House is beautiful."

The balloon rose majestically into the sky in what seemed like complete silence, broken occasionally by the dragon's breath fired by the gas cylinders. And then, like a falcon waiting on, we hung motionless in the sky. A slight breeze whispered through the still air and pushed us northeast at the pace of a sluggish snail. The Bothy appeared far below and I could just see Nick waving as he stood by the aviaries. I could almost hear the birds in the aviaries, see them bating and hacking as the balloon drifted across. Frowning, I cursed mildly and felt slightly upset; they hated hot air balloons flying overhead.

"We're going up a little higher to find a bit more wind," announced the pilot. "Need a bit more speed otherwise it'll be dark before we get to Stanway."

The burners flared, the balloon rose and I began to feel sick. I was absolutely petrified. There I was, over one thousand feet above terra firma in a confined basket under a balloon full of hot air with only a couple of inches of wicker between me and oblivion.

"Are you all right?" asked Beardsmore. "You're looking a bit pale."

"No, I'm fine," I replied bravely out loud while my brain was screaming, 'No I'm not bloody fine, I'm terrified'. "Just a touch of acrophobia for a moment."

"Are you OK to do the interview now?"

"Sure."

She looked at me quizzically.

"Honestly, I'm fine. Go for it."

70

On the one hand, having to concentrate on answering her questions helped to take my mind off my perilous situation. On the other, it made me scrunch into my corner of the basket and every time she paused, the fear returned with double the force. (When I saw the programme broadcast on television some time later, I winced at the sight: I looked as though I'd seen an army of ghosts.)

Eventually, Lord Neidpath's stately Jacobean pile of Cotswold stone appeared, surrounded by beautifully laid out formal gardens. I could see the fountain spouting priapically in the canal whose waters glinted in the sunshine. Relief washed through me as we started to descend towards the safety of solid ground. But the view below suddenly shifted and disappeared. The sight of flat open ground, which was ideal for landing, was replaced by the grasping and menacing branches of an extremely large horse chestnut. Panic ensued as the basket lurched with the impact.

"I can't bloody land here!" the pilot shrieked.

Branches were everywhere and I felt the blood draining from my face.

'This is bloody madness!' I thought.

"It's too tight, we'll have to go up. Nobody told me that the place was covered with trees."

"Then take the blasted thing up again," shouted the cameraman.

Flames shot upwards into the envelope, the roar adding to the cacophony of breaking branches. With a final stomach-turning wrench, the basket cleared the canopy of trees.

"So what are we going to do now?" Beardsmore asked calmly.

"Land in a field with no trees!"

"And then what?"

"You'll have to walk back."

"Mmm. I suppose we'll just have to pretend that we landed in the Stanway Gardens and just do the interview with Lord Neidpath without the balloon. Oh well."

Rising up a couple of hundred feet or more, we drifted back towards a nearby field. As we approached, I spotted a herd of bullocks but the pilot began his descent.

"Oh shit!"

The comment might have been prompted by fear, but was also very appropriate. Naturally enough, the field was awash with the erstwhile contents of numerous bullocks' bowels. And I might not be a pilot but even I could see that we were coming in far too fast. The basket hit the ground with a heavy thump and tipped over on its side, throwing us together in a tangle of bodies and heavy equipment. Absolute chaos. We crawled out into the shit and mud, only to be confronted by the snuffling wet noses of over inquisitive bullocks. By now it was ten thirty, which was the agreed time to meet Lord Neidpath in the gardens, and we were in a filthy field with a bunch of nosey bullocks.

"Could have crawled here quicker," I muttered. "If anybody wants to use hot air balloons as a form of transport, they're insane. I've had enough of this."

Somehow we managed to clean up enough and a few minutes later everything was set up in the gardens to the front of the house. The sun was shining, the sky was blue, we were safely back on terra firma and the camera was ready to roll. Then a door opened and a prim little lady trotted down the steps and across the grass. The housekeeper she said.

"I'm afraid his Lordship is still in bed. Let me get you some tea and biscuits while you're waiting."

She returned some fifteen minutes later carrying a loaded tray.

"Lord Neidpath won't be long. He'll be getting up soon."

Fifteen minutes after we'd finished the tea and biscuits, there was still no sign of the eccentric Lord.

"Bollocks to this," said the cameraman.

"I couldn't agree more," said Beardsmore.

"Leave it?"

"Leave it."

Abandoning the poor pilot to sort out his own problems, the ITV vehicles were called in and drove us back to Sudeley.

"You're still on for flying the falcons this afternoon?" asked Beardsmore.

"Absolutely."

They flew brilliantly and I felt one hundred per cent more comfortable than I had a few hours earlier. Beadsmore and I did a few more pieces to camera. I talked about falcons, feathers and flights while she prompted and questioned.

"And finally Gary, how did you feel this morning in the balloon? Up there, where the birds fly?"

"It was wonderful! And such a marvellous opportunity to see the world as the falcon sees it, to share their view and perspective."

I waxed lyrical and lied eloquently. But I've never been in a hot air balloon since and certainly had no inclination.

However, my run with the media was to continue as the Estate Office maintained its role as an enthusiastic conduit.

"I've been talking to a chap from the Daily Mail," Julie said. "He'd like to watch one of your displays and interview you afterwards. Once you've done that, we thought you could take him up to The Bothy to show him the birds and aviaries over there. You fine with that?"

"No problem."

The reporter showed up one afternoon a few days later, looking the stereotypical hack of the times. The rumpled jacket, badly knotted tie and pork pie hat painted the perfect image, completed of course by the grubby notebook and chewed biro. He reminded me a bit of Arthur Daley, except the Mail man had a photographer in tow rather than a minder. During the display, he took copious notes while the snapper clicked away from every possible angle.

"Good show, mate. Bin doin' it long then?"

To a lad from the Shires, the heavy London accent sounded pure East End, conjuring up visions of Stepney and Whitechapel. Did I have a genuine cockney for an interviewer? It was almost a disappointment not to hear him use one single bit of rhyming slang. Nevertheless, he still seemed the real deal and friendly to boot. My only qualm was how accurate the detail in the article would be since there really isn't much falconry within the sound of Bow's bells. Not that there was any chance of me checking it before the paper went to print.

After the interview at Sudeley, I showed him round the grounds and aviaries at The Bothy and he was clearly impressed. We'd more or less finished the interviewing side of the business, his notebook and pen back in his pocket. He peered through the spyhole in the side of one breeding aviary, hoping to catch sight of a saker or two.

"You breed them birds, do yer?"

"Yes, yes we do."

"Good mate of mine might be interested in wot yore doin' 'ere. You probably 'eard of 'im."

"Who's that?"

"Bloke called Al-Fayhed."

"Mohamed Al-Fayed?"

"That's the geezer."

"Right!"

"Anyway, as I was sayin', 'e's a good friend uv mine and I fink 'e'd be hinterested in this breeding stuff. Tell you wot, when I'm back in London I'll give 'im a bell an' tell him wot yore up to. Might give you a ring, probably. Never know, do ya?"

"Fantastic! Thank you very much."

That was the last I saw of the London reporter and I haven't seen him since. A couple of days later, I picked up a copy of the Daily Mail and flicked through the pages. There it was, the article about the falconer and breeder at Sudeley Castle in all its glory. Me, not the Castle. And it wasn't too bad although there was one sentence that brought a small frown to my face.

'The falcon swooped around the Sudeley fields in regal chase of a piece of Sainsbury's chicken.'

Here was I, trying to create a dramatic image of the historic and noble art of falconry as practised by yours truly and a reporter had the temerity to refer to a falcon chasing Sainsbury's chicken!

'That'll look good on my profile,' I thought.

74

The article let loose the dogs of the press. The Sun, Mirror, Telegraph et al, all suddenly wanted a piece of the action. The phone rang itself off the hook for 24 hours.

"Of course, I'd be delighted … I'm afraid not … It might be possible … NO!"

Basically I cherry-picked the ones I considered were best and left out those that I deemed unsuitable. Being written up in the 'right' papers was hardly going to do my career any harm. In addition, we were expanding the whole falconry experience and had started running hawking weekends at the Castle. Getting national press coverage was seriously good news (please excuse the pun!) and worth money in the bank for Sudeley. Not that I ever got paid for any of the interviews. Thus a stream of articles and features appeared in some of the dailies and the odd Sunday supplement. But it didn't end there.

Chapter 8 – Two hawks for a Sultan

A couple of weeks later, when the immediate media falconfest had died down, I had a call that was not from the Estate Office.

"Mister Gary Cope?"

"Yep."

"You have a few minutes to talk?"

"Yeah. Who's this?"

"Mister Al-Fayed would like to talk to you."

"Ha ha. Very funny. Whoever you are, it's a weak wind-up."

(Quite a few friends had heard the tale of the reporter and the Egyptian magnate.)

"So sorry Mister Cope, but this is the truth that Mr Al-Fayed would like to talk."

"Blimey!"

"Wait please, I will put him on the line."

The new voice was deeper, with more gravel and a distinctive accent.

"Mister Cope. I am Mohamed Al-Fayed. You have heard of me perhaps."

"Er, yes sir, Mr Al-Fayed, indeed."

"I understand that you are involved with the birds?"

"Yes."

"Let me tell you then, I am looking for a couple of eagles for my friend, the Sultan of Brunei, you will understand."

"Well, I don't deal with eagles, I'm afraid. But what does the Sultan of Brunei want with a couple of eagles anyway?"

"I will explain, right? He is setting up a big bird garden at his palace in Brunei and it is for that that he wants the eagles."

"As I said, I don't deal in eagles but I do have a couple of spare Harris hawks."

"And what are they, Mr Cope?"

"They look a bit like eagles, quite a lot in fact, but they're nowhere as big. To be fair, they'd be far better suited to an aviary than a couple of eagles. And they'd travel better. I think they'd fit the bill."

"I see. Perhaps you could send me some photographs of these, Harris hawks?"

"Of course."

The next day I sent a handful of prints in the post to Barrow Green Court, Oxted, Surrey. I didn't have long to wait.

"Mr Cope? Mohamed Al-Fayed. I have received the pictures. They are excellent and, I think, they are what we are looking for, these Harris hawks. And what would you want for them?"

"You're probably looking at five grand each," thinking, 'What the hell? Push it.'

The idea of five thousand pounds dropping into my parlous account was really quite delicious. And I knew that Lord Ashcombe wouldn't be too unhappy about the deal either.

"Good. In addition, can you design the aviaries for these birds? Do not worry about the cost, money is not an issue here."

'Thank you, Lord.' "Yes, of course I can do that for you. I'll have to let you know how much time I've put in and send you the bill. Is that OK?"

"No problem."

"There is one other thing I must tell you," Al-Fayed continued.

'Oh, here comes the catch,' I thought.

"We would like you to install the birds at the palace and it will mean travelling to Brunei. It should be quite pleasant. You will be responsible for taking the birds over there and doing what is necessary. Naturally, we will arrange for your flight to Brunei and onward flights to other places you might like to visit."

"Sounds great. I'll be in touch when I've done the designs."

'Bloody hell!' I thought, 'this is fantastic. Maybe Singapore. I've always wanted to stay at Raffles. Perhaps some sightseeing in Kuala Lumpur. Yay, this is the big time!'

The aviaries that I designed were absolutely fabulous and probably ranked with the best in the world. It was wonderful to have a job where expense was no object and I took full advantage. The aviaries were perfect for the birds and aesthetically stunning. I was all geared up to go until Lord Ashcombe disabused me of the idea.

"No, you can't possibly go!"

"Why not?"

"Because you have responsibilities here, Gary."

Maybe he thought that I'd leave and never return. Perhaps he was worried that I'd be headhunted by the Sultan of Brunei, leaving him with a serious headache, considering the Ashcombes had risked thousands on the breeding project. Whatever the truth of the matter, he was adamant. Not wanting to fall out with the man, I capitulated and phoned Al-Fayed.

"Everything's fine. Obviously we need to paid up front, but the birds are yours. All the designs for the aviaries have been completed so I'll send those with my bill. But unfortunately, I'm not going to be able to take the birds personally to Brunei. Sadly, I'm too busy with my commitments at Sudeley Castle. Pity because I'd have loved to have gone."

"That is a shame. But do not worry, my personal falconer will take them out instead. Stephen Frank is a very good and experienced falconer; the birds will be in safe hands."

"Stephen, really? I know Stephen, we're friends. That's good. What about the export stuff?"

"Do not worry about that side."

"But you'll need export licences."

"No, I do not think so."

"OK, but I think you'll find that …"

"The birds will have diplomatic immunity and so will not require the licences you speak of. Please do not be concerned."

And so it was that, come the day, Joy and I travelled up to Al Fayed's offices on Park Lane in London to pick up the money. Several floors above the hustle of the street where salesmen sold Aston Martins to people who stayed

78

at hotels like the Dorchester, we were ushered into a seriously plush office suite. Al-Fayed himself did not make an appearance but even his assistant was wearing six hundred pounds worth of threads.

"Your cheque, Mr Cope. That is to cover the cost of the two birds and your designs for the aviaries. Mr Frank should be collecting the birds in about a week but, I believe, he will liaise with you in the interim. Mr Al-Fayed would like me to convey his best wishes and his thanks for your assistance in this matter."

It was a long time since Joy and I had seen that much money; we were delighted. Shooting into the first Lloyds that we could find, we banked the cheque before anyone could change their mind. Ridiculous maybe, but we were young and naïve.

Stephen turned up at The Bothy some two weeks later with a pair of expensive travel boxes for the Harris hawks, stayed a couple of nights and flew off to Brunei with the pair. Apparently, all went according to plan and he had an excellent sojourn in Thailand. We didn't begrudge him his jaunt – for once, Joy and I were cash rich. And it all stemmed from a little reporter in a pork pie hat who just happened to genuinely know Mohamed Al-Fayed. One never knows where life may lead.

Back at Winchcombe, the media requests were still rolling. The latest in line was the Illustrated London News.

"They want to run a centre spread on the falconry at Sudeley Castle," said Julie. You up for it?"

"Yes, of course, the more the merrier."

"Oh, and they're thinking of sticking you on the front cover."

"Fame at last!"

A lovely lady reporter and her photographer spent a whole weekend at Winchcombe. At the time, we'd started flying falcons at partridge and the photographer was determined to get some action shots. I had two really good cracking little tiercels which were veritable demons and he faced a tough challenge to get them on camera. We did catch a few partridge but he never quite managed to pick up a kill. During the course of the weekend, he shot 24 rolls of film and although he missed the coup de grace, he still managed to get some lovely images.

One particularly beautiful photograph stood out from the set. A big ball of orange sun was setting in a big red sky over Sudeley Hill and there was I flying a falcon in silhouette. The photographer's timing had been perfect, catching the falcon streaking past the lure at full stretch.

Four of his pictures made it to the double-page spread and the reporter crafted an excellent piece to complement the images. But my glorious silhouette never made it to the front cover as I was totally upstaged by Princess Diana. One might call it a variation on the divine right of kings but at least we made to the middle where it falls open naturally. And a lot of people saw that spread.

Photography, of course, was not limited to the press. Most of the people who came to watch the displays and attend the falconry courses came with that all important visual recorder, the camera. The cameras came in all shapes and sizes but the lenses seemed to be getting longer and longer.

One display was attended by over 300 people, most of whom were duly armed with standard issue photographic equipment. But standing on the front line was one chap bearing a very large camera with an extraordinarily long lens attached.

'That's bloody ridiculous,' I thought as I went through my spiel. 'Get it out of my face!'

It was almost intrusive and certainly distracting but, being always polite, I said nothing aloud. The show must go on and the audience were paying my wages. The talking finished, I put the falcon on the wing and watched her wander around the sky for a while. After a few moments, she started to circle downwards until she was more or less head height. At which point she calmly flew towards Mr Big Photographer, alighted gently on his lens – and muted copiously over the barrel. The crowd erupted with laughter while he turned a fiery shade of deep red embarrassment.

But he wasn't the only onlooker to suffer the attentions of an avian kind. At another display shortly afterwards, I noticed a rather elegant, well dressed lady sporting a type

80

of hairstyle that was fashionable in the 60s called, if I remember, a beehive. Audrey Hepburn had one and so did Mandy Rice Davies who was involved in the notorious Profumo affair. Somehow, the fashion had bouffed on through the next couple of decades and this was a prime example. Although the lady wasn't especially tall, her barnet positively towered over the heads of the crowd.

Morgan was flying superbly and I was enjoying her flights so much that I overcooked it and pushed her just that little bit too far. It happened sometimes. Exhausted from one too many passes at the lure, Morgan decided that she'd had enough. But instead of pitching up in the old oak tree, as most of the falcons did, she swung around the audience and landed squarely on Madame's beehive. And promptly sank, disappearing into the depths of the blown coiffed hair. Only Morgan's head protruded above the lacquered hairline.

Madame Bee was screaming, stamping her feet, waving her arms and generally going totally apeshit. The crowd was in stitches, many bent double with the extremes of their laughter. Which of course added to Madame's embarrassment and overall discomfiture. Morgan just looked rather confused for a while, stomping around in the strange nest in which she'd landed. Finally, she crashed her way through the cover in a similar way to an attack helicopter crashing through the branches when leaving a small wooded landing zone. The beehive was a total ruin and Madame was not a happy bunny. In fact, she was livid.

Unperturbed by all the noise, Morgan came immediately and obediently to the lure, hopped onto my offered glove and pulled happily on the piece of pickup meat. Her behaviour did little abate Madame's wrath and distress.

"That horrible, horrible bird. It's dangerous that's what it is, bloody dangerous."

"Look, I'm terribly ..."

"Look at what its done to my hair. I only had it done yesterday."

She snatched angrily at a wayward tendril that had fallen across her face. New gales of laughter erupted from the crowd.

"It's not funny!" she shouted, swivelling from side to side as she tried to identify the main culprits.

"Look, I'm terribly sorry, this type of thing doesn't normally happen."

"Well it has, to me!"

"I really am sorry."

Putting one hand to the side of her ruined hair, she gave me a murderous look, turned on her heel and marched through the still laughing mass of people. Although even I had to grin slightly, remembering the sight of Morgan's little head bobbing over the beehive, having to apologise in public does not make for good press. On the other hand, they do say that even bad press is better than no press.

Chapter 9 – It's not about killing

"Good piece and some damn fine photos," said Lord Ashcombe, waving an open copy of the Illustrated London News through the fog of cigarette smoke. "Can't do us any harm, can it Gary? I think it's time that we made this partridge hawking a bit more commercial."

"Absolutely."

"Right. I'll make some enquiries. First thing we need to do is to get someone in who knows about game and cover crops. I think Chris Minchin might be our man. Lovely chap and happens to head up the Game Conservancy."

As ever, Lord Ashcombe did everything extremely properly. And he invariably had the necessary contacts.

"I would plant some mustard over there, and some roots perhaps," said Minchin as we wandered around the estate. "Camelina sativa. Sorry, you probably know that as gold-of-pleasure. That's good. Kale would provide with good cover that'll last for, oh, a couple of years but I'd add some quinoa to break it up a little. There's a lot of high protein for the birds in quinoa."

We duly discussed our lessons in agriculture and game conservancy with the estate's tenant farmers. In turn, they talked about crop rotation, fallow fields and finance. But decisions were taken and we jointly agreed which crops were to be planted. Release pens were purchased, poults installed and the commercial partridge hawking project was powering ahead.

My relatively newly hired aide-de-camp, Rob, who helped me out with the birds, acquired the additional title of gamekeeper. Delegation being an important aspect of people management, it was his job to look after the game.

At the time, I was flying two tiercels. One was Brock, a beautiful tiny falcon who flew at a mere one pound, three ounces. Black as soot, he was a cobby little bird but he certainly could fly. The first time that I took him off the creance, he rang up to a pitch of over 600 feet and I genuinely thought he would keep going until he disappeared. He was the high flyer of the two, reaching heights beyond the sight of a human eye and the like of which I have not seen since.

The other was called Byron, which was short for Screaming Lord Byron; so called because – he screamed a lot! Pulling rank once again, I delegated his training to Rob.

Both falcons quickly learned their new trade and were soon catching partridge quite well.

One early October afternoon, Rob and I were at The Bothy preparing to do a little hawking of our own. So far, we'd had no customers for our new project but practice makes perfect and it pays to be ready. Accordingly, the falcons were sitting on their cadge in the kitchen and the dogs were ready and waiting. And we were just finishing our cups of coffee when three visitors appeared unannounced. (Why do people always pop up uninvited in my kitchen? That's a rhetorical question.)

"Good afternoon. By the looks of it, I'm in the right place."

Clasping his hands across a portly stomach only just constrained by the buttons on his sparkling new tweed jacket, he smiled at us both beatifically.

"Martin Furdon-Smythe. You might have heard of me. I own Fenridge Court Hotel."

It seemed vaguely familiar: a large country hotel that had recently been refurbished for vast sum of money in expense-account taste, surrounded by parkland.

"It rings bells."

"And these," he continued, waving one large fat hand at the youngsters at his side, "are my personal professional falconers".

"What can we do for you?"

"Marvellous pair of falcons you have there, on the cadge. They look as though they're raring to go."

Actually Brock and Byron were hooded and barely moving a feather.

"They're pretty fit. As I said, how can we help?"

"Yes, well. I heard that you're doing a spot of partridge hawking down here, which sounded rather interesting. So, I thought that I'd bring my falconers down with our birds

84

and take a look. I wondered if we could come out with you this afternoon."

"Not a chance, I'm afraid, you'll have to make an appointment and come back. I suggest that you phone the Estate Office at Sudeley Castle. Everything has to go through them."

"Right. No chance this afternoon then?"

"No."

Mr Furdon-Smythe and retinue were eased though the doorway as we picked up the cadge and walked purposefully towards them. A few minutes later they drove off in their Range Rover, while we walked out for our private bit of hawking. We caught a brace or two in their absence.

"Gary? I've just had a call from a Mr Furdon-Smythe. Said he popped over to The Bothy a couple of days ago," said Julie. "He'd like to hire some partridge hawking. I assume that's fine with you?"

"Yeah, I remember the guy. Go ahead."

Weather checked and arrangements made, the Castle took a healthy sum from our sporting hotel owner and the deal was done. The following Monday morning, the showroom green gleam Range Rover turned up at The Bothy, disgorging Furdon-Smythe, two personal professional falconers, one lanneret and one peregrine tiercel. And no dogs.

"Mr Cope. Good to see you again. I didn't get the chance to introduce my falconers last time. This is Suzie," he said waving at the young girl by his side, "and this is Alan," he added, indicating an equally young man. "I'll leave you to it then."

Climbing back into the Range Rover, he then drove off down the track while I did the falconer's version of speed-dating. I shook each by his and her free hands respectively and looked at the pair of falcons on their fists. The lanneret would find partridge hawking tough going but maybe the tiercel would have a chance.

"Has the lanneret been entered?"

"She's had a few flights at game."

"Caught anything?"

"Um, no. But she had a good try at a magpie," Alan added defensively.

"What about the tiercel?"

Suzie ran her ungloved fingers through fashion advert-glossy brunette hair and shiny brown-eyed the falcon.

"No, she's untried. But she works well with the lure and I think she's got it in her to be a star."

'Great,' I thought, 'I've got two wannabe falconers, one bird that's a no-hoper and the other's a maybe.'

But they were paying good money for this and they were also our first clients. I sighed.

"Look, to increase your chances, Rob and I will go out with you and I'll bring my dog. You can use Bracken to flush the partridge. So, let's go out and see how it goes."

If they'd tied the falcons to rocks on the ground and hooded them both, they'd have had a better chance. Putting it more politely, we were out partridge hawking and their birds were crap! Covey after covey was flushed, partridge burst through the air like broken pillows in flight but the falcons were not waiting on, stooped half-heartedly or too late and missed every one.

By day three, Suzie and Alan were getting just a little bit annoyed. I wasn't sure whether they were annoyed with themselves, the birds or both. They might even have been blaming the partridge for being too sneaky because they started to insist that we re-flushed the coveys. They insisted that we re-flushed the partridge!

Rob and I shared a common philosophy and it is one that I'll follow as long as I fly falcons at game. If, when you flush a covey of grouse, partridge, pheasant or whatever, the falcon zaps down and nails one that is absolutely brilliant and fine. If not, you don't hound the game because that's not falconry. Frankly, you don't need a falcon to catch a partridge. By constantly re-flushing it with a spaniel or similar, the partridge becomes so exhausted that it loses all of its strength. Once that point is reached, you could pick it up with your bare hands and wring the poor thing's neck. In other words, it's just not done.

But it was clear that what Alan and Suzie wanted was to kill something. And after four days of fruitless hawking, Rob and I had probably joined their hit list along with the partridge. To a degree, the feeling was mutual although, in hindsight, they were probably desperate to impress their boss who was paying their wages. It was pretty obvious that we weren't getting along with these two young falconers. And it finally came to a head while we were out in the field.

"Look, flush the partridge again. That's what we want, and that's what you're being paid for!"

"Stuff you! If your birds aren't good enough to catch a bird on the first stoop, then too bad."

They stormed back in the direction of The Bothy and left. The following morning, I received a phone call from Furdon-Smythe.

"Your behaviour was unwarranted and unprofessional, and the so-called partridge hawking, a waste of time and money. This is totally unsatisfactory and I demand an immediate meeting to discuss the matter."

The meeting was convened at The Bothy the day after. Those in attendance: Mr Furdon-Smythe (nouveau riche hotelier); Suzie and Alan (falconers-in-waiting); Rob and myself. Eventually, Lord Ashcombe arrived to complete the dictated quorum. Once all parties were there gathered and present, Furdon-Smythe stated his case directly to Lord Ashcombe, totally ignoring everyone else in the room. He neither referred to his falconers for detail not asked Rob or I for explanation; we had suddenly become invisible. And that really annoyed me for a moment.

"The bottom line is, Lord Ashcombe, that I paid you a large fee to kill some partridge," said Furdon-Smythe in conclusion. "In my business, I expect a return on an investment, as I'm sure you do yourself. From my point of view, I'm seriously out of pocket and not a blasted partridge in sight!"

Lord Ashcombe had been sitting quietly in his chair, listening attentively throughout the diatribe. While he calmly blew streams of smoke into the air, I was becoming more and more uncomfortable. The partridge hawking was our first go at running a proper commercial project and it was all going terribly wrong. A pregnant silence filled the room as Lord Ashcombe ground the stub of his most recent Marlboro into the ashtray.

"You haven't paid to come here and kill partridge, you've paid to hawk them. And there's a huge difference. Clearly that is a distinction that you do not appreciate. Therefore, I suggest that we give you your money back and you can – kill – partridge elsewhere."

I felt like punching the air, saying: "Yes!" But instead, heaved a huge inward sigh of relief. Lord Ashcombe was nothing short of brilliant. Principles need to be upheld in all things; falconry is a sport and it's not about killing things. Furdon-Smythe and his minions were rank amateurs who viewed falcons as status symbols and a kill as success. It was not Rob's way of thinking, nor mine or Lord Ashcombe's. His support was really uplifting, especially since a substantial amount of money was involved. But it was all paid back and life returned to normal.

Rob had become an important part of the team at The Bothy and we worked well together. A good falconer in his own right, he knew how to take care of the birds and get the best out of them in the field. As far as it is possible to build relationships with birds of prey, Rob had few problems but, as the saying goes, it takes two to tango.

At a time when Harris hawks were beginning to take up airspace in the world of falconry, I acquired a young male from a guy called John Campbell who lived in Shropshire. Although an unknown quantity at the start, Gizmo proved to be a good hunter, very obedient and generally well behaved - until Rob appeared in his sights.

It was a perfectly ordinary day: perhaps a little overcast with a light breeze but nothing untoward. I'd cast Gizmo off to potter round the sky and follow our ground level perambulation. After a while, Gizmo decided to perch on a branch in a tree ahead and wait for us to catch up. He watched and waited until we'd passed the tree before launching his attack. Flying along a well-planned trajectory to the optimum killing point, Gizmo closed his claws in avian fists and hit Rob's head hard in a perfect passing

88

double punch, before flying gleefully onwards. Rob fell forward with a cry of pain while I doubled up with laughter.

"Fucking hell, Gary! It's not funny. That hurt."

He touched the back of his head gingerly and then looked at his blooded fingers.

"Gizmo's just keen," I remarked, still laughing.

It never fails to amaze me how intelligent Harris hawks are and how quickly they learn. The next time we were out with Gizmo, Rob took the precaution of wearing a cap. As soon as Gizmo took a stance in a tree, his eyes would lock on to the bird and he readied himself to take evasive action. The problem is that Harris hawks frequently perch in trees and Gizmo was no exception. But this time, he repeated the fly-and-perch routine until he caught Rob off guard. And nailed him again.

Although a certain amount of separation was possible, unfortunately the pair had to work together as Gizmo was frequently the bird of choice for falconry courses and hawking walks. On one particular afternoon, we were due to set off with a fairly large group but Rob hadn't arrived. A few minutes went by before a figure appeared wearing one of my long coats, a large hat that shadowed the top half of his face and a scarf that covered the remainder. Perfect camouflage.

"Sorry I'm late," said the muffled voice.

"Interesting disguise," I commented.

He buried himself in the centre of the group, maintaining his position carefully as we moved along the path. Gizmo chose a high branch on a tall oak tree as the launch point for his ambush. One by one, the members of the group walked by without hindrance and then it was Rob's turn. And Gizmo struck with unerring accuracy and full force. Whatever he did and however he dressed, there was no way that Rob could evade Gizmo's premeditated attacks. For some bizarre reason, the bird simply hated him and could pick him out every time. And the feeling became mutual.

As the breeding project took a higher profile, Gizmo's malevolent shadow began to fade as Rob's mind changed focus. Whitehead's sakers had been installed and we were waiting for them to come on but before they became active I got a call from John Anderson in Riyadh.

"You picked up a lanneret and a female lugger from Martin Jones a while back."

"Yeah, Morgan and Fay, they're great little birds. Why?"

"It's just that I've got their parents with Martin at the moment. Obviously they're proven breeders and I thought they might be useful before you started with the sakers. And it would help Martin out if you could have the pair at The Bothy anyway. You interested?"

"Yeah well, brilliant."

"They usually produce three or four chicks out of a couple of clutches."

It was excellent news. Since I had no experience at all of breeding, having a proven pair would give me the opportunity to cut my teeth. Rob and I ploughed through the Cornell papers with renewed vigour. The birds were installed and neither of us knew anything about breeding. Suffice it to say that we both spent long hours reading and rereading.

According to Martin, they normally laid their eggs in late February through early March and this time they were early. When the first clutch arrived, we quickly transferred them to the incubator and waited with a mix of emotions. Hammer blows of trepidation tempered my excitement and I was petrified that it might all go wrong. This was the acid test: if I couldn't breed from a proven pair, the whole project would collapse. The eggs would usually pip at between 28 and 30 days, but when we got to the 26th day of the incubation period, I started to panic. Glasier's words on what makes a falconer now had a challenging adjunct that rang loud in my ears.

"You're not a falconer, boy, until you've caught something, and you're not an aviculturist till you've bred something."

"And you couldn't breed a rabbit in a horny warren," added the black imp on my shoulder. "Wait all you like.

Won't make difference. They won't hatch and you're blown out of the water again. Because you're crap!"

The incubators had been set up in The Bothy's large loft and, since I'd decided that the eggs needed watching round the clock, we added a camp bed to make life more comfortable. Sometimes, lying on the camp bed, I'd stare for hours willing the eggs to hatch. Unfortunately, we shared the loft with a large community of great big horrible spiders. Invariably, there would be one that silently descended from a crossbeam on a slender silken thread. It would then make its landing on a vulnerable part of one's anatomy and start to explore. Or one would scare the shit out of me by suddenly appearing in front of my nose and wriggling in that horrible way that spiders have. It will come as no surprise that I'm terrified of spiders, and hate them accordingly, but the eggs took precedence over fear.

Rob and I would sit there late into the night, drinking coffee, smoking cigarettes and poring over Cornell's literature. We'd have little discussions and arguments on the finer points of candling or feeding. Our dedication was total and we maintained our vigil over the incubators 24/7, changing shifts seamlessly; hour after hour, day after day. Surely we deserved success.

And then I spotted one tiny bump on the smooth surface of an egg, and saw a little crack appear. The first egg pipped, a second, a third and a fourth. Four eggs from clutch of four; all of the eggs from our first clutch had hatched. It was a monumental moment. When the second clutch pipped, eight out of eight hatched. It was fabulous success and I was over the moon.

"Bloody hell, I've done it. We've done it," I hissed at Rob in delight. "We've bred birds of prey!"

Suddenly, I didn't feel a fraud and the imp on my shoulder had vanished in the flush of achievement. All the investment in The Bothy, the development of the aviaries and all the hard work took on a new meaning and promise. It didn't matter that lanner lugger hybrids had no particular value in the Arab market and that birds such as these were given to children to amuse them. Our first attempt at breeding at been 100 per cent successful and it augured well for the future.

"Well done, Gary. Outstanding," said Lord Ashcombe as he admired the chicks.

He was clearly delighted and I was finding it hard not to cartwheel around the room, shouting: 'Yeah, I've done it! Bloody good, eh?' Restraining myself, I kept calm and nonchalant.

"No big deal really. Of course, it was extremely useful having Rob to share the load."

(Rob had been brilliantly supportive. He'd been there from the beginning to the end and had made a tough journey that much easier.)

"It's always easier if there are two of you when the eggs are incubating."

(I never did tell Lord Ashcombe that I'd been a breeding virgin beforehand.)

"It all went according to plan. But naturally I'm pleased that our first attempt at The Bothy has been so productive."

In due course, all the birds were sold. The practice run had worked so much better than I'd expected and my confidence was high as I looked forward to breeding the sakers.

Chapter 10 – The impatient patient

One has to amuse oneself occasionally; you can't work all the time and nor can you hurry a breeding season. Nor can you always be in your employer's good books.

Somehow I'd added a female Finnish goshawk to the family and, with my usual incisive wit, called her, Gos. To use the appropriate cliché, goshawks are killing machines with few brains. Once trained and entered, she was murdering rabbits with speed and efficiency. In fact, she was a pretty good bird but shared all the normal traits of goshawks: she was barking mad and looked criminally insane.

One misty afternoon in late October, I took her up to Cleeve Hill where I had permission to hunt bunnies. At 1,083 feet Cleeve Hill is the highest point in the Cotswold range and usually commands a magnificent view of the surrounding countryside. On that particular day, one could barely see the edge of the limestone escarpment let alone the countryside below. However, I was looking for short, hard-hitting flights and dinner.

When the bountiful warrens provided the opportunity, I slipped Gos who immediately gave chase, missed the lucky rabbit and, without changing course one iota, disappeared into the mist. Gos was gone. As she hated having a transmitter fitted, unusually for me, I tended to give her dispensation. I searched all afternoon but without the aid of telemetry, I was looking for a needle in haystack. As ever with the lost bird scenario, you don't give up but after two days of scouring field and wood, there was still no sign. As I booted and spurred for a third day's foray, the phone rang.

"Gary. Have you lost your goshawk?"

The voice sounded none too cheerful.

"Yes, Lord Ashcombe, I have."

"Well the bird's up here."

"Where's here?"

"I'm at Charlton Abbotts. Damned bird has totally ruined the shoot. Come and get it, now."

"Yes, Lord Ashcombe. I'm on my way."

Since Lord Ashcombe was a neighbour, he'd naturally been invited to join the shoot. Apparently the guns had all been at their pegs, the beaters were driving the pheasant from the coverts and what had flown down the line? Gos! A goshawk on a drive is definitely not beneficial. With an aerial killer on the loose, the pheasants froze with fear, hunkered down in the coverts and refused to budge.

By the time I arrived, the shoot had moved on, leaving one rather surly under-keeper to point me in the right direction. Having told me the new locations of beaters and guns, he stomped off leaving me to wander around, luring inanely.

"Oh Go-os. Come on Gos. Come on Gos."

The sound of jangling bells broke into my calls and seemed to come from the depths of a densely wooded copse. As my hearing zoned in, the noise blipped on my mental radar, coming ever closer as I worked my way through the trees. The bells jangled again and there she was, a pale apparition looking down with glaring orange eyes from a branch some 12 feet above my head. Stepping slowly backwards, I threw out the lure and called.

"Come on Gos."

She stared at the lure, then stared at me and blinked.

"Bollocks to that," she seemed to say.

Gos flew off and away. That was the last time I saw her, leaving me mortified by the whole episode. It left me feeling more than a little sick. But that paled into insignificance by the way I felt when the next breeding season got under way.

A clutch of lanner lugger eggs were slowly cooking in an incubator and the sakers were on the brink of breeding. March was going to be a busy month. And I woke up one morning at around six o'clock with a serious pain in my chest. My first reaction was to blame the previous night's rabbit stew. It felt like a case of severe indigestion with a ball of pain cramping and burning at the centre of my chest. Pulling myself off the pillow, I bent forward in an attempt to relieve the discomfort, only to have a broadsword of agony rip through my chest and take my very breath away.

94

Trying to lie down again only made it worse. Suddenly I couldn't breathe and was gasping for breath like a fish out of water. It was truly terrible. Sitting upright once more, I found that it helped if I turned to the right. It required quite an effort to nudge Joy awake.

"'oy, way up, eugh. Way up! Eugh."

"Gary! What's wrong? What's wrong?"

"Eugh got 'is terrible pain in, eugh, my chest. Can't, eugh, breathe."

It was difficult to get the words out and each sentence was punctuated by a rasping groan at each stertorous intake of breath. In a nanosecond she was wide awake and sparking. She knew me well enough to know there was a problem.

"What's going on?"

"I think, eugh, might be having a heart attack."

She was out of the bed and down the stairs like a greyhound from the slips. I could hear the curses and the flurry of pages as she struggled to find Dr Cummings' telephone number.

"Urgent … Yes, he thinks he might be having a heart attack … Pain in his chest and he's gasping for breath … Thank you doctor."

Cummings arrived within minutes, came straight up to the bedroom and immediately got to work. The chill of the stethoscope on my skin was unpleasant and somehow almost morbid.

"Breathe in."

"Eueugh."

I definitely sounded sick.

"And out."

"Neugh." A much weaker sound, like a dying mouse's sigh. "Am I having a heart attack, eugh, Doctor?"

He looked at me dispassionately.

"No, Mr Cope. You've sustained a spontaneous pneumothorax. It's quite interesting actually. Essentially, a tear in the wall of the lung has released the air which is now trapped. I suppose one might compare it to a punctured balloon except the air has nowhere to go."

"Smoking?"

Dr Cummings firmly believed that smoking was the root of all medical ailments. If you went to see him with a broken toe or a sore arm, he would tell you that smoking was to blame.

"Actually, no. Smokers are slightly more at risk than non-smokers but perfectly healthy people, often young people, develop a spontaneous pneumothorax. It quite often strikes fit athletes and tall, thin people."

"What can you do for it?"

"We need to get you to a hospital."

"I can't go to a-eugh bloody hospital. I've got eggs in the incubator and work to-eugh, do."

"You need to go to a hospital," he said, slowly and firmly enunciating each word as though speaking to a child.

"Eugh, 'm I going to die?"

"No, you won't die, as long as you do what I tell you to do. If you don't, then you will die."

"Fuck it!"

He called for an ambulance. The response by the South Western Ambulance Service was amazingly quick, but the two paramedics might have been kin to the Chuckle brothers.

The Bothy had wonderful wooden staircase that climbed its way upwards in staged rectangles. Every few steps led to a quarter landing that bore round to the right, leading on to the next set of steps. And it wasn't that wide.

"It's not going to go, Charlie."

"Take it up vertically."

"Yeah, but we're not going to get it down again with him on it, are we?"

"No, 'spose not."

Two minutes later, they're in the bedroom.

"Mr Cope, can you hear me? We can't get the stretcher up the stairs so we're going to have to carry you down manually. And then we'll put you on the stretcher in your hallway. Do you understand?"

Of course, I bloody understood! I might have been in pain but I hadn't lost my hearing.

"OK, not a problem," I wheezed.

Locking fingers, the paramedics formed a cradle of arms; two under my thighs and two behind my back. As soon as they took the strain, an explosion of pain ripped through my chest and it felt as though my heart was going to burst through the bone. What I didn't know was that one lung had totally collapsed and was pressing on my heart. Any movement was excruciating.

"Down, euargh! Put me down."

"We've got to get you to the stretcher, Mr Cope."

"Doan-eurgh worry. I'll fucking crawl."

Somehow I found a position that was fractionally more comfortable. By turning on one side, I suppose that my heart flopped away from my heart and slightly eased the pressure. And somehow, I managed to crawl and bump my way down the stairs, stopping at each quarter landing to drag in a few agonising breaths of air. The journey down to the wide hallway seemed to take a lifetime but probably took less than five minutes. By the time the paramedics rolled me onto the stretcher at the bottom, I was drained of every ounce of energy. As they carried me out through the open door, Rob's concerned face loomed into view like the moon on a dark night.

"Rob-eaurgh, 'ook after th'eggs. Euargh. Look after the eggs 'n sort out the heu-incubators, whatever you do."

"Don't worry, Gaz, it'll be sorted. Don't worry."

Thanks to Joy, it seemed as though everyone was suddenly there, simultaneously looking strong and worried. Joy touched my arm as the paramedics stretchered me into the ambulance. My lovely sister-in-law, Ali, another stalwart assistant who'd been there on all the early falconry shows, was smiling fondly and once again giving support. And Rob, who'd stuck with me through the highs and lows of breeding the hybrids, had also managed to get up at that unholy hour.

They all disappeared as the doors of the ambulance closed and somebody pushed a rubber mask over my face. And I immediately went into panic mode. Back in the old days, dentists anaesthetized their victims with gas, fed through a tube into the mask that covered both noise and mouth. I was given gas for the first, and only, time when I was about six and almost went into convulsions. Nobody knew that I was allergic to the stuff. I was really quite ill and vomited my way through the following three weeks. Now I had a mask on my face again, hear the hiss of the gas and feel its cool breath on my skin. It was as though I'd been transported back to the dentist's chair under the bright lights and the stare of waiting black eyes.

"What kind of birds do you breed then?" the guy was asking.

"Get the bloody mask off, for Christ's sake, get the mask off." I flapped one hand across the mask in a feeble attempt to remove the hateful thing.

The paramedic easily grabbed my hand and held it gently but firmly by my side. "It's oxygen. You need it to breathe."

"No I don't, I don't."

"Yes, you do. Don't worry mate, you'll be all right. Just try to relax and breathe slowly. You'll be fine."

Cheltenham General Hospital welcomed me with an x-ray that confirmed the spontaneous pneumothorax and the collapsed lung. I was transferred from a gurney into a bed where they pumped me full of drugs and I was out for a full 24 hours. When I woke up the following morning, a large tube protruded from my side which was draining fluids into a plastic sac. Tubes of one sort or another seemed to be everywhere, attached to a variety of bottles and machines. And all attached to me. Needless to say, I was feeling very poorly.

I spent the next 10 days very slowly recuperating but getting grumpier by the moment. Every morning, at precisely seven o'clock, I'd be woken up by a voice telling me that she had my tea. Why do they insist in waking you up at seven in the morning?

"Mr Cope. Mr Cope? I've got a nice cup of tea for you."

(And it's always in that singsong voice that compounds the irritation.)

"What time is it?"

"Seven o'clock."

"Why are you waking me up at seven o'clock?"

"Because it's time for your tea."

(Irrefutable logic.)

"Go away. It's too early to wake up. It's a bloody hospital, for God's sake and there's bugger all to do all day. Go away and let me sleep!"

In the end, they left the tea on the bedside table and quietly crept away. But even the nights weren't always undisturbed. There are often strange sounds on a general ward at night and my next-door neighbour invariably added his notes to the unholy symphony. He looked for all the world like a tramp. He stank like a sewer, used a handkerchief that had become as hard as cardboard through lack of washing and snored like a Gloucester Old Spot pig in a sty. A frequent sleepwalker, one night he decided to take a stroll in my direction, fell on top of my bed and started to pull on my various tubes. But the days were worse.

The days drag out endlessly when you're in hospital, broken only by meals, doctors' rounds and nurses doling out medications. Joy brought in all of my falconry books, so at least I had something to read and, during designated times only, I did have a healthy stream of visitors. Joy, Mum and Dad, Ali and Lord Ashcombe all came in at one time or another. Rob assured me that everything was going well and that the eggs were fine. But I asked the doctors the same question every day.

"When can I get out of here? When can I go home?"

By the eleventh day, I think they were singing a similar tune with slightly altered lyrics.

"Cope really is a pain in the arse. When can we get rid of him?"

On that eleventh day, at about the eleventh hour, my bed was surrounded by a pack of student doctors, one of whom drew the curtains to seal off the area. Enter the Consultant, stage left. It was like a scene from the film Doctor at Large. With the neatly trimmed beard, curled moustache and portly girth, the Consultant even looked like Sir Lancelot Spratt, as played by James Robertson Justice.

"Right Mr Cope, you'll be pleased to know that we're going to remove your drain today. Gather round and pay attention. Nichols, I think you're the man for the job."

Sir Lancelot briefly reminded Student Doctor Nichols of the procedure involved and asked the pretty blonde Student Doctor Dobbs to assist as necessary.

"Any questions? Right, Nichols, proceed."

Dr Nichols grasped the tube and simply pulled it out with a quiet – pop. And farce morphed into catastrophe. Removing the tube immediately broke the vacuum and air rushed into the cavity with the force of a suction pump.

"Stick your finger in it!" shouted the Consultant. "Stick your bloody finger in, Dobbs."

Apparently, the stitches around the hole should have been tightened at the same time as the draining tube was slowly removed. In that way, the hole would have been neatly closed as the final millimetres of the pipe made their exit. Instead, the pipe had simply been yanked out. And the Consultant went spare.

"Don't move a muscle, Dobbs. Keep your finger in the cavity. Simpson, sew the sutures around Dobbs' finger and move inwards."

So I'm lying there, silently praying, with a young girl's finger stuck into one of my lungs while a young man is attempting cross stitch around her delicate digit. It was an absolute nightmare. I could feel the finger slowly ease its way out and finally it was done. I could breathe again.

"I'm afraid you'll have a bit of a scar there, Mr Cope, and we'll have to keep you in for a few more days. Bit of a hiccup, that's all, but then you'll be right as rain. Good morning."

I was livid. As I understood the programme, once the drain was removed, I could be discharged. Now I was facing several more days in the madhouse. They'd fucked up and I was paying the price. I fumed my way through four more days.

"You should take things fairly easy for a week or two, Mr Cope," said the nurse. "You can leave when you're ready."

"About bloody time!"

And off I stomped with Joy to the car. As it turned out, I'd been released only a few days before our second set of eggs were due to hatch.

100

Shortly after I returned to The Bothy, I received a visit from Lord Ashcombe. "Gary, you need a holiday."

'Yeah right,' I thought, 'I'm just out of hospital, totally broke without a penny in the bank and basically just managing to survive. Never mind, I'll pop off somewhere nice and enjoy. In another lifetime!'

"I'm really eager to get stuck back in to work, Lord Ashcombe. I want to get these eggs hatched and ..."

"All of which is fine and you can take a holiday once the eggs have hatched. Now, where would you and Joy like to go?"

It suddenly dawned on me that this wonderful man was offering to pay for us to go on holiday. Turkey sprang to mind. In the mid-80s Turkey was not the commercial destination that it is today; it was a place of exotic adventure where history and banditry lived side by side.

"I think Turkey would be an exciting place to visit."

"Consider it done, Gary. Once you're ready to travel, the pair of you can go off to Turkey and I'll pay for the trip."

I was ecstatic and thanked Lord Ashcombe profusely for his kindness and generosity.

But first I needed to focus on incubators and eggs. March that year was bitterly cold and, on this particular day, the wind was a howling banshee that blew the snow in horizontal icy knives. Cheltenham races had been on and we were watching excerpted replays on television while keeping a weather eye on the incubators. This time we'd brought them downstairs.

We didn't panic when the power went off. I simply shot upstairs, grabbed an armful of blankets and pushed them into the spaces between the incubators.

"That should keep the heat in them until the power comes back," said Rob as he arranged the last of the blankets.

"Yeah, but we're getting so many of these power cuts. I think we really need to consider getting a generator."

After about half an hour, the temperature gauges were dropping dramatically.

"Bugger, this isn't good. We need to get some heat in here."

Despite stoking up the wood burner to generate more heat, it still wasn't enough to raise the temperature to the right degree in the incubators. There was no option.

"I'm going to have to incubate the eggs myself."

"You've got to be joking."

"No, I'm serious it's the only way."

Having cranked up the heat in the room as high as possible, I put on a baggy shirt and made myself comfortable on the green Chesterfield.

"OK, start passing me the eggs. It should only be for an hour or so."

I very delicately placed each of the eggs next to my body underneath the shirt and settled gently down to incubate. Half an hour went past, then an hour and another. Every so often, I turned the eggs as a real falcon would do and sat there.

"What else can we do?" I asked, looking at Rob's concerned expression. "I've got to keep these bloody eggs warm."

"Yeah, I know."

"Everything's resting on this, Rob."

We were total prisoners and the hours ticked on and on. Rob stoked the fire at times to keep the ambient temperature up while I sat almost motionless on the Chesterfield with a shirt full of eggs. Four hours, five hours, six hours. And finally the power returned. We brought the incubators up to the required temperature, replaced the eggs and hoped.

"If those eggs hatch it'll be a flaming miracle!"
But by Christ, they did. Every single one of those eggs hatched safely and I'd actually incubated them myself. Leaving the chicks in Rob's capable hands, Joy and I flew to Turkey, hired a car and drove right through the centre of the country.

In the Golden Age of the Ottoman Empire, falconry was a passion at the court of Süleyman the Magnificent. Falconers were held in high regard, sparrowhawks ruled the skies and quail were their prey. But that was back in the 16th century. By the time I arrived in Turkey, the sport was on the verge of being banned and hunting was done with a gun.

No matter, it was an extraordinary adventure that took us from the Mediterranean coast, through the interior and up to the Black Sea. I returned to The Bothy refreshed to find that all was well, I had two good tiercels and another season of partridge hawking was about to start.

Chapter 11 – Poachers and Partridge

The soft silver light of the full moon shone in the clear night sky, showing the way for those bent on catching unwary prey for the pot. Many's the time when a poacher's moon was witness to such successful rural villainy. But this particular evening was better suited to Gloucestershire poachers who were not so well acquainted with the poetic rules of the game.

Whether gibbous or full, any sight of the moon was hidden behind lowering clouds which leaked constant rain, blown by a steady wind. In fact, it was so foul that I'd brought the dogs inside rather than leaving them out in their kennels. Having been curled up in close proximity to the stove, the dogs were suddenly alert and up on their feet.

'That's a bit weird,' I thought.

Not wanting to mooch around outside in the wet and the cold with a torch, I went up to the bedroom which overlooked the walled garden. Peering though the rain speckled window, I could see the beams of two flashlights cutting lines through the darkness.

"Shit, someone's stealing the falcons!"

I watched carefully for a couple more seconds before I realised that they were nowhere near the falcons; the lights were coming from around the holding pens.

"Bloody poachers! They're after the poults."

In fact there were probably around 200 partridge and 50 pheasant poults out there! Dashing downstairs, I brought the dogs to heel and made for the back door next to which was a small gateway that led into the walled garden. Flipping the switch on the wall by the door that operated the floodlights, I rushed out and through the gateway.

"Right, you bastards."

And released the dogs who shot off like bullets, baying like the hounds of hell. The garden was bathed in blinding white light and there, standing in the holding pens, were two guys holding sacks, half-stuffed with squirming poults. Frozen like rabbits in the headlights, they stood there for a moment with their mouths agape. Until the sight and sounds of the dogs penetrated their obviously thick skulls and panic took over.

"Bluddy 'ell! They nose we're 'ere."

"He's sent dogs an' awl. Fucken 'ell! Jus' lissen to 'em buggers!"

"Sod lissenin'! If we're not out o' yer roight quick, we're bluddy daid!"

It was like watching a bad comedy sketch in a Gloucestershire village a hundred years ago. Their accents were so strong as to be almost unintelligible. And since it had been raining all day, the pens were covered in bird shit. Two hundred and fifty birds in a pen deliver a lot of droppings! They slipped and skidded in the mess, falling down in the stinking stuff until they were covered.

"Yow'd better ger up fast cus hotherwise them devils'll ger us."

"Oi'm bluddy troyen! Oi 'it moy 'ead bad wen oi fell."

"Cum on!"

As the dogs got closer, their exchanges took on a new sense of urgency. I wasn't sure what the dogs would actually do to the poachers, but they didn't deserve to be savaged. Fortunately, they managed to escape through to door of the pen in the nick of time. And once out, they were certainly fleet of foot. They raced across to the far wall of the garden where a ladder was ready and waiting. Obviously they'd originally used it to climb to the top of the wall when they'd arrived, and then dropped it down on the inside.

While they were still on the ladder, the dogs arrived at the bottom, snapping and barking like ravenous wolves. Spurred on by fear, our friendly poachers redoubled their efforts and clambered onto the wall. But such was their panic that one began to fall and, in the process, grabbed the other's shirt, pulling him down in his wake. The double thump of bodies landing on the ground was clearly audible, as were the curses.

"Fucken 'ell Jeff! Yer almust killed me."

"Bluddy lucky yer wusn't killed. Fuck, that 'ert!"

And they legged it, getting clean away - but not quite. My first concern being the welfare of the game birds, I went quickly over to the pen. Although they were clearly upset by the unwarranted intrusion, no serious damage had been done and it looked as though we had only lost a couple of birds through fright. The dogs were still growling and sniffing around the ladder and I called them to heel. As I waited I saw, to my amazement that in their flight, the poachers had left their bags, coats and tools in an untidy pile by the pen.

Gathering it all up, I returned to the house and rifled the pockets. My search revealed an assortment of items including several that clearly identified the two men. I smiled contentedly and phoned the police.

"Have you any idea who they were, Sir?" said one of the two constables as we sat in the kitchen.

"Not personally, but I suspect that this might help. Have a look at this little lot."

I fanned out damning pieces of plastic and paper on the table and sat back.

"I think we've got them. That'll do nicely, Sir."

The policemen's grins were as wide as a barn door.

"Do you know them?" I asked.

"Oh yes. They're well known hereabouts. Been poaching and thieving for years, these two."

Apparently my failed poachers were duly apprehended, prosecuted and convicted. Not that I ever met them again or heard any details of the sentence but at least that was the end of the tale. Partridge hawking would continue as planned. Which sort of started when Lord Ashcombe's face appeared at the window.

"A bit of partridge wouldn't go amiss. Could we possibly go hawking this afternoon with the tiercels, Gary?"

"Of course," I replied, thinking, 'nothing like a bit of forward planning, M'Lord'.

Across the road from The Bothy the lovely open fields were full of winter wheat that glowed greenly in the warm afternoon sunlight. I'd known there was a good covey there and could see their heads bobbing among the sea of six inch shoots. Signalling Lord Ashcombe to stop, I let

Bracken off the lead; he immediately circled round, cut into the wind and went solid on point.

"We've definitely got a point here, my Lord."

"Wonderful, wonderful."

Striking Brock's hood, I cast him off and we watched him climb steadily upwards. Certainly my best tiercel, Brock was a natural and went up to his usual extraordinary pitch. Walking around in a wide arc to face Bracken's point, I knew there were birds between his nose and mine and we easily flushed the covey of partridge. Brock came down in a staggering stoop, cracked one partridge down with a resounding thump and the stunned bird fell to the ground not far from Lord Ashcombe. Throwing up again after his dive, Brock flipped over and gently glided down to land on the stricken partridge. Bracken went in to the kill and lay down perfectly, as he'd been trained to do. It was all over in a couple of minutes. It was a perfect day and I was full of pride as I walked over to them.

Brock was picked up from the kill, rewarded and hooded. With the partridge safely stowed in the hawking bag and Bracken at heel, I walked back to Lord Ashcombe with a big smile on my face.

"There we go," I said.

"Yes, well done Gary. Well done, very good. But I have to say, it all looks rather easy though, doesn't it? It all looks a bit too easy."

That raised a mental eyebrow to heaven. I felt like saying: 'You have no idea of the amount of work I've put in with that pointer and falcon - and getting game out there. You should bloody try it!'

"Thank you Lord Ashcombe. When it all comes together as well as that, it does look easy. Believe me, it's not always that slick."

On the next occasion, the request for a little pleasant Saturday afternoon's hawking came separately from both Lord and Lady Ashcombe. We agreed to meet at the old hill barn, perched nicely on the top of the highest point on the Sudeley Estate. It was one of those gloriously mellow autumn days, warm and scented with the heavenly smells of the season. Buds of cotton wool clouds dotted clear skies and the view from that beautiful place stretched out to a distant horizon. Winchcombe nestled comfortably in the valley below while beyond lay a verdant patchwork quilt of fields and villages, delineated by light grey curling lines of roads. A perfect country idyll.

The winged hunter of the day was Brock's colleague, Byron, while the ever-faithful Bracken served to point. The Ashcombes were positioned correctly, ensuring that they could see all the action. As the hill barn was situated on a very steep bank which invariably produced a perfect updraft, even the most inept of falcons would be able to wait on easily. And partridge were assuredly out there, just waiting to be flushed. A perfect scenario for hawking. Byron was dutifully waiting on and in no time at all, Bracken had got a point.

"Rob, get in behind the dog, head the point and you give the command to flush."

A small covey of about four birds burst into the air and Byron stooped to smack one heavily in perfect style. As tiercels do, he reached terminal velocity, threw up to a stall where he lost impetus, and dropped down to land on the partridge. It was another classic flight and I was chuffed as nuts.

Rob and I walked calmly down towards our successful hunting team. Byron was mantling over his kill while Bracken was lying obediently off to one side. We were around forty or fifty yards away when Spud the spaniel went trundling past. Ancient, deaf as a post and completely unruly, Spud was obviously day-dreaming of his days as a gundog. A time when he was fit, alert and his job description included retrieving game birds that tumbled down from the sky after big bangs from the master's firestick.

"That dog's going to retrieve your falcon as well as the bloody partridge," Rob said, digging me in the ribs.

"No, don't worry. It'll be fine."

"Come on, we've got to stop him."

"Rob, don't! It's going to look terribly rude if we start charging after Spud. Lord and Lady Ashcombe are up there."

108

A few seconds later, it was only too clear that the spaniel was making a bumbling beeline for falcon and partridge. On second thoughts -

"Run!"

The pair of us set off in hot pursuit. We were both fairly athletic and fit: I still kept my hand in playing a little football and Rob was a very good rugby player. And, after all, we were chasing a senile old dog whose legs had long since lost their power and suppleness. But where Spud maintained his plodding progress, I was running out of breath, coughing and spluttering. I had this ghastly vision of the spaniel returning with a mixed mouthful of mangled partridge and falcon. Rob, on the other hand, hit the turbo and literally left me standing. He intercepted Spud with a matter of yards to spare, grabbed the dog by the collar in a brilliant play worthy of a rugby international and got the mutt under control.

Wheezing and spluttering, I arrived on the scene a few seconds later. Carefully making my way in to Byron, I collected him onto the glove with a pick-up piece, bagged the partridge and heaved a huge sigh of relief. Thanks to Rob's turn of speed, disaster had been averted. As we walked back up the bank, I was wondering what on earth I could say to Lord Ashcombe.

'I've got to say something,' I thought. 'My Lord, that really wasn't cricket. Hardly! What the hell am I going to say?'

I needn't have worried. As we reached the top of the rise, Lord Ashcombe greeted us enthusiastically.

"Wonderful flight, wonderful flight." And before I could say a word, "terribly sorry about the dog. Blasted thing slipped the lead. Sorry."

There was nothing more to say but the point was obviously taken. As it had turned out, it had been a successful day's partridge hawking in which Spud had played a minor, albeit momentarily frightening, part. Thankfully, no damage had been done but after that, I always made sure that Spud was on the lead, and kept on the lead!

At the end of the season, Lord Ashcombe decided that it would be a grand idea to arrange a day out for all the tenant farmers, their families and friends. By his way of thinking, we'd asked them to plant game crops and then used the land for partridge hawking; what better reward than to invite them all to a falconry extravaganza and, to finish off the day, a sumptuous feast at the Castle. It all sounded very fine but, of course, it was up to me to provide some exciting partridge hawking for the guests.

The weather Gods were obviously feeling gracious. It was another beautiful autumnal day when the sun shone brightly and warmed the ground but the air had just a touch of that delicious bite that adds a certain tingle. Naturally all of the tenant farmers turned out including some that were interesting and others that one might call idiosyncratic. One guy that I was particularly pleased to see was Bill Hitch. An excellent field sportsman, a brilliant naturalist and a great character, Bill was also a very good friend.

The Scudamores were there, without any dead sheep for Bracken to maul. And there were the Rand brothers from the other side of the valley. There were about three of them as far as I knew, all looking remarkably similar and generally friendly but rather odd. On an earlier occasion, I'd been out hawking and unintentionally landed up in their farmyard. As I stood there with dog and falcon, the brothers and two lumpen farmworkers formed a circular cordon around us and stared – rural kettling, you might say.

"Hi, how are you all doing? Everything all right?"

Silence.

"I, er, think we missed a turning on the path back there and ended up in the farmyard by accident. I hope that's all right."

Silence.

"Yes, well, nice to see you all again."

Silence for a few more seconds.

"Aaargh," one of them said finally.

"I'll be going then."

Getting any conversation out of them was like drawing teeth and you never knew whether you were intruding or not. It was always difficult but one simply had to accept

110

that they were men of few words. So the brothers turned up for our day of falconry, looking alike and dressed in identical clothes apart from the different arrangements of mud stains on their boots. They stood shoulder to shoulder like a line of statues in a colonnade and, like statues, said very little.

Lord and Lady Ashcombe were naturally there, in their capacity as hosts and for the pleasure of watching the prowess of the falcons. And, of course, they had invited a few of their own friends along to enjoy the proceedings.

To get started, we had a few decent flights on the lowland part of the Estate but the few partridge flushed managed to elude the efforts of the falcons. So it was decided that we should try our luck from the higher vantage points of the estate. I felt calmly confident as I knew there were good coveys at the top end. Lords, ladies, gentility and knaves, they all piled into their vehicles and the convoy wound its way up the hill.

Reaching the crest first, I ran Bracken out on the roots and he quickly found a strong point. Rather than wait, I put Brock in the air and watched him mount up to his usual high pitch. That extraordinary little tiercel never let me down. As Brock did his thing, Lord Ashcombe arrived with a few others in tow. What I didn't know was that Lady Ashcombe and her entourage had parked their vehicles further down the hill and were walking up the lane.

"Bracken's on point, Lord Ashcombe. Shall we?"

"Absolutely. Get on with the show, Gary."

Given the command, Bracken goes in, a covey goes up, and down comes the falcon like a spitfire. Brock quickly singled out his target, hunting the quarry down as it fled towards the lane. But instead of overflying the lane, the partridge suddenly banked hard left and took a new line, directly towards Lady Ashcombe and company. Hard on his heels, the tiercel banked in response, levelled out and hit the turbochargers. Closing the gap, Brock hit the partridge hard, threw up and dropped down on the kill less than ten yards from the walking party. Confronted by a falcon mantling over a dead partridge, Lady Ashcombe and company stood there in silence. And then quietly applauded. It was a total fluke, of course, and not something that could ever have been planned, but clearly appreciated.

"Well done, Gary," she said when I arrived on the scene.

It would have been difficult to beat the drama of that flight. Thus we decided to call a halt and adjourned to the Castle to celebrate a great day's sport. The Ashcombes had arranged for a magnificent banquet in the old hall. The long timber table was laden with the finest meats, finest wines and finest everything. Nothing had been forgotten. A massive log fire blazed in the wide stone hearth as we all made merry, our voices ringing under the vaulted stone ceiling. It was as though we had all been transported back through time, to the days of the Tudors when Catherine Parr might have sat through similar revelry. Or so it seemed to me as I sat there laughing and quaffing another glass of French ruby red wine. A wonderful and magical experience, it was truly a great way to round off our falconry extravaganza and an excellent finish to a successful season. How could you beat it?

Chapter 12 – Glorious Moors

Inspired as he was by partridge hawking, Lord Ashcombe felt that it was time to extend the experience and chase a different type of game bird. Grouse hawking appealed for the simple reason that he had access to a grouse moor or two.

"You've done a spot of grouse hawking in your time, haven't you Gary?"

"Yes, up in Caithness."

"Still do any?"

"No, I can't afford it really."

"How do you fancy a touch in Yorkshire? A friend of mine, Brigadier Watson, has a small moor just outside Helmsley and a place called Sykes Cottage. Wondered if you'd be interested in going up there for a week or two's grouse hawking?"

"Definitely."

"And Lord Bolton, another friend, owns Roper Moor which is a lot bigger. We can have a bit of fun on that as well."

"Brilliant. Bracken's a pretty useful pointer these days, so we could take him. And I would like to give Brock a try over grouse."

So it was all arranged. Brock, Byron, Poacher, Bracken and I all piled into my car while John Whitmore travelled in his car with only his Harris hawk, Malin, for company. John, better known as 'Whitty', was an amateur falconer and a close friend of mine. The deal was that he would do all of the shopping, cooking and skivvying as required in return for the experience and the falconry. A character in his own right, he was involved with the restoration of hundreds of longbows, rescued from Henry VIII's warship the Mary Rose after she was pulled up from the seabed over 430 years after sinking in the Solent. Whitty also founded the British Longbow Society and was an avid traditional archer. Legend holds that while in the Army on National Service in Honduras, he hunted a variety of game with the longbow, including alligators and crocodiles.

After making the long trek to Yorkshire, we finally arrived at the drive down to Sykes Cottage itself. The Brigadier's private lane seemed endless, and chopped into sections by innumerable gates. For some strange reason, Yorkshire is blighted by an inordinate number of the damn things, none of which open properly. Each one requires you to stop, get out of the car and open the gate, which inevitably falls over. Once you have driven through the gap, you then have to heave the wreck back into position with one hand while securing it a post using rusting chains, baling twine or unbendable wire.

Eventually (and thankfully) we arrived at a wonderful oasis on the Yorkshire Moors, nestling in a slight valley and protected from the winds. Sykes Cottage turned out to be a rather fine farmhouse with a beck running nearby that was brimming with trout. Lord Ashcombe had already arrived and was standing outside with a trim, grey haired chap with a distinctly military bearing.

"Gary, John, let me introduce you to our host, Brigadier Watson."

"Welcome to Sykes Cottage, gentlemen. Follow me."

Leading us into the cottage, he showed us our billets where we'd bunk and could stash our kit, where the mess was and generally what was what. The Brigadier was a wonderful character in his late 70s, delightfully old school and very polite. He was charming and very welcoming but there were certain rules and regulations. We were clearly told where we could and could not go, and given instructions as to the geographical and political limits of the moor.

"Where's the dog?" asked the Brigadier. "Hear you've got pointer."

"I have, Sir. He's in the truck, outside."

"Well bring him in, young Cope, bring him in. Ah, where d'you plan to keep him while you're here?"

"I was hoping to keep him in the house. He's very well house-trained and he wouldn't be a problem."

'Mmm, not sure, don't normally keep dogs in the house. He could bed down in the barn, which would probably be better."

114

"Of course, as you wish Brigadier. It's just that he's used to being inside at night and he's very good and well-behaved indoors."

"Oh well, bring him in and we'll let it pass this time."

Released from the truck, Bracken needed no invitation and promptly followed his nose inside. Stubby tail wagging and nose snuffling, he skittered around the room, snouting old and new friends alike. And he received succinct greetings in return.

"Hello Bracken, you old rogue," said Lord Ashcombe, giving the dog's head a quick scrub.

"So you're Bracken, are you?" asked the Brigadier, doing the wag-the-dog's-head-by-the-ears routine. "Welcome to Sykes Cottage."

After which brief hiatus, the conversation resumed. As we talked, we lounged comfortably in the fine chairs and sofas arranged at one end of the large room. My eyes flickered round, taking in the pictures on the wall, the beautiful walnut bookcase, the highly polished expanse of the dining table with its leonine feet and the other wonderful pieces of antique furniture. On which Bracken was progressively pissing! Moving from teak to mahogany, Bracken was cocking his leg on every piece of valuable furniture available. And I was the only one who had noticed. Until, a second later, when they all noticed!

'Why are you screwing this all up for me?' I shouted telepathically. 'You stupid fucking dog!'

Lurching from my chair, I grabbed Bracken by the scruff of the neck to stop any further urinary perambulation. Not for the first time, I wished that the earth would open and swallow me whole. But that wasn't an option.

"Brigadier Watson, I am so, so sorry. He never does this at home; this is so out of character. I am really sorry."

I was expecting an artillery barrage, running along the lines of 'Take the bloody dog outside immediately' and 'I knew I should never allowed the blasted dog in the house'. What I got was a winning smile and a tolerant nod.

"Don't worry. He's not the first dog to come in here and take a piss. Don't worry about it, he's simply marking his territory."

So Bracken was not dismissed, barely disgraced and the potentially stormy waters were calmed. After an uneventful night's sleep, we were out on the Brigadier's moorland backyard with several days (hopefully) successful hawking ahead. However, as well as being somewhat small, it was not a terribly good moor for the purpose. Situated as it was on the lee of a hill, the resultant downdraft of wind negated any possible lift for a falcon and made it a difficult moor to fly. On the other hand, an abundance of bunnies provided plenty of sport for the Harris hawks and a lot of fun for the humans.

Whitty's Harris hawk Malin was an experienced and battle-hardened hunter. In contrast, I had my young Harris, Poacher, who was still wet behind the primaries and spent most of her time fumbling rabbits rather than catching the things. On one occasion, Malin caught an eight and a half pound hare with great style and aggression. Poacher caught heather. Over dinner that night, the tale was retold ad infinitum and the analysis was not in my favour.

"So what kind of heather did Poacher kill? Was it the tough purple or the slightly bluer and more elusive variety?"

"Whitty, would you consider lending Malin to Gary as Poacher's mentor?"

"Taking everything into account, if Malin can nail a monstrous hare, Poacher should be able to catch the odd kit, don't you think. Can you get glasses for hawks?"

People should be allowed to have their glory, and be a butt for their jokes. At least the ridicule only lasted for one day. On another, I was flying Byron when Bracken went rigid on point. Whoops! The bane of all falconers, Bracken's point turned out to be false and he skulked off looking rather ashamed of himself. Meanwhile, Byron was floating around, waiting for someone to do something.

"Are you going to call him down?" asked Whitty, looking skywards.

116

Although I knew that there weren't many grouse on the moor, I wanted the falcons to keep fit.

"No, I'll leave him up there for a bit, let him stretch his wings."

The words had hardly left my mouth when an attack flight of feathered Hurricanes came tearing across the sky with the sun behind them and Byron in their sights.

"Kik-kik-kee-kik, kik-kik-kee-kik."

The cries of the two merlins sounded just like high-pitched machine guns in miniature. Byron was obviously on their territory and they had no compunction about taking the fight to the larger intruder. My instinct was to bring him down immediately; it was unlikely that hurt him but they could well drive him off and I'd lose him. But I was mesmerised by the aerial dogfight. Those wonderful little falcons were full of courage and their brilliant manoeuvres were just amazing to watch. I just had to watch this duel of falcons play out for a little longer. Common sense kicked after a couple more minutes.

"Bring him down," said Whitty. "We don't want to be going home without the falcon."

As soon as the lure was out in the open, Byron dropped down immediately, stepped easily onto the glove and tore at his reward. At one point, he looked me in the eye and I swear I could hear him saying: 'You took your time! It wasn't a lot of fun up there with that foul pair. I hate bloody merlins!' So much for gratitude! But it had been a wonderful display and showed me what fabulous little falcons they are, and how special.

A few days later, we were invited to hawk at Duncombe Park, owned by Baron Feversham and only a mile southwest of Helmsley. Over the years its 300 acres of parkland had seen quite a bit of hawking and falconers. But while the adjacent grounds around Nawton Towers provided fine game hawking for pheasant, partridge and grouse, Duncombe Park was under the dominion of rabbits.

Malin and Poacher had a reasonably successful few hours rabbiting in the company of Lord Bolton and other assorted dignitaries on the beautiful estate. John Masterman, Head Keeper for Lord Ashcombe's Helmsley shoot, had also joined the throng. But the weather was not that kind. Yorkshire being what it is, the skies were a moody grey and the wind whipped the heavy drizzle into a foam. By the time one o'clock arrived, Lord Ashcombe called a halt to the proceedings.

"I think it's time for luncheon," he announced.

As though by magic, the Range Rovers and 4x4s regrouped into a tight laager formation. And out from his Lordship's vehicle appeared a fully attired waiter, complete with black suit, bow tie and starched white shirt. Opening a large bag, he produced laundered white tablecloths which he spread carefully across a number of bonnets, securing them with large stones. A necessary precaution since the wind was blowing a hooley! Several hampers followed and opened to reveal a cornucopia of delectations. A tureen of warming soup, delicate canapés, smoked salmon sandwiches cut in precise diamonds and French wines were just few of the delicacies that emerged.

That luncheon was truly surreal, bringing to mind images from the film, The Shooting Party. Oh, the indulgences of the aristocracy! It was a true Edwardian theatrical production in which I was a bit player with few lines. Not that I didn't enjoy the part; I thoroughly enjoyed every bite, sip and moment. Wonderful but strange, this was a million miles out of my league. I was more accustomed to dining on more prosaic fare while out hawking, such as one rough-cut cheese sandwich with a touch of pickle.

And, once the hardy diners had sated hunger and thirst, the remnants of our repast were packed away with the same sorcery that had made it all appear at the start. Tablecloths were folded and stowed, a few marks polished from one or two bonnets and the vehicles broke formation to line up in waiting. Malin and Poacher took to the skies once more while the bunnies presented themselves to be hunted. With so many rabbits running about, even Poacher gave a good account of herself.

Food being an important feature in Lord Ashcombe's way of thinking, he decided that lunching at the Black Swan would be an appropriate garnish for our final day. An inn of some renown, after the stagecoach route linking Leeds to York was started in 1838, the Black Swan became a regular stopping point for The Helmsley Flyer. Our vehicles had a little more horsepower than the Flyer.

"We'll be in the Ashcombe Suite," his Lordship instructed. "Lunch will be served at one o'clock. Be there."

As the plan was to follow lunch with some grouse hawking on Roper Moor, Lord Bolton was naturally there with a few friends and members of his family. Lord Ashcombe had invited quite a few more and thus it was quite a gathering that met in the formal surroundings of the eponymous suite. Indeed, most of the guests were clad fairly formally too, apart from Lord Bolton who was dressed a little more modishly. As behoves a young man in his 30s, my Lord Bolton sported an old checked woodsman's shirt, tight blue jeans and trainers. And while his attire might have raised one or two eyes among the traditionalists, they were far too polite to comment.

Luncheon turned out to be an elaborate three-course meal accompanied by vintage wines, each costing approximately 2,333 per cent over my three pound budget for vin plonk. Nevertheless, far be it from me to complain and, once again, I was extremely happy to dine so regally. The only fly in the sorbet was a rather serious lady with a long face framed by clashing red ringlets of hair.

"You're Lord Ashcombe's falconer, aren't you? Phoebe Arrowsmith," she said, holding out her hand to be shaken. "I train setters, professionally of course. Lord Ashcombe invited me to join you for the grouse hawking this afternoon."

"Excellent. Well, I hope you enjoy the afternoon."

We chatted idly about dogs for a while, trading opinions on pointers versus setters. Apparently, Ms Arrowsmith had trained some of the best dogs north of the Watford Gap, to which shoots across the country could bear testimony. Which finally sent alarm bells ringing in my obviously muddled brain.

"So since he was so impressed with the dogs, Lord Ashcombe suggested that we work together this afternoon - my setters flushing for your falcons. He thought it was a jolly good idea and I think it'll work rather well, don't you?"

'She's a hired gun," I thought. 'He's hired in some dogs and trainer and he didn't mention a bloody word! My team is my team and I know how it works. He can't just bring any old person in at the eleventh hour. But he fucking has!'

"Really, I see. So have your dogs got any experience of working with falcons? Or hawks?"

"Of course not, they're shooting dogs."

"So, your dogs have no hawking experience at all?"

"No."

"Phoebe, there's a big difference in flushing for falcons and flushing for guns."

"Nonsense! Flushing is flushing. The dogs go in and the birds go up. That's it! The grouse aren't going know the difference, are they?"

"That's exactly what I'm saying. It doesn't matter whether it's a grouse, a pheasant, a partridge or a duck, if they see the silhouette of a falcon waiting on they sit tight. That's their best form of escape, doing bugger all very quietly! What I'm saying is, they don't flush easily. It's different with guns: all the dog has to do is bumble around in the heather. The grouse is disturbed and gets up because it doesn't understand the danger. Fear of shotguns isn't in their DNA but falcons are their natural enemies and the birds know that a silhouette is bad news."

Arrowsmith leaned back in her chair, squared her shoulders and folded her arms.

"First of all, Mr Cope, my dogs do not bumble! Secondly, my setters are among the very best trained in the country. Frankly, I think that's all rubbish. Don't you worry about my dogs, they'll produce grouse, they always do. You just get your falcon to do what it's trained to do and everything will be fine."

'Christ, here we go!' I thought.

Roper Moor was a wonderful place which was quite flat but dropped off dramatically at one end for some 200 feet. The result was a strong updraft that would provide lift for the falcons and help them to wait on. What I hadn't expected was the size of our audience. Rather than a small

120

hawking party, at least half of Helmsley was present. The estate workers had turned out en masse, bringing several generations along for good measure. Seemingly, the only people missing were Catherine Earnshaw and Heathcliffe. Even the track at the end of the moor was lined with people, some 60 or 70 strong. The whole thing was rapidly turning into a circus but, when the Ringmaster calls, the show must go on.

The lady with the well-trained gun dogs was given the sign to release the setters. Bracken watched mournfully from the side-lines as they flowed silkily across the heather. In all fairness, the elegant setters were a magnificent sight, ranging effortlessly over the moor. I watched and waited with my star performer hooded and primed on the glove. Unlike Caithness, you didn't have long to wait in Yorkshire for a dog to find set or point. And sure enough, within minutes the dogs went on set and Arrowsmith's arm shot up like a lightning rod. It was time for Brock to show his metal.

Unhooded, Brock headed straight for the stars, going up and up and up. He mounted to such an extreme pitch that he was barely a speck on the sky's blue canvas. I was so pleased that my heart was pounding. The huge audience waited with bated breath for the contest between falcon and grouse. And I gave the signal for Arrowsmith to send in the setters.

"Get 'em up, get 'em up."

Nothing. The dogs ruffled around in the long heather but to no avail.

"Come on! Get 'em up, get 'em up."

Still nothing. Arrowsmith is getting more and more exasperated. In the meantime, my tiercel was up at this extreme pitch and my heart was beginning to sink. We couldn't let her down. It's the worst of crimes not to produce game when a falcon's waiting on and the setters were not coming up with the goods. I looked at the two Johns, Whitmore and Marston.

"Bugger it! She's not producing the game. Come on, let's form a line and see if we can at least walk something up."

We walked out in a line across the heather but not a feather was to be seen and the dogs were on a false set. With one eye on the ground and the other on Brock, I suddenly saw him flip over. At the same time, about a half mile away, I spotted a single grouse get up, which was no thanks to any of our efforts. Brock dropped like a teardrop exploding from heaven, in a magnificent stoop carrying unbelievable speed. Across the undulating heather, I saw the grouse go over the top of the rise and disappear, followed closely by the falcon.

'At least she was served,' I thought.

Then I realised that something was terribly wrong. When a falcon hits a grouse, or any prey, she'll normally throw up before dropping back to land. But there'd been nothing. There was nothing. Not a sign. The two Johns and I made our way to an old hawthorn tree on the ridge. I climbed part way up the tree, marked more or less where Brock should have come down and walked towards the spot, flipping open the yagi. There was not the slightest bleep in any direction, not even on the top of the hill, and I was getting desperate. I asked Arrowsmith for help.

"Phoebe, the telemetry's not working. Can you get the dogs to work the ground over here. The falcon's probably sitting on a kill somewhere but we haven't spotted her and could do with a bit of help."

The setters spread out across the moor, efficiently crisscrossing the heather but to no avail. Others joined the search that continued until sunset, but it was fruitless. It was as though Brock had flown into Yorkshire's version of the Bermuda Triangle. Whitty and I were due to drive back the next day but delayed our return. The following day, we searched from dawn to dusk without seeing or hearing one single sign or signal.

Necessity forced me to drive south since there were matters that needed sorting out at The Bothy. It was impossible to concentrate or think of anything else but Brock. I was totally distraught; I'd lost my pride and joy and the pain was intense. There was no option other than return to Roper Moor. Whitty volunteered to go with me, Brigadier Watson offered accommodation at Sykes Cottage

122

and the search continued. For a whole week, John and I searched every nook and cranny, widening the search from Roper across adjacent moors. Searching for a lost falcon is grinding and heart-breaking. You stand there, inanely swinging the lure and calling while every second your eyes search the skies and landscape. You pray for just one tiny bleep from the telemetry receiver, a minute glimmer of a single red light on the row of ten. But there was nothing.

On the return drive from Gloucestershire to Yorkshire, there were positive words that kept repeating themselves in my mind, over and over again.

'I'm going to get him back. He's there and I can't lose him. I'm going to get him back. He's there and I can't lose him.'

On that final long, long drive back to Winchcombe in the dark, there were no words. There was just a vast black void that swallowed the light and the massive pain of loss. I had failed, and lost him.

But the tale does have a codicil. Mike Dorgan was the Head Inspector for the Department of the Environment and he loved coming to The Bothy to make his mandatory checks. In his opinion, our breeding chambers were the epitome of what breeding chambers should be like and run. So much so that he wanted to feature them in the department's magazine. But that would have been a touch unfair since they'd been built on an unlimited budget and most people are not quite so fortunate. Not long after I'd returned from Yorkshire, another check was due and, in the course of conversation, I told him the story of how I'd lost Brock.

"Where were you?"

"On Roper Moor, near Helmsley."

"You don't have a photograph of the falcon, do you?"

"Actually, I do."

Rummaging around inside, I soon found a photograph that had been taken shortly before we'd left. As far as I was concerned, Brock was the image of a perfect gamehawk. I passed it to Dorgan.

"Quite a short, stubby little fellow. Looks as though he hasn't quite moulted out when this was taken."

"Yeah, that's right. If you look carefully, you can see that he's got several immature feathers down his wing."

"I see what you mean."

Although Brock was generally a dark slate-blue, the immature feathers meant that a brownish V-shape ran down his wings.

"Can I take this?"

"Sure. But why do you want it?"

"I can't tell you at the moment but I'll get back to you," Dorgan said mysteriously.

A couple of weeks went by before Dorgan returned to The Bothy. And he had news, of a sort.

"I know where your tiercel is, Gary."

"You're joking?"

"No."

"But that's brilliant. Let's get him back."

"We can't."

"Why on earth not?"

"Because I can't prove that he's your bird."

"What do you mean?"

"The DoE was contacted by a guy, near Helmsley, who asked for a cable tie ring. His story was that his tiercel had contracted a bad case of bumblefoot, so he'd had to cut off the closed ring and need a cable tie replacement. Anyway, it just so happens that he's pulled a few scams with us before and the department's got his number. The upshot was that I was sent to investigate and see whether his request was genuine. When I got there, the bird was a perfect match for your falcon."

"So who is he?"

"I can't tell you that. The problem is that we can't prove that it is your bird. I think it's your bird but I can't be 100 per cent certain. I'm guessing that he's had a tiercel of his own in the past. That probably died or was killed somehow, so he cut off the ring but kept it registered with the DoE and now he's come up with a replacement tiercel. Which is probably yours, but there's not a damn thing that we can do about it. I'm really sorry, Gary."

124

And that was the end. Without modern day DNA testing there was no hope of proving that the falcon was really mine. Hope finally died and I never saw Brock again.

Chapter 13 – An importance of visitors

Brock's loss was devastating but time, sometimes sadly, moves on and even the team at The Bothy realigned. Rob had decided that commercial falconry was not for him and had gone to pastures new to run his own business. Nick had made his way through the pain of the Youth Training Scheme and was now working with me full-time. And I'd taken on a guy called John Bennett who was already a reasonably experienced falconer. So now there were three of us running the project.

"Do you fancy having an English pointer?" John asked, one day out of the blue.

"No, I don't at all. Why?"

"Well, these friends of mine are getting divorced and they've got this English pointer. Basically, the poor thing's an orphan. Pete's work means that he travels round the country a lot and Carole's decided to move abroad. And the dog's, sort of caught in the middle."

"Nah, I'm not interested. Anyway, what would I want an English pointer for?
The only thing that English pointers are good for is grouse hawking. They're no good for lowland ground because they range too far. And as for grouse hawking, that's pretty much limited to what I'm doing with Lord Ashcombe."

So the mutt got the thumbs down.

"No, no, no, no."

And then Joy pipes up in orphaned dog support.

"Oh go on! The dog needs a home."

"Joy, we've got enough going on here as it is."

"Puleese! Please, please, pretty please. Just have a look at her."

Beauty and badgering must be a powerful combination; I caved in and admitted defeat. So one afternoon, Carole turned up with the pointer and as soon as I saw it, bells started ringing. It was short, squat and close to being downright ugly but it was distinctly reminiscent of the strain of dog owned by Stephen Frank. Not that I said a word. And Carole brought the miserable, skulking little bitch into the house.

126

"Would you, could you possibly give Candy a home?"

'Candy! That's an awful name for an English pointer,' I thought.

"Well, I really don't know."

Candy by this time had scoped out the place and already found a comfy spot on the Chesterfield.

"Um, I simply don't need another dog."

"She's no trouble and she's really well trained. Listen, I'd be really thrilled if you could give her a home because I don't know what we're going to do with her otherwise."

'Warning, warning,' cried the little voice in my head, 'you do not need another dog. You do not want another canine mouth to feed.'

Joy's sharp elbow made a pointed impact with my ribcage.

"She's lovely. Come on, give her a home."

The phrase was beginning to sound like a bad refrain to a weak song. But it was only fair to find out a little more, given my earlier suspicions.

"OK, what's the dog's background?"

"Well, she's very good, extremely obedient. She's two years old and she's been spayed."

That at least was a point in Candy's favour. Bracken was a male with big balls and I certainly didn't want English/German blood crosses with all the hassle that they bring. Not that I was changing my mind!

"And she comes from the Embercombe line," Carole continued.

"Hmm. Sorry, what line did you say?"

"The Embercombe line."

Opposing thoughts are now rattling around in my head.

'What am I going to do with an English pointer?'

'Never know, it might come in handy."

'I'll have to feed it which'll cost money."

'Cheapskate! It's not costing you anything. Embercombe dogs don't come cheap and this one's a freebee.'

Joy took up the cry once again.

"Come on, give her a home. She's so sweet, she needs a home and she's heartbroken. Go on."

"Oh, all right then."

Done deal. I took the dog out into the paddock, followed by Nick and John who both had broad grins on their faces.

"Knew you'd cave in," said John.

"And so did I," added Nick.

"Bugger off, both of you. Buggers! All right she can stay. But the first thing we're going to do is change her name. If you think that I'm rocking round the countryside shouting 'Candy, Candy', then think again. The name's got to go."

John and Nick gave it their best, but my talent for names and experience with dogs won through!

"Becky," I announced, "we'll call her Becky."

"Becky? Why?" asked Nick, scratching his head.

"Dogs relate to sounds, not names," I said rather pompously. "Beck-ee sounds a bit like Cand-ee. See? It's important for training."

"Right," said Nick, "of course."

She was an unattractive, moody little bitch and for several weeks I really wondered why on earth I'd agreed to keep her. I had absolutely no use for an English pointer and, as predicted, she was simply another mouth to feed. Ironically, the ugly duckling would never turn into a swan, but she would prove to be an outstanding asset. Becky was there for the duration but, for a short time, I had another guest who came to stay.

One afternoon, Nick, John and I were drinking coffee in the kitchen when our conversation was interrupted by a sudden racket which appeared to be coming from the walled garden.

"Eek-eek-ekek, eek-eek-ekek."

"Kek-ek-eek-ekek, eek-eek-ekek."

Thinking it was some of our birds in distress, the three of us naturally went out to investigate. But what we found was two wild kestrels crabbing on the ground. Claws locked and beaks hacking, the pair were so entangled that they formed a balled mass of agitated feather. Trying to separate the tiny gladiators was no easy task as they clung to each other like grim death in their murderous battle. But after a while, we managed to prise them apart and assess the damage.

"This one's fine. Although it's a bit pissed off! Ow."

John happily released the unwounded victor and watched her fly off over the treetops. The other bird had clearly sustained some harm to one wing which was drooping and slightly damp.

"We've got a spare aviary," I said. "Why don't we put in there to recuperate for a few days, see how she gets on."

For the next two weeks, we left her alone and undisturbed in the aviary. Since she was a wild bird, it was important that we didn't make any contact apart from ensuring she had food. Fortunately we had a reasonable stock of mice to feed her, mice being a natural prey for kestrels. (You don't get many day-old-chicks wandering around in the wild!) After a full fortnight, it was clear that she was getting stronger. Her wing had regained its strength and flexion; she was feeding well and was obviously, generally comfortable.

"She looks ready," I said to Nick. "It's about time we released her back into the wild."

Which is exactly what we did and I didn't think anything more about the little falcon who'd stayed for a while. Until a couple of nights later, when I was lying in bed pondering those great thoughts that come in the hours of darkness and heard the sound of tapping.

Dit, dit, dee-dit, dit, dit. Something was tapping on the window. I rolled over and ignored the sound. But whoever, or whatever, was insistent that I paid due attention.

Dit, dit, dee-dit, dit, dit.

"No peace and all that," I grumbled as I poured myself out of bed and onto the floor. I drew the curtains and peered through the window to find myself eyeball to eyeball with our erstwhile guest.

"This is ridiculous!"

Slowly and carefully, I opened the window and the kestrel promptly hopped through the opening. She perched on the windowsill, on the inside, cocked her head slightly to one side and waited.

"This is bizarre!"

Quietly part-closing the window behind her, I shot downstairs to grab a mouse and, once back in the bedroom, laid it on the sill beside her. Miss Kesterelle tucked in with gusto while I retired to my bed. There was plenty of space for her to leave without saying thanks or goodbye. But the following morning, there she was, sitting calmly on the windowsill.

"Good morning."

She cocked her head to one side as though in acknowledgment. I walked slowly over to her and pushed the window wide open. Feeling the breeze on her back, she turned round, bobbed her head twice and flew away. I didn't see her for the rest of the day, but when night fell and I was comfortably tucked up in bed, I heard it again.

Dit, dit, dee-dit, dit, dit.

This time I didn't hesitate and went straight to the window.

"Bugger me!"

To my utter disbelief, there was Miss Kesterelle, tapping impatiently on the glass, waiting to be let inside and fed. With a smile of wonderment on my face, I opened the window and in she hopped. Once she was settled on the windowsill, I went downstairs for a mouse, returned to the bedroom and putting it beside her, went back to bed. After sleeping the night away undisturbed, I woke up to find her still there, flung open the window and off she flew.

This extraordinary routine continued, night after night for about two months. Each night she would tap on the window; and each night I would let her in, feed her and retire. Having spent the night, in the morning she would fly off to spend her day elsewhere. But finally, one night there was no tapping and no kestrel and my platonic affair with Miss Kesterelle was over. Our sakers, however were more productive.

Two of the four pairs of sakers bred successfully that first season, resulting in five females and three males. All of them were good birds but one of the females was absolutely massive, dwarfing her siblings. Given the average size of sakers, she was positively Amazonian. Lord Ashcombe was understandably thrilled with the quality and

130

number of birds. Not to mention the prospect of potential sales.

"An outstanding success, Gary. Outstanding. I'll invite Prince Khalid over to take a look at them. As you know, he's been interested in the breeding project since we started and he could well be our first customer. And I'm sure he'll like her," he added, nodding towards the Amazon.

Later that day, I got a call from Lord Ashcombe.

"He sounded rather enthusiastic, I'd say - very keen. He'll be over on Tuesday so that'll give you a couple of days to everything ready."

Tuesday! This was late July and over the previous few weeks we'd had a good mix of sun and rain. The grass was lush and verdant, weeds had insidiously worked their dark magic and serried ranks of nettles formed dense bulwarks around the perimeter of the paddock. The Bothy had extensive grounds in addition to the walled garden itself. There was suddenly a mass of work to be done in a relatively short time and we went into overdrive. As well as Nick, John and I, two estate workers were conscripted to tackle the list of chores. Grass was cut, nettles strimmed, weeds pulled, aviaries cleaned; everything had to be perfect. Lord Ashcombe even gave me a brief lesson in etiquette.

"Do you know how to present yourself when you meet a prince, Gary?"

"Well, no, not really. I can't say that I've ever met a prince before."

"Yes, well there is a certain protocol, a way to behave properly, you know." (And Lord Ashcombe was nothing if not a stickler for protocol and correct behaviour.) "Let him approach you. You can't just walk over to him. When he approaches you, wait for him to put out his hand and then you put out yours. You bow, from the waist, and say, 'Good afternoon, Your Royal Highness'."

'Can't screw up on this one,' I thought, even though the whole business of bowing and scraping stuck in my throat.

Needless to say, I practised the hand-bow-and-Uriah-Heep routine until I was appropriately humble and obsequious. By two o'clock on the day, all was pristine and in place. The sun had obeyed the Royal command and spread its glorious warmth across our beautiful oasis. We did not have long to wait. At precisely two thirty, two polished black Range Rovers growled up the drive to The Bothy. Leaving Nick and John in the kitchen, I went out to the porch, readying myself to greet our very important visitor and his retinue.

Four doors opened in perfect synchrony and out stepped four identically dressed people. Black suits, navy blue ties, white shirts and mirror sunglasses were obviously de rigueur. The only variation was betrayed by distinct curves in the lines of one suit. Three of them were male but the fourth was definitely a lady.

Without a word of greeting or even acknowledgement, Prince Khalid's close protection squad immediately dispersed across the grounds, quartering their sectors as they moved. Each took station at strategic points, one of which was under my favourite apple tree and another close to the outbuildings. Still non-communicative, they stood in their chosen positions looking darkly menacing like black jaguars waiting to spring into action.

A few minutes later, Lord Ashcombe's Range Rover rumbled up the drive followed by a silver Bentley Mulsanne Turbo. As the vehicles were parked, I could feel my heart pounding and my nerves sparking.

Lord Ashcombe was out first, looked quickly across to make sure I was there and then back at the Bentley. The first man out of the Bentley had a similar physique to the men in the security squad but boasted a blue suit and white shirt, nattily set off by a red tie and braces. Once out, he too looked at the Bentley and watched as a short neat man in an expensive charcoal grey suit, complemented by a lilac shirt and tie, stepped from the car. Prince Khalid had arrived. Flanked by red tie and braces on one side and Lord Ashcombe on the other, the Prince walked across the lawn towards me. Meanwhile, I'm silently rehearsing my lines and moves.

'Good afternoon, Your Royal Highness – bow, bow.'

As he approached, all I could see was a wonderful endearing smile and the light glinting on the large gold-rimmed thick glasses that magnified his twinkling eyes.

"Hello Gary, I am very pleased to meet you."

The pitch of the voice was slightly higher than I'd expected and only lightly accented with a warm smokiness. As Lord Ashcombe predicted, Prince Khalid stretched out his hand. His handshake was firm and the skin dry. I bowed, somewhat stiffly.

"Good afternoon, Your Royal Highness."

His eyes blinked slowly behind their glass barriers, making the long face with its large nose and neatly trimmed moustache seem slightly mournful for a moment. But as soon as the eyes reopened, the smile relit and he looked almost mischievous.

"Shall we look at the birds?"

"Of course, Sir."

Indicating the doorway to the walled garden, I allowed Lord Ashcombe and the Prince to lead the way. I brought up the rear, following red tie and braces. As I knew that the Arabs do not like tame birds, Nick, John and I had been up at first light putting all the sakers out onto the weathering. All the saker falcons were jessed, hooded and perched on wakars (Arabic for the Arab block that resembles an oversized drawing pin).

As Prince Khalid entered the garden, he saw the saker falcons holding pride of place in prime position, and wild as hell. As the supporting cast, my birds were also out there and the chorus line included a great big, horrible female red tailed buzzard tucked into one corner. Joining Prince Khalid at the front of the group, we walked along the line of sakers.

"Could you pick that one up?" he asked, pointing at one bird.

Collecting the bird on the glove, I held her up for the Prince to inspect. He felt the bird's body firmly with both hands in a way that showed confidence and knowledge.

"Yes, yes, good conformation, Thank you. You may put her down."

And then his eyes lit on the jewel in the crown, the Amazon queen with her subjects and ladies in waiting. She was the biggest saker that I have ever bred and must have weighed at least three pounds. Strong, wild and beautiful, she had never been handled apart from the time she was picked up from the aviary some six hours earlier.

"Ah. Could you pick that one up?"

As soon as she was on the glove and ready for inspection, the Prince began to maul the falcon.

"Oh yes, this one has very good conformation, oh yes."

By this time, the falcon was getting seriously agitated, raising her wings and hissing with anger. As his fingers felt around her breast, she arched her head, opened her beak slightly and I envisioned that beak hacking back downwards and into his hand. And then what was I meant to do?

"Very good falcon, very good. Perhaps you would take off the hood."

At which, I practically filled my pants. This was a seriously pissed off wild bird as big as a house and the man wanted me to take off the hood! But the man was a Prince and, willy nilly, the hood had to come off. How I was going to get it back on again would be an entirely different matter. Striking the braces with teeth and hand, I carefully removed the hood. As often happens with wild birds, she stood motionless on the glove, mesmerised by the myriad sights around her and totally bewildered. The seconds ticked by so slowly that it seemed like an hour had passed before Prince Khalid made any further comment.

"Yes, is definitely a very good falcon. Thank you. You may replace the hood."

'Think, Cope!' I silently commanded.

I thought. The last thing I wanted was a war of attrition which would inevitably lead to a messy scene and would not look good on my resumé. And then it struck me – shout! The one thing I remembered from reading various treatises on Arabian falconry was that when handling a totally wild bird, the Arab falconer shouts at it. The falcon is so taken aback and by the aggression and noise emanating from the giant that, for a short time, she's totally tractable.

"Haah! Haah! Haah!"

Taking advantage of the moment, I quickly slipped the hood over her head and tightened the braces. And sighed quietly with relief. Prince Khalid held me in his eyes for a second and seemed to nod once briefly. I suddenly realised the importance of that moment; my professionalism and skills had been on the line. I replaced the bird on her wakar and looked back at him. He stood back, looked down the line of sakers and started to point.

"Yes, I like that one, that one is too small, but I like that one, that one and that one. Good. What is that?"

Having decided on which of the sakers he liked, he was now focused on the redtail tucked away in the corner. A huge and extremely powerful female, she was the only bird that I've ever flown that could catch and kill a rabbit with one foot. In a nutshell, she was a great big murderous thing, the size of a small eagle. Prince Khalid walked up to within three feet of Big Red and peered, rather disdainfully.

"What is this?" he asked again.

"An American red-tailed hawk, Sir. Some Americans call them chickenhawks."

"Does it hunt chickens?"

"Rarely."

"I thought not. Sometimes the Americans are not so clever with words. I think we shoot these in the desert."

"I think that's unlikely, Sir. Redtails are indigenous to the States. It's more likely that the birds you shoot are eagles and the redtail does look a little like an eagle."

"Maybe. When we fly the falcons at houbara, the falcon catches the houbara and then the eagle comes. So we shoot it. But this bird, you fly this?"

"Yes, your Royal Highness. We fly them at rabbits and hares."

"Hmmm."

By this time, Big Red is taking an unhealthy interest in the man standing less than three feet in front of her bow perch and invading her space. She's leaning forward, tipping her head to one side and flaring her cheeks. I'm thinking that any moment she's going to lunge at the Prince's legs and grab him - game over, career over, end of. And then what was I going to do? In an attempt to lure him away from the danger zone, I walked back towards the sakers.

"What about this bird here?" I asked.

Without shifting position, Prince Khalid simply turned around to look in my direction, which still left him vulnerable to attack. But now, he was unsighted and less than a leash length away from the monstrous redtail.

'Any second now, the bloody bird is going to nail the back of his legs,' I thought.

Thinking on my feet, I moved along the saker line to the Amazonian that he'd liked so much, and picked her up.

"Would you like another look at this one, Sir?"

Finally, he moved out of range and disaster was averted. As we walked back along the line, I noticed that three of the close protection squad had slipped ninja-like into the garden and taken up position. It suddenly seemed like a Tudor court: the Prince taking his regal time while the courtiers watched and whispered. And red tie and braces was hard on our heels.

"I would like to see the breeding falcons that have produced these birds."

"Certainly, Sir. Of course. Follow me."

As we walked towards the breeding chambers, the close protection mob converged to the rear and began to follow in our footsteps. Hearing the footsteps, Prince Khalid turned around and simply raised an imperious hand which stopped them in their tracks. And he and I went forward on our own.

The circumstances were truly extraordinary. Here was I, a lad born in rural Worcestershire, coming from a humble background walking alongside a Prince of the Royal family of Saud. This guy was from a different world. Extremely rich and powerful in his own right, Prince Khalid was the nephew of King Abdulaziz who founded the Kingdom of Saudi Arabia and brother-in-law to King Fahd, the ruler of the day. But as we walked down that aviary block, that vast canyon of circumstance that would normally divide us,

136

closed and levelled. For a few minutes, we were just two falconers looking at breeding chambers and chatting about falconry.

He talked of hunting houbara in the desert from 4x4s, how they flew the birds, prepared them and cooked them.

"The houbara is a very clever, intelligent bird. Sometimes you English call them bustards. I say why? Such an unpleasant name for this wonderful quarry. And the houbara is very good to eat. The men, they make some pressure cooker and put the houbara in with water with spices and cook this on the fire. With some savoury rice, it is very good."

And I told him about the breeding programme, the displays at the castle and of grouse hawking in Yorkshire. I was with a kindred spirit who shared my enthusiasm and love of falconry. The conversation flowed so naturally that all my earlier nervousness evaporated. Once we had finished the tour of the aviary block, we returned to the weathering ground and the waiting retinue. It was time for business and the Prince was back to pointing.

"So, Gary. I do not want that one," he said, indicating a small female. "But, I will have this one, that one, that one and that. You can arrange it?"

"Yes, of course I can."

"Lovely, thank you. Wonderful."

As the gaggle returned to the parked vehicles, red tie and braces slotted into position beside me and kept pace. The powerhouse of a man was clearly Prince Khalid's right hand and used to issuing commands himself. He put a hand firmly on my arm and stopped me when we reached an apple tree, weighed down by good old English Bramleys.

"Schwarz," he said by way of introduction. "Thank you so much, Mr Cope. Prince Khalid was very impressed by your project and the birds, as are we all. So, on His Royal Highness' behalf, I would like to thank you for your time and your courtesy. Before I go, would you mind very much if I had one of your apples?"

"Of course not." I looked at the large green cookers hanging from the branches. "I don't think that you want one of these, though. Some of the others are better for eating."

"No thanks, Mr Cope, one of these will do just fine. Yup, I want one of these."

"Help yourself."

With that, Schwarz plucked an apple from the tree, bit deep into the bitter flesh and chewed happily. God knows what American teeth and gums are made of but his were certainly acid resistant.

"Marvellous," he pronounced. "Reminds me of when I was a kid. This is genuinely fabulous. Thank you so much."

And off he went to join the group around the cars. A moment later, Lord Ashcombe appeared.

"I'll be back in about half an hour, Gary. I'm just going to see Prince Khalid off and then I'll be back. I think that all went rather well."

The Prince and Schwarz returned to the white sheepskin upholstery of the Bentley Mulsanne Turbo while the close protection crew were absorbed by the two black Range Rovers. Once the Royal convoy had rolled down the drive to disappear from view, Lord Ashcombe reappeared. He had a great big beaming smile on his face.

"Well done, well done. Where are the boys?" he asked as we walked into The Bothy. "Bring them in." And once everyone was assembled, he continued. "Thank you all for a job well done. I don't think that it could have gone any better. That was a jolly good team effort so once again thank you all. And I'm sure that you'll be delighted to know that Prince Khalid is going to buy four of the sakers. Gary, what you'll need to do now is to sort out the export permits and transportation."

Of course I was delighted, but I now faced a mountain of paperwork. The Department of the Environment had reams of rules that had to be adhered to and regulations that could not be broken. Under the Convention on International Trade in Endangered Species of Wild Fauna and Flora – commonly known as CITES – there were a lot that included permits, forms and checks. The paper trail was endless. And then there were travel boxes to consider,

138

the logistics of transportation and the care of the birds themselves.

The travel boxes were the least of our worries. Danny, the Estate carpenter, produced superb boxes from my designs which provided state-of-the-art travelling accommodation. Carpeted inside constructed from good timber, they were brilliant. The complexity of paperwork took a little longer but was finally completed. Everything was organised and arrangements were made for the birds' flights to Riyadh. Unfortunately, the Royal flight was unavailable as the Prince's private jet was already commissioned to transport racehorses. The sakers would have to fly steerage with KLM, a lowly commercial airline.

The birds were hooded, primaries and tails secured with parcel tape, and boxed. I arrived at Heathrow's cargo terminal with several hours to spare. Finding the appropriate office was a task in its own right but I got there in the end.

"What you got mate?"

"Four birds of prey in traveling boxes."

"Bleedin' 'ell. Where they goin'?"

"Saudi Arabia, Riyadh."

"Got yer papers there? Ta," he added as I plonked them on the counter.

Flick, check, tick, cross. Delete, tick, check, tick. It seemed to take him ages to go through everything but the process probably only lasted a few minutes. Finally satisfied, he tidied the stack up again and then started stripping it down, handing half of it back.

"That's it, mate. Toast. Where're the birds?"

"Outside."

"Right, you bring 'em in 'ere and we'll pop 'em in the warehouse until they're ready to go." He looked at his watch. "Yeah, they're not due for boarding for another three hours. Might as well leave 'em 'ere and we'll load 'em later. No point in you hangin' around."

"No chance, mate. Not a chance."

"What d'you want to do then?"

"No offence, but I'll sit with them till they're ready to board."

"Up to you, mate. There's a coffee machine over there if you want one."

"Cheers."

There I sat for three hours, jealously guarding the sakers and drinking plastic cup after cup of vending machine coffee.

"These the birds for Riyadh?"

"Yeah."

"We're ready to go."

"Please be careful."

"Don't worry, this ain't the first time we've stuck boxes of birds on a plane," the cargo loader said with a grin. "Probably won't be the last neither."

It was really quite emotional watching the boxes disappear down the corridor. These were my babies, flying off to a strange place that I'd never been and to a world I'd never known. I'd bred them, brought them into the world and now they were leaving. It was strangely difficult but the deed was done and my sakers were off to a royal future. But I still felt quite sad at the loss.

I trucked my way home and that night I doubt that I slept at all. Questions kept looping through my head in perpetual motion. How were they doing? Have they still got their hoods on? Is the packing tape on their tails and wings still holding up? Would they arrive in perfect condition? Around and around they went in constant circles, without end or answers.

The following morning, as instructed, I phoned the Riyadh number that I'd been given to call. I was to talk to a man with an unpronounceable name that sounded like Kinafarti.

"Have the sakers arrived?"

"Yes they are here."

"Was all the paperwork in order?"

"No paperwork is necessary."

"Sorry?" I'd spent days sorting out all the papers and forms.

"We need no papers for the birds. We have vehicle on tarmac ready for them and then they are taken to the Royal Mews."

140

"So they're arrived safely and everything is fine?"

"Yes, Mr Cope. All is very fine. Thank you."

And that was the end of that. I didn't hear anything more for about six months, when I did get some feedback. Apparently, three of the four falcons had proved their worth in the desert, had flown well and caught houbara. Sadly, one hadn't made the grade, had been injured and died. However, the three successful falcons had been retained in the Royal Mews which was wonderful news. At the end of the season, Arab falconers usually take off the jesses and release the birds back into the wild. Falcons are only retained through the off-season if they are really good. Having three out of four housed in the Royal Mews once the season had ended was true testament to their quality and worth. At that point, and with that knowledge, I knew we were embarking on a grand new adventure.

Chapter 14 – Lock, stock and barrel

A grand adventure indeed. Everything seemed to be touched with magic. We were breeding sakers for wealthy Arabs in the Middle East, other birds for the British market and making a nice little profit. The hawking weekends and falconry courses were well subscribed and running smoothly. Partridge hawing was still on our menu, although more of an expensive amuse gueule than a profitable main course. Joy and I both had sports cars plus a 4x4 to share, considerable disposable income and a lovely home.

Since The Bothy was fairly isolated in terms of neighbours, it was an ideal place for extravagant parties. Seventy or eighty guests would converge on the place for those wonderful parties that were invariably fancy dress. It was just 'The' place to be and we were riding on the crest of a wave. We were untouchable, marvellous creatures, so what could possibly go wrong? And just when you're thinking that, something does!

One foul Friday night, Joy, Ali and I were hunkered down in front of the fire watching some mind-numbing 80s movie. The birds had all been locked up for the night and out of harm's way. Which was all to the good since the wind was howling like a banshee while the rain lashed and whipped everything in its path. It was a fine night to watch rubbish and then curl up in a warm bed, protected from the wrath of the weather outside.

By the time the sun peered through the window, the storm had abated but had left the world in a sodden mess. After a night like that, it was prudent to feed the birds early and get some food inside them. Having loaded my bag from the hawk larder, I went out to the breeding chambers and fed the birds there, pleased to see that they looked none the worse after the gales of the night.

From there, I walked round to the block of four nursery pens where we usually kept surplus youngsters and a few other birds. And as they came into focus, to my horror I realised that the doors were wide open, swinging gently in the breeze. The heavy-duty padlocks lay uselessly on the grass, the chambers silent and empty.

One chamber had held four tribrids which were really quite unusual. I'd been breeding one of John Anderson's female lanner-lugger crosses with a sakerette for some time and produced quite a few lanner saker-lanner-lugger tribrids.

"A lanner-lugger cross won't breed with a saker," said the experts. "And even if they do breed, the eggs won't be fertile."

So much for their expertise. The birds I'd bred were smaller than sakers with the conformation of hybrids but perfectly serviceable and excellent birds to fly. The four birds in the chamber were due to be sold but now they were gone.

Another chamber had held a bird that I'd actually been flying for the past year. I'd called her Goda after the Anglo-Saxon princess, daughter of King Ethelred the Unready, and she was a lovely bird. I only put her there for a few days as I'd been too busy and now she was gone as well. Totally shell-shocked, I rushed back to the house.

"Geez, you're white as a sheet!"

"What's happened?"

As soon as Joy and Ali saw me, it was clear there was something badly awry.

"The birds in the nursery pens have all gone. They must have taken them last night. Didn't hear a bloody thing in the storm. Not one's left."

Once I'd stopped babbling, they had the gist of the story and I phoned the police. About 45 minutes later, Sherlock and Watson duly arrived in plain clothes and an unmarked car. And keeping conversation to a polite minimum, I took them to the scene of the crime.

"Mmm, yes, it looks like you've been raided, Mr Cope."

"Yes, I have."

"They were locked, these cages?"

"Yes, of course! The padlocks are there on the ground. They obviously chopped them off somehow."

"Boltcutters, Holmes?"

"Boltcutters, Watson. Yes, if you look here Mr Cope, you can see that they cut them off."

"I can see that," I said, trying to keep the exasperation out of my voice.

"And the contents have all gone, have they?"

"Yes, they've taken all of the birds."

"Did they take anything else from here?"

"There wasn't anything else they could take!"

"Ah. So it's just the birds then?"

"Of course."

"I see. Oh dear. Valuable are they?"

"Yes, but it's not just that. I'm concerned about their welfare."

"I understand. Mmm. Where do you think they got in?"

"Well, looking at the crushed brambles over there by the roadside wall, I would suggest that they got in there and that they had their vehicle parked outside on the lane."

"You're probably right, Mr Cope, you're probably right. They could have hurt themselves on those brambles."

"We were raided by poachers a while back so I've let the brambles grow fairly wild. The thought was that if anybody dropped over the wall in future, they'd end up waist deep in the things. Serve them bloody well right. Plus we've had some good blackberries from them. Two with one stone, if you know what I mean."

"I don't think that letting the brambles grow for the purpose of deterrence was quite appropriate. You have to consider the consequences of your actions."

'For God's sake,' I muttered as the pair wandered off to search for tyre tracks and other incriminating clues.

Holmes shuffled about in the grass and poked at stones while Watson took notes. Their enquiry was quite obviously going nowhere at a very slow rate of knots.

"Having made initial investigations, we'll file the case with lost and found pets, Mr Cope."

"They're not pets and they're not lost! Someone's bloody stolen them!"

"I understand Sir, but that's the procedure. Naturally we'll keep our ears to the ground and see if we come up with anything."

'Great,' I thought. "What do you suggest I do?" I asked aloud.

"I suggest that you contact the RSPCA and improve your security, Mr Cope."

'Thank you for that pearl of wisdom!' "Perhaps I'll get a pair of blood great Dobermans."

"Oh no, no, no Sir. You can't possibly do that. I couldn't possibly recommend that avenue."

"Why not?"

"Well, it's like this Sir. If somebody were to come over your wall and was savaged by your dogs, you'd be liable for prosecution. You see all they'd be doing was to trespass. Until they actually took something, they'd have been savaged for trespassing and could therefore seek damages."

"All right, we'll go for Plan B. How about if I cemented broken glass along the top of the wall? Or maybe it would be better to run razor wire along it."

"No Sir. I can't advise either of those two since the same thing applies. Just imagine if somebody was to climb over the wall; they could cut themselves extremely badly. And they'd be within their rights to prosecute again."

"You have got to be joking? Surely, glass or razor wire is a deterrent?"

"It may be Sir, but think of what might happen if someone did try to climb over. You wouldn't want to be prosecuted for something like that."

I was beginning to wonder who the criminal was and who the victim.

"What do you suggest then?"

"From a professional point of view, I would strongly recommend approaching a reputable company and installing a good security system."

"Thank you for your help, Inspector."

'And for your totally useless time,' I added silently.

Shaking my head in despair and amazement, I watched Sherlock and Watson drive into history. I never heard a word from them again, nor was I ever contacted by anyone else in the force. After the two detectives left, I was overwhelmed with sadness and concern.

Fortunately, the young sakers which were due out were still with their parents in the main block; better that the tribrids were stolen than the sakers. But that commercial, practical thought did little to mitigate their rude and abrupt loss. And to think that someone had forced their way in to Goda's chamber, grabbed her with rough hands and simply shoved her in a box. What was she thinking now that her life had collapsed? She must have been terrified. Losing a bird that you've trained and flown is especially heartbreaking.

All of the birds were naturally registered with the Department of the Environment, which might make life difficult for the thieves if the plan was to sell them. And that thought led to an even more ghastly and grisly one: it was strongly rumoured that there was a horrible trade in stolen birds to be used for taxidermy. I shuddered. And then I remembered something that had happened a few weeks before which set me wondering.

About three weeks earlier, I'd placed an advert in a well-known avian publication with the intention of selling a few birds. When someone phoned to say – I want to buy a falcon – they were always vetted very carefully.

"What are you going to do with it?" I might ask.

"I'm going to fly it at rooks."

"Fine. Where?"

"Oh, in my local playing fields, in Wednesbury."

At which point I'd terminate the call. I was invariably very careful and extremely choosy as to who bought my birds.

This one guy from London did sound fine on the phone but I immediately had my doubts when he arrived at The Bothy. I heard the roar of the exhaust well before the car drove into view. The rear end was jacked up and adorned with a large spoiler while the front was so close to the ground that it was almost grading the path. Tinted windows concealed the identity of the occupants who only revealed their full urban dress sense when they emerged. Four of them got out of the car, each wearing a baseball cap, branded Ts, low slung baggy jeans and trainers. Alarm bells were clamouring a warning.

'What am I going to do now?' I thought as I looked at the quartet in some dismay.

146

"All right, mate? You're Gary, right? We spoke on the phone about the birds for sale?"

"Yeah."

"Darren. Good to meet ya."

"Hi, Darren. Umm, look, I'll be honest with you. The birds you've come to see -I'm afraid that they're not going to be for sale after all. I'm terribly sorry to let you down. Umm." Thinking quickly on my feet, I continued, "There's this friend of mine you see, I owe him a massive favour and he could really do with them. I'm really sorry."

Strangely, he didn't seem at all perturbed by the news even though he'd driven all the way from London on a wild goose chase. If it had been me, I'd have been seriously pissed off and said as much.

"Don't worry mate, these fings 'appen, don't they? Tell you what though, don't mind if we look at the birds anyway? Maybe your mate'll change 'is mind. We'll give you a ring in a couple of weeks, all right?"

Caught on the back foot, there was little option but to give the urban warriors the guided tour. When the memory of their visit returned, my gut instinct was that they were the culprits. They'd simply come up to case the place and had then come back two weeks later to filch the birds. Maybe it was them and maybe not, but I never did find out what had happened to my precious birds.

However, my musings on the whys and wherefores were going nowhere. It was time to talk to Lord Ashcombe, break the news and discuss a way forward. He was quietly pragmatic and decisive.

"It's rotten luck, Gary, but it could have been worse. Look at it this way, at least they didn't take any of the saker pairs, they're all still here. On the other hand, it's pretty clear that we do need a good security system installed. I'll leave that to you to organise."

Thus a number of company representatives visited The Bothy, each clutching his or her glossy brochure, printed in full colour, with warnings, cautions, recommendations and numerous reasons why their company was the best. There were cameras, floodlights, sensors, trips, klaxons, sirens and a wealth of other technological gadgetry from which to choose.

In the end, we settled for the installation of an infrared system at a cost of £9,500, which assumed that yours truly would undertake all the groundwork. Nine plus grand was a lot of money in those days, so it seemed only reasonable that I showed willing. Therefore it was up to me to dig the trenches for the underground cabling, fix brackets and all the other necessary things. Nevertheless, it was going to take between five and six weeks for the installation to be completed. I needed an interim security solution.

'Poacher alarms might do the trick,' I thought.

Clever little things, your basic poacher alarm comprised a metal rod with a container at its base into which one inserted a shotgun blank or live shell, depending on your intent. A wire was attached to the top of the rod which was then fastened to another pole, the side of a building or a wall. As soon as someone walked into the wire, a catch would immediately be released, allowing the hammer to strike the firing pin on the cartridge. And – kerboom! Brilliant.

"Have you got any of those poacher alarms?" I asked Kerry Wiggett, the Estate gamekeeper.

"Yep, I've got some of those."

"How many?"

"About eight or nine."

"Can I borrow them for a few weeks?"

"Course you can, Gary."

"Excellent!"

Once acquired, each alarm was strategically placed and trip wires carefully stretched across vulnerable pathways. But the trick was to remember the exact position of each location and that was an absolute nightmare.

While changing my shirt in the bedroom one afternoon, I happened to look out of the window and saw Major Lawson wandering towards the walled garden. Major Nicholas Lawson, previously Private Secretary to HRH Princess Anne and formerly an officer in the Life Guards, was the new Estate manager. We got on well enough but the major had the annoying habit of turning up at The

148

Bothy uninvited. And once he'd arrived, would simply wander round as he pleased which did not, however, please me one little bit. If I was honest, I would have to admit that I didn't like anyone walking around without Nick, John or I in attendance.

So there I am, watching the Major tootling about and making his way towards the aviaries. The sixty-four thousand dollar question was whether or not I had enough time to open the window and shout a warning.

"Watch out, you're heading towards a tripwire!"

Suffice it to say that by the time I'd considered the question, it was already too late. The Major blundered straight through a tripwire, simultaneously firing off two separate charges. Unfortunately, Nick had loaded the alarms with live shells the night before which simply compounded the situation. The detonations not only resulted in mighty explosions but also threw huge clods of earth into the air. Lawson followed suit, leaping upwards in fright like a startled hare. The violent noise died away, leaving the distinctive acrid scent of nitro-glycerine to fill the void. Ashen faced and wild-eyed, with his normally tidy floppy hair awry, the Major stumbled away from the devastation caused by our anti-personnel mines, towards the house. I met him outside, stifling my laughter with some difficulty.

"Ah, Major Lawson. Everything all right?"

"Yes, I think so. Obviously set off one of your damned booby-traps. Bloody near frightened the life out of me."

"Yeah, well we have to have security, I'm afraid. Best that people don't go wandering around on their own, without somebody being with them."

Live shells do have an impact and certainly the Major never repeated his error. And it wasn't that long before the basic poacher alarms were replaced by a somewhat more sophisticated system. Several men from the Bristol based company came up to install and commission our posh new infra-red security spies and eyes.

"Done and dusted?"

"Yessir. All finished. An' it's all wurkin' fine."

"So we should be pretty secure now?"

"Oh, you'll be secure enough. Bloody moth won't git past 'ere without you knowin' abowt it!" the foreman said prophetically.

"Great, that's exactly what we want."

Or so I thought until 145 decibels of blaring klaxon screamed frenetic warnings at two-thirty in the morning. The main siren was fixed to the outside wall next to the bedroom window. For the next four or five weeks, at least once or twice a night, something would trigger the system. I'd be fast asleep until the klaxon went into full howl mode as though World War Three had been declared and The Bothy was about to sustain airborne nuclear bombardment. Floodlighting banished even the smallest sliver of darkness and bathed the walled garden in enough glare to illuminate a football stadium.

I'd leap out of bed, drag on shirt and trousers and rush downstairs. Then, arming myself with a gun or other nearby weapon with which to confront the intruders, I'd dash outside. To find that it was a false alarm: nothing and no one. Turning the sirens and lighting off again, I'd re-arm the system and return to bed, only to be woken again an hour or so later.

Night after night, week after week, it was blaring sound and glaring lights, but no action. The security system was so sensitive that when a moth, a bat or even a leaf was caught by the sensors, the alarm would rip the night open. After all these weeks of broken, sleepless nights, I was a nervous wreck and was beginning to dream of air raids. Finally, I phoned the boys from Bristol.

"It has to be desensitised."

"We can lower the system's sensitivity, Mr Cope, but you have to understand that it will compromise the efficiency to a similar degree."

"Of course, but we need a security system that'll go off if there's an intruder. What we don't need is an infrared bloody mosquito net. Please come and lower the sensitivity."

The company complied, albeit with written provisos with regard to efficiency percentages and trigger tolerances. Although we still had a few false alarms when

150

something as large as a fox crossed the sensors, the problem was substantially diminished. At last I was able to get some shut-eye, safe in the knowledge that the birds were secure.

Not that our spanking new and moderated security system deterred visitors during the day. Trip wires and shotgun shells were now part of history's rich tapestry. Every weekend saw a constant stream of VIPs rolling up to The Bothy. Lord Ashcombe maintained his coffee and Marlboro habit during our mandatory Saturday or Sunday morning chats and would often have a guest or two in tow. Many of the guests would spend the weekend at Sudeley which often meant taking them out hawking on the estate. Usually it would be a spot of rabbiting and maybe a bit of partridge hawking if it was in season.

One elderly but sprightly gentleman who came to stay had an interesting way of introducing himself. He was a blood relation of Franz Ferdinand who was assassinated in 1917 and might have been a nephew or similar. And while he shared both name and title with the deceased, he obviously did not share his politics.

"Ja, I am called Archduke Ferdinand, like Franz Ferdinand. Maybe you have heard of him? He was responsible for starting the First World War."

I remember thinking that it was a brilliant way of breaking the ice and the Archduke was quite delightful company.

As indeed was Rocco Forte who was a close friend of Lord Ashcombe and, of course, named a suite after his Lordship at the Forte-owned flagship, the Black Swan in Helmsley. It was a natural progression that Rocco Forte would accompany us on one or two hawking excursions on the moors nearby but his dress code was rarely commensurate with being in the field. He'd appear in a pristine white Puffa jacket which might have been synonymous with style in some sporting circles but was hardly the best camouflage when out hawking.

It was on one of those jaunts to Sykes Cottage with Lord Ashcombe for some grouse hawking that life took another downturn. A few days before leaving for Yorkshire, I noticed that my star demonstration falcon, Cid, had developed a tiny bump on the outside of one of his toes. It looked like a touch of bumblefoot and, although it wasn't on the ball of his foot, I wasn't taking any chances. Accordingly, I took Cid to see the renowned avian specialist vet, Neil Forbes, who was fortunately based in Gloucestershire.

"I'm probably being paranoid Neil but Cid's such a valuable bird. He's a real breadwinner."

"Prevention's always better than cure. It's not a severe case but I'll give you some antibiotics which should tidy it up fairly quickly."

"Brilliant. I'm away for a while but Nick can administer the drugs and Cid'll be in good hands."

As I expected, Nick was quite happy to take care of Cid in my absence and give him his antibiotics. Which is why I was shocked to hear the tremor in Nick's voice when he phoned me in Yorkshire a few days later. He was clearly upset and shaken when I took his call.

"I've got some terrible news, Gary. I'm so sorry. He was fine last night and then when I …"

"Nick, slow down. OK, tell me what's up?"

"Last night. I left Cid in the kitchen as usual and he was absolutely fine. Then when I came down this morning, I found him lying on the floor, dead."

"What?" I almost shrieked the word at the phone.

"Honestly, he was right as ninepins last night. Business as usual. And then this morning I found him dead. He was just lying on the floor, lifeless."

I felt the blood drain from my face and the air sucked from my lungs. Nick's news was shattering but I needed to know the cause of death.

"You'll have to put him in the freezer and we'll get a post mortem done."

Examination and analysis showed that Cid had died from kidney failure following an allergic reaction to the antibiotics. Not that it was Neil's fault as he couldn't have known, but Cid's death was a game changer. The show has to go on and the falconry shows recommenced the following season with a different falcon and other birds.

152

But it wasn't the same without Cid. That wonderful little lanneret had been such a joy to fly and he delighted audiences time after time because he was truly extraordinary. The team that I now had was good, but not one of those birds was extraordinary.

For me, the displays were routine and colourless with little drama or spark. They followed a pattern that was predictable and unemotional. I could still bring the enthusiasm to my voice as I gave the audience my spiel but I could talk without thinking and my mind would drift.

'I wonder what we should have for dinner tonight? We could have lamb chops, pork chops or there's even a bit of steak in the fridge,' I thought as I was halfway through my talk.

I suddenly realised that I'd been on autopilot. It was like that feeling you get when you've driven several miles, then get to a certain point and realise that you can't remember one bit of the journey.

'Bugger, have I been boring people with what's on tonight's menu?!'

From the looks on their faces, they hadn't heard words like chop or steak but the fact that I wasn't concentrating was not good. And falconry displays had become so common. Centres had grown up like mushrooms in a field of cowpats. Every Tom, Dick or Harry was flying Harris hawks over the pergolas for sale at the back of the garden centres. Everywhere seemed to have falconry bolted on to the line-up, diminishing the impact. I had been doing displays for quite some time, so there was an element of burn-out, constantly have to keep the public face in place. And Cid's death had been so hard to accept. Somehow the whole thing had lost its magic.

"I almost told them what we were going to have for dinner today. I'm not quite sure when. I think it was just after flying the Harris. Joy? I think it's time for me to quit this."

The two of us talked it over for a while, or rather, I picked at the problem while she listened intently to all I said. And then, when I'd run out of steam and I'd stopped mentally juggling all the pros and cons, she said:

"Listen to yourself. Look if your heart's not in it then so be it. You know what you feel, so follow your heart."

The following morning, I rang Lord Ashcombe and started to tell him about my thoughts on giving up the displays. Stopping me in mid-trickle, he said he was on his way.

"So what do you want to do?"

"I think I'd like to continue running the courses. But there again, I don't know. There are so many people doing falconry courses these days for pennies. Some people are even running them from home over the weekend for pin money! I don't know. The whole thing's really become oversubscribed but ours do work well. What I really want to do is concentrate on the breeding. I think that's it really. I'd be happy to continue with the falconry courses but focus on the breeding side."

We talked around the subject for a while longer, pushing thoughts around the mental table.

"Let me think about it for a while as well," he said. "Might just be able to come up with a few ideas."

A couple of weeks later he was in the chair in the kitchen, sipping his coffee and lighting a cigarette.

"OK. If you don't want to do the shows, fine. Maybe they've had their glory days anyway. But I'd like you to stay with the courses. You happy with that?"

"Fine but …"

"You were going to mention the breeding." Steepling his fingers together on the table, he looked me straight in the eyes. "I suggest that you buy the project."

"Buy the project?" I asked in some amazement. "Umm, I hadn't really thought about that one. Wow."

"Gary, you buy the breeding project from us and the profits from the sales of any birds bred domestically you have in toto. Naturally, we would want a cut of any birds sold in the Middle East since the contacts are really all mine. The money you take for any courses that you arrange is all yours and if we arrange them, again we get a cut. On top of that, we'll let you have The Bothy, the breeding chambers and everything that goes with them for a nominal fee. What do you think?"

154

"Lord Ashcombe, that all sounds marvellous. What sort of money are we talking about? Getting down to the basics."

The figures were extremely fair and I think that we were both happy with the deal. And that was it: I hung up my show glove for the last time, turning my focus on falconry courses and breeding.

But it didn't take long before I realised that prices for birds on the domestic market had plummeted. By the early 90s, a lot of people were breeding birds of prey and the competition was tough. It was suddenly apparent that what I'd thought would be my main stream of revenue was shrinking rapidly and the numbers weren't adding up any more.

'Oh crikey, what have I done?' I asked myself. 'What have I done?'

Chapter 15 – Falconer Royale

'Something's bound to come up sooner or later,' I thought as I looked through the window at the monochrome blankness.

Thick fog shrouded the landscape beyond, blurring the lines of walls and turning trees into wraiths. The world was a damp grey place in which sights were dreary and sounds muffled. Not one small ray of sunshine had managed to seep through the impenetrable layers of mists; nor were they disturbed by any whisper of wind. Somehow the scene was a visual approximation of my mood and did little to raise the spirits.

But the sight of Lord Ashcombe emerging from the gloom was really quite cheering. He stopped outside the window and blinked at me slowly from the other side of the glass. I nodded and grinned.

Although we'd kept in touch after making our deal, I hadn't been seeing quite so much of Lord Ashcombe. The continuity of our habitual coffee and cigarette mornings had fractured a little and I missed the comfortable regularity.

"It's good to see you, Lord Ashcombe. Coffee?"

"Of course," he said, tapping a Marlboro out of the packet. "How's everything going, Gary?"

We spent a while catching up with the news, chewing the fat and shooting the breeze. And then he got down to business.

"I've got proposition for you."

"What's that then?"

"Well, I was having dinner with Prince Khalid last week and, in the course of conversation, he mentioned that he's looking for a falconer. Naturally the Prince employs a falconer in Riyadh and this chap's been with him pretty well all of his life. Anyway, it turns out that he's due to retire fairly shortly and the Prince is looking for a replacement falconer - seems like you're at the top of his list."

'Riyadh! Bugger, how's that going to work?' I asked myself.

Joy was running a successful business at Gloucester Docks called Tourism Works. Both our families lived in the area and this was where all our friends were. I had this vision of them all gathered in a group at The Bothy and I was standing in front of them. Drinking down the last dregs of my wine, I smiled and announced: "Right then, I'm off to Saudi Arabia - following in Lawrence's footsteps. 'Bye."

Apart from the pregnant pause and my slightly disconcerted look, I was giving nothing away. Perhaps Lord Ashcombe saw something in my eyes or had taken up mind reading. Or, more likely, he'd anticipated the slight reticence and confusion.

"However, I suspect you might be relieved to know that it's not in Riyadh. He's looking for someone to be based over here, in Britain."

"Right," I said with relief that was only fractionally tinged with disappointment. "OK. But why me?"

"Do you remember when Prince Khalid came here a couple of years ago to see the sakers? Bought four of them, including that bloody great big one?"

"How could I forget? Man, that bird was a monster and wild as hell! The worst part was when he asked me to take her hood off. I really didn't think I'd get it back on again quite so neatly."

"Exactly! The Prince was rather impressed by that. According to him, he'd decided to give you a test, see how you'd manage to handle a wild bird, work under pressure in front of everybody - that sort of thing. Anyway, you obviously passed and that's why you've been offered the job."

"Who'd have thought it? Wow! I mean, brilliant but what happens next?"

"In the first instance, you'll be liaising with one of the Prince's representatives from Carter Jonas. They're a rather big company of land agents who cover estates across the country. Anyway, the chap you'll be seeing is Richard Carter Jonas. He's one of the family, but he's also a Director of the Fairlawne Estate Company which more or less runs the Prince's place in Kent. I'll give him your number and he'll be in touch."

Despite the impressive credentials, Carter Jonas was not a business suit type and clearly comfortable in a rural environment. I liked him from the outset and the conversation flowed easily until we got down to the details.

"So, what's the deal?" I asked finally.

"As you know, Prince Khalid would like to employ you as his falconer. However, we envisage a division of labour, in so far as, when you were not engaged in falconry, you could undertake general work on the Estate. The post would be based at Fairlawne, Prince Khalid's estate in Kent and a nice little farmworker's cottage has just become vacant so you could live there. Lovely place, Fairlawne. We propose an annual salary of twelve-and-a-half thousand pounds. So, what do you think?"

I just looked at him for a moment, then shook my head.

"Not a chance."

"Is there a problem?"

"Yeah, unfortunately quite a few. Firstly, twelve-and-a-half grand comes nowhere near to what I'm currently earning. Secondly, as you can see, I have a rather nice spacious abode which is more than a few notches above a small worker's cottage. And thirdly, I don't do Estate work; I'm an aviculturist and a falconer."

"Ah, I see. What terms would you find acceptable, Mr Cope?"

"I would suggest that you come back with a revised offer, Mr Carter Jonas. And I'll let you know."

Lord Ashcombe assured me that they'd be back with a better offer. And two weeks later, Richard Carter Jonas was once again sitting in the kitchen at The Bothy.

"As you can see," he said, indicating the salient paragraph on the page lying between us on the table, "the annual salary has been raised considerably. Your concerns on the division of work as previously outlined have been understood and appreciated. Therefore, your work will only entail those duties that pertain to the practise of falconry and ancillary functions. Now, as to the living accommodation -there's a derelict farm on the Estate with a house and barns, which might be ideal for you. Of course it needs a bit of work on it but before we rush in, perhaps you'd like to come down and have a look?"

"OK, I'll come down."

The idea of moving to Kent didn't really appeal. It was too close to London, full of hops, neatly squared fields and upwardly mobile people driving 4x4s that never left the tarmac. I just didn't like the county and the 'considerable' rise in salary was still not bringing it up to the level I needed. But, not wanting to seem constantly obdurate, I decided to at least see this derelict farm. To be fair, it did have a lot of potential and the place could have been brilliant provided Prince Khalid spent a huge amount of money. The house itself was quite nice and there were plenty of outbuildings and cowsheds, but it all needed renovation. The cowsheds, for example, hadn't been used in living memory and were knee-deep in petrified dung.

"I'll give it some thought and let you know," I told Carter Jonas at the end of the viewing.

And I did give it some thought, but didn't make contact for quite a while. Nothing was really gelling in my mind on the Kentish front and then another idea dawned. It made much more sense to stay at The Bothy. I invited Lord Ashcombe over for coffee and conversation.

"To be honest, I'd prefer to stay here anyway, rather than move down to Kent. But it would be insane to spend a vast amount of money on a derelict farm down there when everything I need is already here. We've got state-of-the-art breeding chambers, solidly built and with one-way glass. There are aviaries, a protected weathering ground, a modern security system, the works. We've even got the best vet in the country living up the road - Neil Forbes in Stroud. It's all set up here."

"So what exactly are you suggesting, Gary?"

"Why can't Prince Khalid take over The Bothy? You could let the whole place to him for a decent commercial rent which would obviously be much more than I'm paying. Which I know was a special agreement because of the circumstances, but it does make financial sense to let it to him. Prince Khalid covers all the bills and pays my salary because he's my employer. Doing it that way, the

Prince actually saves money and gets everything going that much faster."

"Your plan has distinct merit, Gary. Distinct merit."

A few days later, Lord Ashcombe invited himself back to The Bothy, ordered coffee and lit a cigarette.

"Your plan's been approved. Prince Khalid agrees that it's a sensible way forward so it looks like you're about to be a Royal Falconer and remain in situ."

"Wonderful. But where does it go next?"

"He wants to meet us in his office in Cadogan Square, so you'll have to come down to London. He'd like to do some grouse hawking and he's considering some of the Yorkshire moors."

"Right. He wants to rent some grouse moors."

"Good God, no! The Prince isn't renting, he's buying. Oh yes, there's another thing. Forget about the sakers. Now he wants white gyrfalcons."

"Bloody hell, gyrfalcons?!"

"Mmm," his Lordship said, taking another gulp of coffee. "You'd better get your thinking cap on about pulling a grouse hawking team together - and where to get white gyrfalcons."

"I know there're a lot of people with domestic breeding programmes in the UK but they're mainly Harris hawks, peregrines or whatever. Gyrs are like hen's teeth."

"Be that as it may, that's what the Prince wants. Bit of research needed there, by the sound of it, but I'm sure you'll manage to track a few down. Anyway, if you could work out a brief and prepare a short report for Prince Khalid, I'll give him a ring and arrange a meeting."

Making good use of Joy's brilliant administrative and writing skills, I managed to produce a fairly comprehensive report which, I thought, read rather well. In the meantime, Lord Ashcombe had been in contact with the Prince's Private Secretary.

"The meeting's on Thursday at about eleven. I'll be at the house in Holland Park, so you'll have to catch the early train to London. That should get you in to Paddington around nine and then get a taxi to bring you to Holland

Park. That will give us enough time to get to Cadogan Square."

The thought made me shudder. Getting up at 5.30am, in the dark, was bad enough. But the idea of a high-profile meeting in the metropolis, which might change my life entirely, was nerve-jangling.

Outside, grey clouds crept hesitantly under an ashen sky, spitting intermittent sprays of cold drizzle. Inside, my reflection looked back at me from the mirror, awkward and uncomfortable in the unaccustomed suit. The old but serviceable Christian Dior that only emerged for weddings or funerals felt constricting and unnatural. I ran my finger under the too-tight collar and grimaced at the poorly knotted tie that stubbornly refused to sit in its assigned position.

'Mutton dressed up like lamb,' I told my mirror image, 'Time for this country lad to go up to the Big City."

'More bumpkin than broker!' it retorted.

The seven thirty commuter train from Cheltenham Spa to Paddington, London was already fairly well tenanted by suits armed with briefcases and newspapers. Climbing on board, I wormed my way through the collective smog of passengers in second class. Fireflies of cigarette tips glowed and dimmed through the pall of smoke in every carriage, reducing visibility to a matter of feet. Conversation was limited to the occasional mumbled grudging apology for toe crushing or shoulder pushing. Unfriendly and isolating, the only warmth on the train was generated by the proximity of bodies. Though I'd travelled the world, it was the first time I'd been on a train since I was seven and it was all a bit strange.

'How do they do this every day?' I asked myself. 'It's horrible.'

Eventually, I found my reserved seat in first class and thankfully flopped down, feeling a total alien. At least it was slightly more civilized: more space and less smoke. Rubbing a hole in the layer of condensation on the window revealed little more than rain-streaked glass against a grey-green film. The syncopated rumble of the train played a baseline to the rustle of papers, catches flipped on a briefcase and someone's hacking cough.

I looked across at the overweight man sitting opposite and briefly wondered what he did for a living. Perhaps he was 'somebody' in the City or a corporate lawyer. Shutting his case on a pile of papers, one podgy hand rifled an expensive pocket and produced a courgette-sized cigar. While he concentrated on cutting and lighting the horrible thing, I fled to the safety of the concertinaed gap between coaches. Yanking down the window, I gulped in the rain-washed fresh air with relief. It had only taken two clouds of billowing acrid smoke to make me feel sick.

"Why am I here?" I muttered.

The sodden countryside gave way to damp urban vistas, followed by drab lines of terraced houses, begrimed warehouses and rusting rolling stock. Ealing Broadway, Ealing, Old Oak West, Westbourne Park, Royal Oak – black print on white boards that flashed past, ignored by our fast intercity train. As we finally ground to halt under Paddington's vaulted roof of glass and steel, doors were flung wide and the train vomited its human cargo onto the platform. The clamour of noise and crush of people was almost overwhelming. Clutching my small leather folio of papers close to my chest, I joined the chaotic river of people that rushed towards the exit. Suddenly, and unfortunately, I felt an urgent need for a pee.

I dodged around women dragging suitcases, tourists who had paused to scrutinise maps and packs of businessmen blocking the way. There were people everywhere, all determined to slow me down and stop me finding the loo. When I finally spotted the magic words, 'Gentlemen's Toilet', I managed the steps with a groin-clenching walk, only to be confronted by a turnstile and a slot that demanded one ten pence piece. Fumbling in my pockets for the required coin, I paid the toll and rushed forwards to blessed relief. Phew!

Leaving the chap who was shaving, the suit straightening his tie and the prototype chav combing his hair, I went in search of a taxi. And the queue was immense, zigzagging back and forth with the sinuosity of a

162

digesting python. I glanced at my watch and frowned nervously. But Paddington's taxi rank operates like an oiled machine with turbo-chargers and within minutes I found myself sitting on one of London's ubiquitous black cabs.

"Where to mate?" the driver asked as he wrenched the cab into the stream of traffic.

"Erm, Holland Park Road, please."

"Seein' friends? Nice place to live, Holland Park, an' full of toffs. Takin' you round the sights, I s'pose. Gimme a call if yer need transport."

He passed a card over his shoulder.

"Thank you. But no, I'm here on business."

"What you in then?"

"I'm a professional falconer."

"What's that then?"

I gave him a low-key falconry spiel, avoiding too many 'toff' references, which passed the time as we squeezed out of Westbourne Street and stuttered along the Bayswater Road. A dense mass of cars, bikes, vans and trucks all vied for position and not one was prepared to give quarter.

"I've never seen anything like this. How do you deal with this traffic ever day?"

"It's all 'bout keepin' calm, mate, innit?"

At which point a BMW Three Series screeched out of a side road, cutting straight across the front of the cab.

"Stupid fuckin' git!" the cab driver shouted uselessly, "Learn to bloody drive." Having leaned halfway out of the car to vent his spleen, he returned to a more normal driving position and continued as though nothing had happened.

"As I was sayin', it's all about keepin' calm and not getting upset."

'It's a total nuthouse,' I thought. 'They're all insane!'

And to prove the point, the cabbie promptly swung a hard left, narrowly avoiding a pedestrian crossing the road. A few minutes later he pulled up at the kerb, outside a fine redbrick building with contrasting light granite entrance and high-gloss black painted door.

"You're 'ere, mate."

My fare paid plus a small tip, I stood on the pavement, looked at the piece of paper in my hand, look backed at the door and rang the bell. Like a stone dropped in a well, the sound took time to travel, ringing back seconds later from the bowels of the house and accompanied by the frantic yapping sounds of a small dog. It had to be Ziggy.

"Rff, rff, reep, reep, reep, reep."

After Spud died, Lord Ashcombe has replaced the aged springer spaniel with a young cocker spaniel called Ziggy, who was just as nuts as her predecessor. As the yapping got closer and louder, I could hear her claws skittering on parquet flooring. And then the sounds changed. The yapping suddenly stopped, the skitter turned into an uncontrollable full-blown slide and a moment later she thumped into the door.

"Ziggy! Ziggy, you bloody idiot! Come here," shouted Lord Ashcombe from the depths. "Won't be a moment," he called through the door, "just sorting out the damn dog."

Opening the door with one hand while the other was hooked through Ziggy's collar, he looked up at me and smiled.

"Found it all right then. Come in, come in."

Regaining his composure, he took me into a beautifully appointed spacious lounge and indicated a seat. Then he shook his head.

"Right. On second thoughts, I just need to take Ziggy out for a brief run in the park, so why don't we take a quick walk. You've got your report I assume?"

"Yes, Lord Ashcombe."

"Fine, let's go."

Fifteen minutes later, we were in another cab, driving up Cromwell Road towards Knightsbridge. Once in Cadogan Square, Lord Ashcombe took the lead and rang the bell outside an imposing residence complete with portico and columns. A young man, very formally dressed in a black suit, starched white shirt and tie, opened the door.

"Good morning, Lord Ashcombe. And Mr Cope, I believe. Please follow me."

He escorted us to very plush, oak-panelled anteroom.

"If you would wait here, gentlemen, I will notify His Royal Highness of your arrival."

Both of us were silent, pacing slowly around the room on independent routes. I was certainly apprehensive and not a little nervous but I was surprised that his Lordship appeared to having the same feelings. Neither of us said a word and the profound silence was only broken the sound of slow soft footfalls.

"Gentleman, good morning," said a voice from the doorway. Neither of us had heard him enter the room. "I'm Ian Gibbs, one of His Royal Highness's aides. The Prince will see you now. Please follow me."

Turning out of the anteroom, we walked down a similarly panelled corridor and then climbed up the grand staircase that seemed to curve upwards to the ceiling several floors above. The wall to our right was covered with obviously valuable and original paintings, many of which were of racehorses. I had already discovered that Prince Khalid's Juddmonte Farms had produced some of the best racing bloodlines in the world. Khalid Abdullah's racing colours – pink sash on green with white sleeves and a pink cap – appeared on more than one of the jockeys portrayed. I'd made a mental note to remember that he probably knew a lot more about breeding than I'd given him credit for when he visited The Bothy.

Leading us away from the stairs, Gibbs grandly opened huge double doors and let us into the palatial room that the Prince called his office. The vast space was surprisingly sparsely furnished, dominated by a huge desk on the far side of the room.

The man himself sat behind the desk on an upright gilded chair upholstered in white brocade and beneath a portrait of an Arab who I assumed to be his father.

And standing to one side, wearing the familiar blue suit, red tie and braces was the redoubtable Mr Schwarz. Despite the smile and nod, he still looked every bit the personal bodyguard.

Prince Khalid stood up and smiled as well. "Good morning, Lord Ashcombe, Gary. Please."

He motioned towards two seats in front of the desk which were similarly gilded and upholstered to the Prince's own, but just a little smaller. Remembering the etiquette, I bowed and reached across the desk to grasp the extended hand before falling back on the chair.

"Good morning Your Royal Highness."

"So, it seems that I have acquired not only a new employee, but also a fine property in Gloucestershire. I am pleased with the arrangements. Now to the other matters: you have a report for me I believe, Gary."

"Yes, Sir," I said, leaning forwards to place the sheaf of papers within his reach. "I've outlined all the facilities available at The Bothy, together with all the services and utilities. There's a brief on the situation with grouse hawking in Yorkshire, on the terrain, environment and ..."

"Of course, you know that I am seeking to buy one of your grouse moors. How are we to progress with such a purchase?"

"I'm afraid that they are quite difficult to find, Sir, and rather expensive."

Prince Khalid waved a hand in the air as though dismissing an irritating fly.

"There has been some progress on that front," Lord Ashcombe chipped in, "as I have already made some enquiries on your behalf. Fact is, I went to see a grouse moor near Leyburn in North Yorkshire a few weeks ago. I think it's a couple of thousand acres or more and it looks ideal for the purpose. And apparently there's a pretty reasonable population of grouse."

Lord Ashcombe talked for several minutes, waxing eloquent on the potential for grouse hawking. Given the fact that his knowledge of the sport was limited to spending a few trips with me over a period of years, I was really quite surprised at his erudition.

"Chap's sending the rest of the details to me in the post this week," he concluded, "and once I have those, I'll be able to give you a more comprehensive report."

"Excellent."

"Excuse me, Your Royal Highness, if I could just go back to my report for a moment?" He nodded his

166

agreement. "As I was saying, I've also included some notes on how grouse hawking is practised in England which I think you'll find interesting. I know that there are quite a few differences between the way we do things and how Arabic hawking's practised, as we discussed a couple of years ago when you came to The Bothy. I do have an English pointer that I think will be very useful but we may need to acquire one more, and then there are the birds to consider."

"I look forward to reading your report, Gary," the Prince interjected, "however, as you have been informed, I wish to use gyrfalcons. You are able to obtain these birds?"

"Captive breeding has been booming in the UK but unfortunately that really doesn't apply to gyrs so …"

"In which case, where might they be found?"

"Sorry, Sir. There are a couple of people in Nevada who are breeding white gyrfalcons. From what I've heard, they do have a very good reputation and the birds are meant to be excellent but probably rather expensive."

The repeated error of mentioning cost was again dismissed with a wave of the hand.

"In that case, it appears that you will have to make a visit to America. And could you breed gyrfalcons at The Bothy?"

"I see no reason why not, Sir. As you know, I've successfully bred sakers, peregrines and even tribrids, so I don't think it would be a problem."

Our 'conversation' with the Prince lasted only a few minutes longer. He glanced down at the chunky gold Rolex on his wrist.

"Gentlemen, I'm afraid I have another appointment to attend. Thank you both for coming and I am sure we will meet again in the near future. Mr Schwarz will be finalising a few details with you before you leave. Schwarz, if you please."

Bidding farewell to Prince Khalid in the manner to which I was becoming accustomed, I bowed my way out of the room with the dual escort of Lord Ashcombe and Schwarz.

"Welcome on board," Schwarz said and closed the front door behind us.

I'd signed my name on various papers, Schwarz had provided us with several more and then we were back on the streets of London.

"Coffee at the Carlton I think," said Lord Ashcombe.

It was a long walk but little more was said. Actually, nothing was said; it was all rather quiet as we both mulled over our meeting to the sound of our feet on the pavement. It was the doorman, who was standing to one side of the Carlton's grand entrance when we arrived, who finally broke the vocal silence.

"Good morning gentlemen. Are we staying or looking for refreshment?"

"Just popping in for a cup of coffee."

For some reason I found both man and interchange ridiculously funny. I suddenly had a vision of the chap standing outside the White Lion in Winchcombe, complete with top hat and tails. And the locals throwing eggs at him for his trouble. Obviously he couldn't share the joke and simply bowed briefly at the waist, an outstretched arm indicating the doorway.

Revolving doors require a certain technique which demands a fine degree of arm, foot and eye coordination. The trick is to push the glass on the far side of the open quadrant, nip in quickly to avoid being smacked in the back by the following divider and shuffle forwards in the manner of a penguin while maintaining constant pressure on the glass in front. Armed with that knowledge, we should have had little difficulty in negotiating the obstacle.

Lord Ashcombe naturally took the lead and put his best foot forward, stepping into the beckoning opening with one hand readied to push. At which point, my system was alarmed by the violent report of a car backfiring loudly. My head flew backwards, my chest pulled forwards and my legs threw me straight into his lordship's back. Since there was only room enough in any one quadrant for one person, I found myself intimately squashed against Lord Ashcombe's derriere. To add to my embarrassment, my reactive lurch into the small space meant that the movement of the door accelerated.

Our conjoined shuffle rotated through the necessary arc and, on reaching the apex, the revolving beast ejected us unceremoniously into the calm of the lobby. It was not the most decorous of entrances and attracted more than one disapproving glance from the very posh people drinking their beverages in that terribly genteel way. As we tumbled our way out onto the floor we looked more like a pair of drunks than a member of the British aristocracy and a prince's falconer.

"Gentlemen, may I take you to a table?" asked the waiter, totally unfazed.

I could feel the colour suffusing my face with embarrassment but Lord Ashcombe didn't say a word. And, once we were seated, our presence was forgotten by all but the waiter.

"Coffee for two, please."

"Certainly Sir."

Moments later a silver coffeepot appeared on the starched white tablecloth, accompanied by porcelain cups and saucers. The waiter poured each cup half full and departed, leaving us to add milk and sugar as we wished.

"Probably the most expensive coffee you'll have ever drunk," Lord Ashcombe quipped. "Fine place, on the whole, but they do overcharge desperately on some things. Anyway. All in all, I think that went rather well, Gary. How does it feel to be a Royal Falconer?"

"I don't think it's really sunk in yet," I replied. "There's so much to think about."

As we drank our coffee, we picked over the details of our meeting with Prince Khalid and Lord Ashcombe was clearly happy with the outcome.

"This business with the gyrfalcons? Of course, you know that you can go to America."

"Good. Well it's fine as long as it's all paid for."

"I don't think money is going to be much of a problem," he said, waving one hand dismissively in imitation of the Prince. "You're catching the train back from Paddington, I assume?"

"Yeah, I'm going back to Gloucestershire fairly soon."

"Fine. I'll love you and leave you then."

Suffice it to say that we left the hotel in a far more elegant fashion than the way in which we'd arrived. The two black cabs headed off through London's streets, one to Holland Park Road and the other to Paddington. By two o'clock, the cavernous station had long since escaped the noise and chaos of the early commuter attacks. It had regained its composure in the relative quiet of the early afternoon and was somehow more sedate. The low rumble of trains and murmurs of human sounds simply added to its grandeur.

Unusually, my train was on time and gloriously empty. I settled down gratefully in my first class seat, luxuriating in the space and the lack of fat men smoking large, rank smelling cigars. As the train rumbled on towards my beloved Gloucestershire, it left the grime and greyness of London's suburban sprawl behind. As the fields of England's green and pleasant land took their place, the sun finally broke through the clouds. And as I gazed at the passing scenery, my mind seemed to mirror the sky, full of bright beams of sunshine and a few menacing black clouds.

It had all happened so quickly. Suddenly, I was looking at setting up a breeding programme for gyrs, acquiring the falcons from the other side of the Atlantic, pulling a team together to take a Prince and his VIP guests grouse hawking. And those were just a few of the mass of things to consider.

"You've never bred gyrs," sneered the gremlin. "You haven't even bred gyr hybrids. How do you think you're going to manage that? No chance. Forget it. Why don't you just admit it now, that you can't do it? Bit out of your comfort zone is it? It is! Give up. Before it's too late."

"Piss off!"

I almost heard him scream as I mentally punched him hard in his ugly twisted face and watched him vanish. Of course I was concerned about the weight of my new responsibilities but the sun was shining and the excitement took over. And that was a good feeling, a damned good feeling. The rhythm of steel wheels on steel tracks was

170

comfortably mesmerising, sending daydreams of childhood days.

For a moment, I was that 12 year-old boy again, searching for slowworms in an old churchyard in Worcester. I heard the kee-kee-kee calls scything through the air and stared, searching the air around the church's tall spire. And remembered being inspired by a pair of humble kestrels.

Chapter 16 – Bugs, birds and one bear

"The two main guys are Dan Konkel and Dave Jamieson," said Martin confidently. "Dave runs Sky-Out Falcons, north of Reno in Nevada. Dan's based in Sheridan in Wyoming and runs Sage Country Falcons. Both of them breed brilliant gyrs although Dan's probably got a wider range. He's probably the biggest gyr breeder in the world. White, black, purple, green – you name it, the man breeds gyrs! Amazing."

"You know these guys?"

"Sure. I'll give you an introduction and you can take it from there."

"Martin, you're a star."

Martin Jones, the fount of knowledge for all things falconiforme. Whenever I needed help, I ran to Martin and was never disappointed. Armed with his endorsement and contact details for the two American breeders, I started working on making arrangements.

"Sure, you all get over here. Welcome. Come see us in Sheridan and maybe we'll get us a little sage grouse hawking."

"You're good to come to Reno. Bring your boots cuz you're going to be doing some desert walking."

Working out all the travel plans with flights, a detailed itinerary and costs took a little more time. After innumerable phone calls, I finally had everything neatly slotted into place and then the Fairlawne Estate office took over the baton.

"Send me all the details and paperwork," said Richard Carter Jonas. "We'll book everything on your behalf and I'll arrange for you to have some money for expenses. You should have all the documents and tickets in a few days."

"Prince Khalid needs a detailed report when you're back," growled Shwarz. "Enjoy the ride but come back with the goods. Have nice day."

And suddenly I'm flying out of Heathrow on my way to the United States of America to research buying falcons for a Prince. By the time we landed at Chicago's O'Hare International Airport, my lungs were crying out for

172

nicotine. My last cigarette had been hurriedly smoked in one of Heathrow's designated pariah lounges and it had been a long flight. Having a more aggressive health policy, the Americans had decided that smoking was contraindicated and O'Hare was smoke free! Having negotiated my way over the hurdles of passport control, immigration and customs, there was just enough time to dash out of the terminal before my connecting flight to Denver. Suck, inhale, blow, suck, inhale go.

After the relative luxury of a jumbo jet and a Boeing 707, in Denver I was faced with flying on an aged twin-engine prop plane that was little more than an air taxi. It being my first flight on a light aircraft, I embarked with more than a little trepidation.

"Welcome aboard this Convair CV-580. I guess you all know that we'll be dropping down up the road in Cheyenne, Laramie, Casper, Buffalo, Sheridan and Billings, so don't you go getting too much sleep now. We'll be flying at around 340 miles per hour at about nine thousand feet and some. Once we're in the air, Kelli'll be round with a few refreshments. Now sit back and enjoy your flight."

At least, it went something like that. Suffice it to say that I was scared out of my wits. As we flew through the clouds, the turbulence buffeted the plane as though we were in a washing machine with wings. The service provided by the lovely Kelli, complete with blonde hair and short skirt, extended to a small bag of peanuts washed down with a paper cup of coke or orange juice. I stared out of the window at the spinning propeller, watching for any sign of smoke or stutter. It would be hard to describe which I found the most terrifying – the take-offs, landings or bone-shaking flights.

My nerves only started to unwind when we finally touched down at Sheridan County Airport. Which was small, windblown and somewhat tired; I empathised. I walked in to the airport's sole building and flashed my ticket to the one man on duty.

"Thank you Sir. Welcome to Sheridan. You have a nice day now."

If the cowboy hat, boots and holstered gun hadn't given me a clue to where I was, the diorama behind him the foyer was a clear giveaway. Major General Custer's last stand against the combined forces of the Lakota Sioux and Cheyenne warriors was graphically depicted in 3D and full technicolour. The Battle of Little Big Horn was fought only 70 miles north of Sheridan.

'How quaint,' I thought, 'and how American.'

Turning back to my tooled-up friend, I asked, "Can you tell me how to get to the Sheridan Hotel, please".

"Sure thing, Mr Cope. It's right there, across the parking lot."

I trudged over to the hotel feeling absolutely shattered after all the flights and changes.

"Would you like to have dinner after you've freshened up, Sir?" asked the receptionist once I'd checked in.

"No, I'm too knackered. I just want my room and crash. Do you have room service?"

"We sure do, Mr Cope. You ken have any-thing you want. You wanna look at a menu?"

"Sure."

I studied the list for a moment.

"OK. Can I have a Wyoming half-pounder with onion rings, mushrooms and fries? In about half an hour?"

"You got it."

The hot shower powered down with the force of a water canon, washing away the grime of travel. When the burger arrived only moments later, I realised that I was starving and devoured the lot with the haste of a starving waif. After living on airline food (which I hate), the Best of America lived up to its name. Having gorged myself silly, I flaked out on the bed and called Dan Konkel.

"Hey Gary. Guess you got here safely? Good flight?"

"Yeah, not so bad but now I'm trashed."

"Yup, I'm not surprised. Get some shuteye 'n then I'll swing round in the morning and pick you up. Where you at?"

"The Sheridan Hotel, next to the airport?"

"I know it. I'll meet you outside in the parking lot, say around ten."

174

"How will I recognise you?"

"Don't worry, I'll recognise you."

"Fair enough."

My head didn't hit the pillow before I was fast asleep, letting the tiredness seep away into the dark night. Feeling refreshed the following morning, I tucked into breakfast with a vengeance. Grabbing my rucksack, I checked out and took up station in the car park outside the hotel. A white blanket of snow covered everything and it was bitterly cold. Five minutes went by, ten minutes and then, after waiting for fifteen minutes, an oversized Dodge pickup slalomed over the iced tarmac. A hard turn pushed the truck into a power slide, bringing it neatly to a halt within a matter of feet. And out came a big man in boots, jeans, a checked shirt, a baseball cap and wearing a big smile.

"Dan Konkel," he said as he crushed my hand in greeting. "You must be Gary."

"Yeah? How did you guess."

"Well, that's maybe because you look like a Brit. And maybe because you're the only sucker standing on the snow outside the hotel with a backpack and looking like you're sucking lemons," he added with a grin. "Good to meet ya."

Throwing my rucksack into the back of the truck, he reached in and produced a crate of Budweiser.

"Get in and out the cold," he said, chucking the beer into the cab before hauling himself into the driver's seat. "Fancy a beer?"

I considered telling him that I didn't normally drink at that time of day but, hey, this was Wyoming and one didn't want to offend.

"Sure."

Dan cracked open a couple of Buds, tossed one to me and fired up the engine. We chugged our beers as he drove away from the airport, through the outskirts of the mid-western town and into the prairies. It was only a few miles to the ranch on Beaver Drive and we were there within half an hour despite the slick road.

"Wow, that's a wild house!" I exclaimed as it came into sight. "Why is it built on stilts? They must be at least six feet high."

"That'd be a little more. We get snowdrifts eight foot deep out here, so that's why we got stilts underneath."

Parking up outside, he pulled my bags from the back of the truck and walked up the stairs.

"Come on in and meet the family."

Who were really welcoming; we sat in the vast lounge, dominated by an enormous moose's head mounted on one wall, and chatted away as though we'd known each other for years.

"So what d'you wanna do? You wanna chill some or take a look at the facilities?"

"Yeah. Umm, I'd love to see the bird facilities."

"Well, come on then."

I've seen some pretty extraordinary complexes for birds of prey in my time but Dan's setup was out of this world and truly magnificent.

"These are the breeding barns," he said as he climbed a set of stairs built onto the outside of the building.

A doorway led onto long corridor which was totally enclosed. I glanced up at the roof, some 20 feet above my head, before following him down. One-way glass provided a window into each chamber, allowing clear views of the breeding ledges. I peered at white gyrs, black gyrs and a few more besides. As Dan showed me the various pairs, I scribbled frantically in my notebook in the knowledge that I'd have to write it all up in a report for Prince Khalid.

"Whoa there little buddy! There's no rush. Give your fingers a break. While you're staying here, feel free to take a wander round, have a look see and take your notes. You can come up here any time, whether I'm around or not. The place is yours to explore. Just one thing: be very, very careful."

"About what? I mean, why in particular?"

"You gotta watch out for the black widows."

"Excuse me?"

"You're excused - black widow spiders. We're infested with the damn things, and that includes this here breeding

176

barn. Just be careful not to lean on anything and keep your eyes open. Otherwise, one of them little ladies is apt to jump down and bite you."

"Shit, I hate spiders. I've got an inherent fear of spiders. It's not that I've got arachnophobia as such, I just don't particularly like them," I finished lamely.

"There's a widow right there."

He pointed to a shiny little black spider with red markings on its body, about the size of a dime. I only had a couple of seconds to peer nervously before, to my total disbelief, Dan squished it with one large thumb.

"You don't want to get bitten by one of those evil bitches. You get bitten, you come straight to me and I'll drive you to hospital."

"Hospital! They're that dangerous?"

"Weeeell, let's see. Black widow venom's about 15 times more toxic than a rattler. You probably wouldn't die but believe me it ain't nice. People get bit can have bad muscle aches and nausea and the stuff paralyses your diaphragm, right here," he said, pointing vaguely at the centre of his torso. "Makes it difficult to breathe. Not pleasant, no sirree."

"Thanks for the information! But isn't what you just did, squashing one like that, isn't that dangerous?"

"Yup, unless you know what y'all are doing. And I do. Must've killed thousands of the bastards in my time but the damn things keep on coming back."

For the remainder of the tour, I kept one eye on the wondrous facilities and the other on lookout for treacherous black widows. The first filled me with awe and the second with dread. Fortunately, the former took precedence. Even so, I felt a bit more comfortable sitting back in the lounge, nursing a beer under the beneficent eyes of the moose.

"What are we doing from here?"

"Well, some of the guys are comin' round later, we're going to eat something n' do a bit of moth huntin'. You interested in moths?"

"Well, I like moths. But moth hunting?"

"Yup."

Eating 'something' translated to a vast banquet that covered the table in a multitude of dishes. Nor was there any shortage of beer, wine or liquor. Working out what was what, was a little trickier. Somehow, everyone else was perfectly aware of what each dish contained. Fortunately, my new best friend Ken was on hand to help.

"Ah'm pretty sure them steaks are elk. Wyoming's a belter for elk hunting. And ah'm guessing that haunch is from a white-tail. Hey, Dan, is this white-tailed deer?"

"Yup," said Dan, sauntering over. "There's elk, white-tail, that's bison, those fellers are sage grouse. And all the vegetables are organic. All this stuff is hunted or grown locally, Gary. Pretty fine, huh?"

"It's amazing," I said, helping myself to the smallest elk steak I could find on the plate. And even that looked as though it might weigh at least 14 ounces.

"You seem to know your way around the table," I said to Ken once I'd finished chewing a few delectable mouthfuls of perfectly grilled elk. "So does that mean, you go hunting?"

"Not as much as ah'd like to but, yeah, I get out some. There's a lot of hunting in Texas – mule deer, pronghorns, rabbit, quite a few game birds – but it ain't the same as Wyoming, going on to Montana."

"So whereabouts in Texas?" (As though I knew the State that well!)

"Dallas. Used to be a veterinary back in the day but ended up training animals rather than fixing 'em."

"You mean like dogs. Or falcons? Brilliant."

"Not quite," he said laughing. "Most of 'em are just a teen bit bigger an' a lot more dangerous. No, I train animals for the film industry. Ah've got mongooses and cobras, a couple of pythons, alligators. You ever eat alligator? They're good eating."

"Um, no, I haven't. And wow!"

"Anyway, the bigger stuff's lions, bears, tigers. It's a big business and kinda fun."

It was a truly wonderful evening shared with interesting people. And once we had feasted and drunk copious amounts of alcohol, we adjourned to the veranda that ran

178

around the outside of the house. Once everyone was happily installed in the numerous chairs, Dan erected a large wooden frame over which was stretched a white sheet. Behind it, he positioned a very powerful lamp which shone a blindingly white light through the material.

"Dan, what on earth is that for?"

"I said we're going moth huntin'? Well, this is it! Fix yourself another bourbon, then sit down and wait."

I'm actually rather fond of moths, although I don't know a great deal about them. In England, we're used to the greyish-browny fluttery things which seem to leave dust trails behind them. But when Wyoming's finest came in from the prairie, I was stunned. Hundreds of them fluttered onto the sheet in sizes that ranged from a thumbnail to small saucers.

"See that one there? That's an American Dagger moth," Dan commentated. "That's a Waved Sphinx and there's a Bedstraw hawkmoth. Cute little lady, ain't she?"

Obviously Dan's expertise was not just limited to falcons. Now it was moths! I wondered what would come next. With no further information forthcoming, I would have to wait until morning. It was time to crash out and, although it had been an exciting day, my body was still suffering from jetlag.

"Up 'n at 'em, Gary. You want breakfast? Sure you do. And I'm hungry."

I glanced at my watch: six o'clock in the morning, for God's sake!

"Yeah, all right," I said, somewhat wearily.

My brain didn't know whether it was the middle of the day or the depth of night. But willy-nilly, in Wyoming it was time for breakfast and we were heading back to Sheridan in Dan's pickup.

'Why do they have to get up so early?' my mind complained.

Bacon and scrambled eggs accompanied by several mugs of black coffee served as an excellent reviver. I started again to wonder what was on the day's agenda. Maybe we were going to a rodeo where I'd learn about the gentle arts of riding bucking broncos, wrangling steers and how to lasso a recalcitrant heifer. I'd seen plenty of cowboy types in Sheridan the day before, complete with boots, hats and ropes.

"What's the crack today then? Are we going to a rodeo?"

"Nope, up into the mountains. Some of the guys from last night are coming too. Plan is do some butterfly huntin'. You ever hunted butterflies?"

"I can't say I have," I said, "but I'm looking forward to the experience."

Butterfly hunting? Not quite what I expected to be doing in Wyoming.

"How far is it?"

"Ah, it's just up the road a ways - shouldn't take that long to get there."

One thing I learned about Americans is: when they say 'not long', think longer. Three and half hours later, we'd climbed up from the prairie into the mountains and had been joined several other 4x4s forming a small convoy. The air was crisp American alpine and the views, spectacular, when we finally stopped and got out. I felt that this was possibly the most beautiful place on earth. Until I was issued with a butterfly net and joined everyone else in the hunt.

Running across an open hillside which was sprinkled with glorious wildflowers, and chasing butterflies with a net on a pole together with a load of grown men was positively surreal. It was like tripping on acid in a good way – brilliantly coloured lunacy, with motion, natural sensurround and elemental energy. Here were skippers, whites, sulphurs, gossamer wings, brush-footed butterflies and many more. Iridescent rainbows, patterned silk watercolours and delicate matt designs – all flutterbyed before our nets. Surreal but fantastic fun.

In typical American style, barbecues were fired up and steaks grilled to fuel us for continued chase in the afternoon. And then, once again, we were back in the hunt. Not that I personally caught that many butterflies and those that I did were apparently not that rare.

180

"That golden girl with the black markings you got there? She's an Aphrodite Fritillary. Nice, but we get quite a few of those up here."

Most of the ones that I netted seemed to be one sort of fritillary or another and all fairly common. On the occasion that someone caught a more exceptional specimen, the butterfly was duly trapped in jar in which it asphyxiated and, presumably would end up on a board. I thought it was rather sad to kill such beautiful creatures for the sole purpose of acquisition and display. Nevertheless, it was a day that will remain in my memory forever and at least my butterflies lived to flutterby for a while longer.

"You wanna take a look around town?" Dan asked me the following morning.

We were back at his favourite breakfast bar in Sheridan, me keeping to eggs while he munched through a stack of pancakes, liberally smothered with maple syrup and cream.

"Sure, it looks interesting."

Interesting in the mid-western state translated to – as long as it's anything to do with the rodeo. Wyoming is big cattle country and rodeos are taken very seriously. It seemed that almost every shop sold related goods and clothes. Needless to say, we had to go into at least one. I felt the rope of lassos and the leather of chaps, tried on cowboy hats, peeked at boots and smiled at checked shirts. And then I tried on a pair of calfskin leather gloves; supremely comfortable, wonderfully supple, a perfect fit and, by British standards, remarkably cheap.

"Can I take these, please?"

"Sure thing sir. Those are mighty fine gloves and they'll give you good service."

"Absolutely. I think they'll be ideal for flying merlins."

"I'm sorry Sir?"

"Just the left one, of course."

"Of course," said the sales assistant, clearly bemused. "You have a nice day now."

Obviously Dan regarded shopping as thirsty work.

"Guess you're done, huh? You fancy a beer?"

"Yeah, why not?"

Swinging in through saloon doors that reeked of the old Wild West, we pulled up a couple of stools by the bar. And two pegs to the right was a man who, judging by his size, would have fitted right in to those violent days. I couldn't fail to notice the man; he was huge. The cutback tank top served to emphasise the muscles of his arms, which were bigger than my thighs, and his thick woolly beard could have nested a congregation of starlings. He caught my eye for a moment, I quickly looked away and he returned to his beer.

Dan ordered a couple of Buds and we whiled away the time, shooting the breeze. Then Dan announced that he was heading for the restroom, and did so. Barely had he disappeared through the door at the end of the bar than the Bear turned his stool in my direction.

"You British?" he growled.

"Yeah. Yes, I'm from England."

"Ha, you seen them mountains out there?"

"Yeah, I've seen them. Wonderful."

"D'you know your fucking Queen owns them mountains?"

"Actually, no. I mean, no, I didn't know that."

"Well what the fuck d'ya think about it?"

Bear was clearly not at all happy about this state of affairs.

"Um well, that it's part of the British thing, to own things in parts of the world where we, um, shouldn't own them. Which is apparently the case, um, in this case. So, I apologise unequivocally, on behalf of the British people to all of the people in Wyoming. And Montana. And any other state in which we might have, err, made the same mistake."

"Ah."

Bear was suddenly joined by two of his equally large friends who stood behind him and definitely weren't in the mood for smiling.

'Why the fuck did I say all that?' I asked myself, feeling like a real little Englander. Looking back at the Bear, I suddenly thought, "Bollocks to it!'

"What are you like at arm wrestling?"

182

"Say what, boy?"

"What are you like at arm wrestling?"

Weighing in at eleven and a half stone, I stood up to my full skinny height of five feet ten and tried to look menacing.

"You kidding me, boy?"

"No. I should tell you that I'm one of England's premier champion arm wrestlers. And I'm telling you that I can beat you eas-i-ly. No problem!"

There was a moment's silence as he looked at me, narrowing his dark black-brown bear eyes. And then he started laughing.

"I like you, boy. You got balls bigger thun a black bear. Let me buy you a beer, and for yer friend."

By the time that Dan got back, the four of us were chugging Buds and chatting a storm.

"Looks like you've been finding a few buddies while I've been away."

"Yeah, we're good. Mike bought the beer."

So the tension had been diffused reasonably quickly and we ended up having a good session with Bear and his buddies. But the story might have had a very different end. Needless to say, had he taken me up on my challenge, I wouldn't have stood a chance. On consideration, if he hadn't taken the arm wrestling route, he might have taken another option but the result would have been the same. Bear would have chewed me up and have spat out the pieces.

So my days in Wyoming were interesting, to say the least, but were coming to a close. It was time for Dan and I to talk business. But there was a minor problem.

"Gary, Dan's gone and done something to his back," his wife told me. "Can you get his chores for the day?"

So there I was, on the penultimate day of my stay, sorting out rows and rows of gyrfalcons in the massive mews. I set them all out in the covered weathering Dan had there and stared at them all in admiration. Just standing there, seeing the quality of the birds, I could see why Dan was a major exporter to the Arab world. His birds were truly the crème de la crème. Taking responsibility for his stock for a few hours was a distinct pleasure and the least that I could do for the man.

"Bottom line is, all my birds are spoken for, they're sold for this year. You wanna come back next year, it'll be my pleasure to sell you some. Sure we can sort out something for you then but this year's a no-no."

But at least I saw some of them fly. Dan suggested a bit of sage grouse hawking for my last day and I eagerly accepted. It was bitterly cold but he had me kitted out in equipment designed for sub-artic temperatures: a voluminous puffa jacket, big furry boots and monster thermal gloves were all key components in my elegant ensemble. Together with a few other guys, we drove out over the snow-peppered prairie in search of grouse. Our weapons: two glittering white gyrs, one big American Peale's peregrine and a couple of English pointers.

"Dan, why do you put telemetry on the dogs?" I asked him as we stood on Wyoming's version of frozen tundra.

"With 300 square miles of sage brush out here, dogs can go a-wandering. A man can easily lose a dog out here and tele's the way of finding the critters."

Watching the birds flying over English pointers at sage grouse was a magnificent experience. But it was damn cold even though I was wrapped up like the Michelin man. At one point, someone asked me to take hold of the yagi and, without thinking, I took off my glove and complied. The metal immediately welded itself to my hand. I manfully managed to prize flesh from metal with only a few yelps of pain. And at least the birds nailed a brace of grouse.

At the end of the day, Wyoming and Dan Konkel had done me proud; it had been wonderful even though there were no birds for sale. Nevertheless, I had plenty of material for my report to Prince Khalid and a lot of suggestions. So I bid a fond farewell to Dan and his family, thanked them for their hospitality and said maybe, just maybe, next year would be the one.

But now it was time for the flight down to Reno and to look for gyrs in the Nevada desert. Dave Jamieson was waiting.

184

Chapter 17 – Dealer Wins

'Welcome to the Biggest Little City in the World' read the legend under a sign vaunting the joys of gambling. Even from the baggage claims hall, I could hear the whirr and rattle of the slot machines. Collecting my rucksack from the carousel, I headed for the exit feeling tired but excited. Seeing the security personnel dotted around, it suddenly occurred to me that I hadn't been pulled over once since I'd first arrived on American soil. Wherever, and whenever, I'd travelled previously, I'd been stopped. Never roll the dice when you're winning.

"Excuse me, Sir? Would you mind stepping out of the line and come over here please?"

It wasn't a question. Not wanting to seem unfriendly, I immediately acquiesced and walked across. On the whole, I believe it is unwise to argue with burly uniformed men who wear handguns.

"How can I help you?" I said, thinking, 'Here we go – it had to happen sooner or later.'

His eyes took in the long hair and Arab scarf round my neck, moving down across my colourful quilted jacket to my rather grubby jeans and trainers. And then he reversed the process, which made it feel as though I was being scanned, recorded and would subsequently be filed. This did not bode well.

"May I ask you what you are doing in Reno, Sir? Are you here on business or pleasure?"

On another occasion I'd have probably given the expected one word answer; I've always been a bit coy about divulging all my secrets. But this time round, I considered it totally appropriate to pull rank and show my full colours. After all, I was travelling on a royal remit and, if truth be admitted, was feeling bloody proud of myself. This guy was going to get the full package.

"Business."

"And may I ask the nature of your business in Reno, Sir?"

"I'm here to buy falcons for His Royal Highness, Prince Khalid bin Abdullah al Saud. As his name might indicate, the Prince is a member of the Saudi Arabian royal family."

His blank look, coupled with the pregnant silence, indicated a distinct lack of comprehension.

"That's the feathered kind, rather than second-hand business jets originally made in France," I continued. "Falcons - as in birds of prey?"

"O-kay," he said, clearly not being any further on the road to knowledge and awareness.

"Right. I'm hoping to buy some falcons from a breeder here in Reno. You have quite a few wild birds of prey in Nevada: golden eagles, red-tailed hawks, American kestrels, prairie falcons? OK, some birds of prey are trained and used for hunting."

Little lights finally switched on in his eyes at hearing the word 'hunting'. So I expanded on the subject and found myself giving an impromptu talk on falconry. The only things lacking were a few display birds to fly loops around the terminal.

"All right! That's great. You know, I always wanted to have a try messing with that stuff, flying hawks and falcons and such. Problem is, there ain't a lot of things to hunt in the desert hereabouts, so you have to travel quite a ways before you get somewhere you can. Anyway, where're you staying in Reno? Downtown?"

"No, near the airport I think. The Best Western?"

"Surely, that's out on the perimeter road. You can catch a taxicab right out there by the sidewalk or you can walk over to the hotel, it's not that far."

"A cab sounds better. Thank you."

"Thank you too, Sir. Enjoy Reno and hope you get your falcons OK. Have a nice day."

Outside the terminal building, the mandatory line of taxis ran along the kerb, the mustard yellow of their coachwork shining dully in the dark night. It had been another long flight which entailed dropping down in Denver before flying west to Reno and I was shattered. I dragged myself to the first cab in the line.

"Can you take me to the Best Western hotel, please?"

186

"No."

"I'm sorry?"

"It's just over there, buddy. If'n I take you to the Best Western, that means driving out of the line and losing a fare downtown. That just don't make sense."

"Give me a break. I'm knackered and you're cutting me out?"

"Yup. I'm not leaving the line for a dime. You can walk there faster 'n I can drive."

"Shit. So where is over there?"

"See them lights twinkling?" he said, pointing into the darkness. "That's where it's at."

Great! Hitching my rucksack higher on my shoulder, I trudged across the car park with matchsticks holding my eyelids open. It seemed an eternity before I reached the welcoming lights of the hotel. I checked in, ordered room service and gratefully fell into my room. The heat of another power shower relieved the worst of my tiredness. Donning one of the chunky white dressing gowns that all such hotels kindly hang behind the bathroom door for guests, I slumped on the bed.

Room service duly delivered the largest seafood platter that I'd ever seen. As I tucked into my marine delights, probably caught on the Californian seaboard or further afield, I flicked on the TV to find The Mission showing on cable. So there I was in one of Nevada's high desert valleys eating shellfish and watching a film about Jesuits in South America. I ignored any sense of irony and finally went to sleep.

"Glad you arrived safely," said Dave, "I'll come and pick you up. You ever been out in the desert before?"

"Not really."

"It's a treat. And we've got some pretty fine falcons out here. What say I pick you up in a while, takes the birds out in the desert and get us a little hawking?"

"Sounds great."

Listening to his warmth and enthusiasm on the phone, I'd warmed to him instantly. And I'd done my homework on the guy. One of the pioneers of artificial insemination together with Cornell and the Peregrine Fund, Dave had been breeding top quality falcons since 1970 and claimed to have one of the world's oldest breeding programmes. While I collected my thoughts, I pigged out on another mountainous breakfast of bacon, eggs and coffee.

The ride out to Newport Lane in north Reno took less than 20 minutes. The conversation was easy and comfortable, reinforcing the impression that I'd got on the phone. And he knew what he was talking about; the man was a mine of information. We pulled into the drive, next to a single storey ranch style house on an unremarkable street. But where Dan Konkel's place was a magnificent gyr factory, Dave's had a concentrated specialist breeding setup.

After a brief tour of some of his spectacular birds, he carefully picked up a beautiful white gyr-peregrine tiercel and put it into the back of his truck. And then he loaded a large crate which he handled with equal care.

"Let's go do some hawking," he said, pulling out of the drive onto the concrete strip that called itself a lane.

"Where are we going?"

"Out to one of the salt flats. Big wide open space and plenty of room out there to fly. We don't have quarry round here for the falcons to fly at; we'd have to travel miles to get at some of that."

"So we're not actually going hawking as such? Meaning you're going to fly to the lure?"

"Nope, we're going hawking sure enough," he said chuckling. "Just that we have to provide somethin' for him to try and get."

"You've lost me."

He turned to me, grinned broadly and nodded his head backwards.

"That crate in the back there contains everything we need for some pretty excitin' flying, Gary. See, I don't just breed falcons, I breed pigeons as well. And I got us four of them babies in that crate raring to go. We get out on the flats, we'll put the falcon up, release the pigeons and we got us some flying, hunting style."

"But surely, the falcon will kill one pigeon and you'll lose the others? Or something like that."

188

"Nope. I call these birds super pigeons and they never get caught."

"So what happens?"

"Here's the story. When that falcon stoops, man he'll be on a mission, but he'll miss every one of the pigeons. And they'll just fly home to the loft."

The salt flats stretched out into the distance before us; a harsh landscape baked hard by the heat of the sun and flanked by the stark mountains of the Sierra Nevada. Dave lifted the crate out of the truck and put it down on the cracked, peeling ground. Then he put the falcon up which climbed rapidly upwards into the clear blue sky. And vanished.

"Bloody hell, I've seen a lot of falcons fly but ... where's it gone?"

"He's up there somewhere, that's for sure," Dave said, producing the telemetry.

"So how do you know when to serve the bird?"

"It's not that easy but using telemetry about the best way to find out where he's at and whether he's in position." He flicked the switch on the yagi and pointed it skywards. The familiar bleep, bleep, bleep sounded strident in the desert air. "Yup, I think he's about right. OK, when I release these babies, don't go looking at the sky 'cuz you won't see nuthin'. You just keep your eyes on the pigeons."

Walking over to the crate, Dave flipped the catches on each of the four compartments and the birds exploded into the air like missiles out of silos. The pigeons drove forwards with strong wingbeats that took them speeding across the flats at low altitude. Within seconds, they were half a mile away and still pumping. Of course, the falcon had begun his stoop as soon as they had been released. But Dave's super pigeons were no slouches and well aware of the potential danger from above. Already they were taking evasive action, jinking and turning at every possible moment.

And then down he came with incredible speed, the like of which I'd never seen before. I could hardly believe that a falcon could fly that quickly. At the risk of waxing lyrical, this was – blue sky, white death – incarnate. Flying in like a fighter jet with its targets firmly in its sights, the falcon quickly closed on its prey. But these were super pigeons and they definitely lived up to their name. They flipped and then, perfectly synchronised, they spread simultaneously in four different directions while falcon blasted through the empty space in the centre. Undeterred, the falcon threw up, flipped over and stooped once again, executing the same manoeuvre. And once again, the pigeons easily eluded its attack.

The open terrain of the flats afforded us a perfect view of the aerial battle in which the pigeons were clearly the winners. Or rather, the falcon was the loser and, accepting defeat, he peeled off without catching a thing. By this time, Dave was swinging his lure and calling the bird back. The falcon dropped lightly onto the lure, roused briefly and glared a few daggers before being put back in the truck.

"That was one of the most amazing waiting-on flights that I have ever seen. Quite extraordinary. But what about the pigeons?"

"As said, they're on the way home, virtually there by now. By the time we get back home, they'll be squirrelled away in the loft and begging for food. And they'll get a good feed then; they worked for it."

It was a fantastic day but, sadly, that was the only hawking I was able to see in Nevada. My time was going all too quickly. While we were taking a longer look at Dave's breeding facilities and birds, we got down to a proper business discussion.

"What we're hoping to do is to establish three naturally breeding pairs of white gyrs. So obviously what I'm looking for are six unrelated young falcons. I'd like to get them for imprinting with a view to establishing an AI project."

"You've just seen Dan in Wyoming, right? OK, if need be we can all liaise but I'm sure we can do something for you next season. I noted down a few prices for you and what I think you can expect. Here you go."

He gave me a single sheet of paper which I added to the pile of notes that I'd already taken. And that was it. I thanked him for his help, he said it had been a pleasure and he drove me back to Reno airport for the long flight back to foggy England. I spent much of the time mulling over the experiences, conversations and annotating my notes that had already been annotated several times during the trip. Certainly it had been worthwhile and I had plenty to put in my report for Prince Khalid. In principle, I was sure that between Dan and Dave, I could get some exceptional birds to kick-start the project. And as both of them knew who the paymaster was, Messrs Konkel and Jamieson were seeing big dollar signs whirling in front of their eyes.

Once back in Gloucestershire, my report was typed, edited, retyped and then needed to be passed to Lord Ashcombe for appraisal. After which, he would forward the report to Prince Khalid and copies to Fairlawne and Schwarz as appropriate. A few days later, Lord Ashcombe duly turned up at The Bothy.

"Good trip, Gary?"

"Excellent. Those guys really have some fantastic birds."

"Give me a rundown on the whole thing, but in sequence."

So I told the tale, sticking more or less to what I'd seen at the two facilities and the hawking days. One or two anecdotes crept in from time to time as we slurped from the usual coffee stream. His Lordship nodded, grunted, laughed and blew train stacks of smoke into the atmosphere.

"And here's the information for Prince Khalid," I said, handing over my carefully prepared and bound report. "The bottom line is that I think we can get exactly what we want from the States, between the two of them."

I grinned at him with satisfaction, knowing that I'd done a good job. He didn't look quite as cheerful; his look in return was a weak attempt at smiling, conveying gloom rather than approbation. And then he dropped the bombshell.

"Ah, there's been a slight change of plan," he said, frowning briefly at the slim folio in his hands before looking up. "The thing is, the Prince doesn't want to wait for the birds to breed."

"Fine. I may be pretty good at aviculture but not even I can persuade one-year olds to breed. He might not want to wait but there's not a lot that we can do about it."

"No Gary, I think you're missing the point. Prince Khalid wants proven breeding birds."

Immediately, alarms and sirens were clamouring in my head. 'Oh no, No, NO! Please, do not go there,' screamed the voices in my head.

"Lord Ashcombe, honestly, that's a possible road to hell with pitfalls at every step of the way." Calm, calm. "The first problem is whether we can get any to begin with and the second is cost. Yes, I know you'll tell me not to worry about the cost," I said as he opened his mouth to interrupt. "Buying breeding birds is going to be seriously expensive, and I mean seriously. Bear in mind that you're asking someone to sell you a slice of his business. At the moment, the going rate for your average white gyr eyass is around ten grand; God only knows how much a proven breeder would cost.

"And then there's a third hurdle. The logistics involved in getting the birds over here, and getting them here safely, is the stuff of nightmares. Gyrfalcons are notoriously delicate, they're prone to lung problems and easily stressed. And like humans, if they're stressed, they're extremely vulnerable to a whole raft of illnesses and ailments. Speaking bluntly, it's an awful idea."

"Thank you for the lecture, Gary. Look, I'm sorry but that's what the Prince wants to do."

"So the whole trip to the States, to Wyoming and Nevada, was a total waste of bloody time. Why did we bother?"

"No, it wasn't a waste of time. Call it reconnaissance. The objectives have changed but you've still got the contacts. Get in touch with them and see what you can do."

Thus, I was in the somewhat embarrassing position of having to phone Messrs Konkel and Jamieson with Prince Khalid's new wish list.

"No way, José. Not a cat's chance in hell," Dan said. "Sorry Gary, I never sell proven breeding birds an' ah'm not going to start now."

192

And, sadly, that was the end of my brief conversation, and our connection, with Dan Konkel. With one down and only one to go, I started panicking. If Jamieson said the same thing, we wouldn't just be back to first base, we'd be wondering how to get there. I crossed my fingers, phoned Dave and told him the story.

"'They're not exactly usual requests, are they?"

"Ah, no. But can you help?"

"Well, let's see here. I'm thinking about shaving off a little on what I'm doing right now, meaning maybe I could cut you a little slack. Best I can do is let you have one white semen donor and let you have that silver female you saw. Remember her?"

"Yes I do, of course. What kind of money are we talking about?"

"I'm goin' to have to think on that one, but I tell you what, you're not going to get them for sixteen thousand bucks a bird. You appreciate that, don't you?"

"Yeah, naturally."

A few days later he came back to me with a price that made me wince and both my eyes water. Suffice it to say that for that kind of money, you could buy a nice little house on the prairie and a 4x4 to park up in the drive. Ouch!

"What I will do," he added as a sweetener, "is throw in a three quarter gyr, quarter saker as a gift."

"Thank you. But there's nothing else that you can do?"

"As I said, that's as far as I'll go and no further."

There was more than a frown decorating my face when I phoned Lord Ashcombe to update him the latest news.

"And that's a lot of dollars," I said when I'd finished with the details. "Just think of how many youngsters we could have bought with that kind of money."

As I said it, I was suddenly aware that my greatest fear had been realised: we literally had all our eggs in one basket. So my report was revised and Lord Ashcombe fed it down to Prince Khalid. The message that came back gave a green light to Dave Jamieson's proposition with the headline – go for it.

"What about the eyasses?" I asked Lord Ashcombe.

"Forget about them, they're not, um, required."

So basically there had been a budget and Dave's figures had obviously reached its ceiling. In a nutshell, I was underwhelmed and less than chuffed. All I could see were problems, pitfalls and pain. Not that there was anything that I could do about it since I was simply being paid to do the job, not take decisions. If my royal employer chose to ignore my advice, that was his prerogative; but I didn't have to like it!

Chapter 18 – Two eggs, one basket

Thus, armed with the royal command, I called the man, several thousands of miles away in Nevada, who was prepared to sell one horny male gyr, a hopefully receptive silver lady and a crossbreed to watch the play. Given the amount of money involved, Mr Jamieson was soon going to have a big smile on his face.

"Hi Dave, how are things in Reno?"

"Good Gary, good. So, what's the story?"

"Prince Khalid would like us to go ahead. So we'd like to buy the birds as agreed."

"Well, how about that? I guess you're planning to come out again pretty soon then?"

"Yeah, I'll let you know dates and times once it's all booked. By the way, Lord Ashcombe would like to come out as well, to meet you and have a look at what you're doing out there. Is that OK with you?"

"Fine and dandy. I got no problem with that, and anyway, I've never met an honest-to-God English Lord before. Jest might be fun."

Since I flew out to Reno the day before Lord Ashcombe arrived, Dave insisted on accompanying me to the airport to greet his Lordship. But the sight that greeted us when he appeared in the arrivals hall was not what I'd expected. Jet lag was one thing and I could understand that he might have been tired but Lord Ashcombe's face was positively ashen.

"Is everything all right?" I asked, somewhat needlessly.

"Not really," he replied in a querulous voice. "I've been robbed."

"What on earth do you mean?"

"When I picked up my suitcase from the carousel, it was strapped up with tape. I assumed that the catches had broken in transit but thought I better check inside. Which is when I discovered I'd been robbed."

"You had something valuable in your suitcase?"

"Well, um, yes. Rather stupidly, I put quite a large sum of money in it, in cash. I know, I know it was silly of me but I didn't think anyone would really break into a suitcase. It's just a bit of a shock, you see. Bugger!"

"Damn! Ah'm sure sorry about that, Lord Ashcombe. An' sorry that it had to happen on American soil. May sound a bit lame in the circumstances but hell, welcome to Reno. Dave Jamieson, Sir, 'n pleased to meet you. Should I call you 'your Lordship'? Sir? Or whatever."

At least that provoked a small smile.

"I'm pleased to meet you as well, Mr Jamieson."

"Hey, call me Dave."

"Dave. And simply 'Lord Ashcombe' would be fine."

This time there were no discussions with recalcitrant cab drivers; Dave drove us over to the Best Western in his truck. While he drove back home, the two of us headed for the reception desk.

"Hi, how are you today? How may I help you?"

"Good afternoon, I have a room reserved for a few days. The name is Harry Ashcombe."

'Interesting,' I thought. I could just see the headline in the Reno Gazette: 'Robbed British Lord books into Reno Hotel as Common Man'.

Apart from looking admiringly at the falcons, praising the breeding programme and cementing the deal on the purchase of the birds, for the next few days we became tourists. Absolutely thrilled at having a member of the British aristocracy for company, Dave insisted that he showed us some of the area's natural wonders. The electric blue millpond of Pyramid Lake with its curious eponymous rocky island was wonderfully peaceful. The road that sort of followed the Truckee River wound its way through part of the Sierra Nevada and took us past craggy awesome scenery. High in the mountains, Nevada's end of Lake Tahoe to the north was beautifully stunning but cold. As for the visit to the Paiute native American reservation around Pyramid Lake, it was interesting. Somehow, that seemed vaguely voyeuristic, which made me feel slightly uncomfortable.

"Hey, don't sweat it, Gary. The Paiute own the damn lake. Every nickel and dime you spend out here goes into the tribe's pockets. Makes you feel better, buy your wife

196

something nice with 'Made by authentic Paiute' on the back."

But it was fun being a tourist for a while. In return, Lord Ashcombe organised a veritable banquet at the Best Western and his Lordship was the main attraction. Generally speaking, Americans are not great travellers, perhaps because the United States is so vast. Accordingly, they think of Britain as Shakespeare's small 'sceptred isle,' believe that we all live in London and know the Queen. However, the Jamieson family had clearly done their research: the conversation inexorably turned to things aristocratic and royal.

"D'you really live in a castle?"

"Actually, I do, Sudeley Castle in Gloucestershire. Great old place built of stone in the 1400s which means it's bloody cold in the winter. Henry the Eighth's last wife lived there – Katherine Parr. She was the one who survived."

"You're related to the Queen of England, right?"

"Not exactly but I do know her fairly well. She serves excellent tea."

"Is that Camilla really having an affair with Prince Charles?"

"Since Camilla is my niece, I do know her rather well. Lovely woman. She and Charles have been friends for years but as to an affair? I couldn't possibly comment."

"Is Lady Di as beautiful as she looks in the photos?"

"She's having an affair too, isn't she?"

"I wouldn't believe everything you read in the gutter press. Rumours of the royal family's affairs of the heart have been touted around for hundreds of years. It's part of British history, and part of the country's fiction. And for Princess Diana, she is a delightful young lady and photographs don't do her justice."

The questions came thick and fast. Lord Ashcombe answered every one with tact, diplomacy and wit. In fact, he handled the whole conversation quite brilliantly but he became truly eloquent when singing the praises of Diana, Princess of Wales. He waxed lyrical about her grace, beauty and charm; lauded her for her tireless charitable work and her wonderful communication skills. And then went back to her beauty which was complemented by her superb dress sense and natural elegance. Family Jamieson was enthralled and dazzled.

So the deal was done and we'd had our fun. All too soon we were back in Gloucestershire and I was faced with the daunting task of organising everything necessary to import three birds of prey from Nevada. My experience of sending sakers to Riyadh had been child's play in comparison. Riyadh may have generated a mountain of paperwork, but Reno threw up a complete sierra. Essentially it was a full-time secretarial job – but I didn't have a secretary. I shall paraphrase.

Under the Convention on International Trade in Endangered Species of Wild Fauna and Floral Controls: import and export of protected species (code named CITES), both the exporter and importer is required to obtain said permits from those countries where the said exporter and importer resides. Permits granted by CITES are not valid unless supported by appropriate export and import permits from the said countries.

The British Department of the Environment would issue the CITES and import permits subject to the importer providing an export permit and detailed information on the 'endangered' species in question. Meanwhile, the US Fish and Wildlife Service, Department of the Interior, would issue CITES and export permits, subject to the provisions of the Migratory Bird Treaty Act (1918) and the exporter having the appropriate import permit as assigned by the country of importation.

I assume you followed all of that with relative ease. The sheer volume of paperwork combined with the high levels of bureaucracy on both sides of the Atlantic was mind-numbingly boring. The bird's antecedents had to be proven and authenticated, numbers to be recorded, processing time allowed for and veterinary inspections to be recorded. It seemed to go on forever and was further complicated by the differences in time zones.

Even when the falcons had arrived in England, they would have to be quarantined and checked before they

198

could be released. And The Bothy wasn't equipped with the appropriate quarters. Fortunately, I knew a man who did: Nick Havemann-Mart, ex-director of the British Falconry Club, Vice-President of the Welsh Hawking Club and supplier supreme of raptor food. And it just so happened that Honeybrook Animal Foods was based in nearby Evesham. I explained my predicament.

"You can use mine free of charge."

Without the constraints of the international tangle of red tape, all it had taken to organise quarantine was a simple phone call to a friend. And, when I was due to collect the falcons from Heathrow, Nick volunteered to ride shotgun.

"Listen, I've been there and done it. I'll go with you, show you the ropes and, hopefully, we can speed things up a little."

Heathrow's Animal Quarantine Centre was just off the south perimeter road, separated from the main cargo areas. Not the pleasantest of places to wait, it had a vaguely drab antiseptic feel and a strange chemical smell. Two timber wolf pups, in transit to a German zoo, looked dolefully through the heavy wires of their cage, visibly shaking from with the trauma of displacement. It was a long way from the liberated wilderness of the Mackenzie Valley in Canada.

"Mr Cope? Can you come with me, please."

I glanced at my watch; the plane wasn't due for at least another hour.

"Sure. Is there anything wrong?"

He took us into a small bare room with a plain wooden table and two chairs before answering.

"Possibly," he said, running his fingers through thinning hair. "We've just had the pilot of the 747 on the radio and he's worried."

"Worried? About what? Has something happened?"

"Apparently there's a problem with the heating system in the hold. He realises that your birds are very valuable and … so he's very worried."

"OK. But what's actually happened to the heating system?"

"Um, it's stopped working entirely. Basically, he's frightened that the birds could freeze to death. Under normal circumstances, the hold's around ten degrees lower than the passenger cabin but if the heating system's down it would be a lot colder. At 30,000 feet, the skin of the plane is around minus 40 degrees. Of course, the hold is insulated and the temperature wouldn't drop anywhere near that but it's still going to be bloody cold. I'm sorry, I don't really know what to say," he ended lamely.

Nick and I started to smile before he'd even finished.

"It's not an issue, mate. They might be coming in from Nevada but gyrfalcons are actually arctic birds and they like it cold! If it had been the other way around and the heating system had cranked the temperature up, we would have had a problem: we'd be getting hold-roasted birds. Anyway, you can tell the pilot that it's not an issue and he doesn't need to worry. Just land the bloody plane safely, is all I ask."

He did, and the gyrs were brought into the quarantine area to be checked by the duty vet. She pulled at the lapels of her lab coat and eyed the travel boxes, clearly hesitant.

"I need to carry out a visual check on these, um, birds of prey."

From her demeanour, she obviously knew nothing about raptors or had any experience handling them.

"Carry on," I said, "you're the boss."

Flipping the catches, she slowly opened the door to reveal the silver gyr female. Understandably pissed off after her long dark flights, Tina went ballistic. Miss Veterinary snapped the door shut as fast as her trembling fingers would allow.

"She's fine," the vet squeaked.

She repeated the same process with the other boxes, with the same conclusion.

'Let me out of here,' I prayed, 'let me get back to Evesham and get them safely into quarantine at Honeybrook.'

As I moved in to pick up one of the boxes, a man's cough made me turn around. A little chap with grey hair and a grey suit was waving a clipboard of forms in the air.

200

"I'm afraid you can't take them away just yet. The import duty has to be paid before they can be released."

"Import duty?!"

"Yes, I'm afraid so. Let me see. Ah, yes, three birds of prey, imported from Nevada, USA, travelling separately as a collective, I believe. I think the duty is around £3,000 but I'll just double check that for you."

"Oh please, let me just check. No, I don't believe I have £3,000 in cash in any of my pockets and I'm damn sure I haven't got enough credit on my card to cover it."

"You understand that the import duty will have to paid?"

"By me? Not a chance, mate. Listen, I wasn't told anything about any import duty."

"You should have been, and it is a legal requirement. Unfortunately, until the duty has been paid, the birds will have to remain …"

"Let me put this clearly," I said interrupting the flow of pomposity, "I assume that you know who owns these falcons? Not sure? I'll remind you. The owner and importer is Prince Khalid bin Abdullah al Saud, whose brother-in-law is King Fahd who just happens to rule the whole of Saudi Arabia. Somehow I do not think that the Prince is short of a penny or two!"

"I see," said the official, quailing in the onslaught. "I suppose …"

"So, if you let these birds go, do you really think it's likely that he's going to do a runner over three grand?"

"Perhaps, you could contact the Prince and make him aware of the situation. But until the duty's paid, I really don't think I can authorise you to remove them."

Sensing he was weakening, I said: "Forget it. You don't have the facilities here to take proper care of the falcons and if anything went wrong with them, it would cause one hell of a diplomatic crisis. Are you wiling to take that responsibility? If you are, then let's get something official typed up in your office stating the fact, and you'll have to sign to the effect that you accept full responsibility. On the other hand, you can let them go and I can assure you that you'll have your import duty within 48 hours."

After much scratching of heads and consultation with higher powers, we were finally allowed to load the birds and drive back to Gloucestershire. As we drove away from the Centre, I felt a wave of relief flow over me, thankful that the whole tortuous process was over. Back at Honeybrook, the birds had to be installed in their quarantine quarters. Nicknack, the young gyr-saker cross, jumped cheerfully out of the box, onto the perch and preened as though he'd never been away. Silver Tina hissed balefully as I took her out, to show that she was not a happy bunny and was seriously pissed off with the whole affair.

Last out was Magnum, our semen donor. About seven or eight years old, he was white as the driven snow and a stunningly handsome creature. To my amazement, when I got him out of the box and onto the glove, I swear he blinked at me lecherously.

"Tuk, tuk, tuk."

This bird had travelled in a box, by road and air, for a zillion hours and now he was displaying to me in no uncertain terms. It was quite extraordinary but one thing I now knew for certain, Magnum was going to be the jewel in the crown.

But for now, all three would have to spend the next 35 days in the isolation of quarantine. Every other day, I trailed over to Evesham to see my new charges. Although I was prohibited from entering the chambers, I could still peer through the chamber windows and interact with them to some degree. However, it was with Magnum that the bond grew and was strongest.

"Wow. You are so special, so fantastic!" I mouthed at him through the glass.

In a bizarre sort of way, I think that he chose me as much as I chose him, but whatever the truth, we developed a fantastic, lasting relationship. Tina, on the other hand, worried me a little because she was still very stand-offish and snooty. If she'd been a Mississippi southern belle, I'd have been the downtrodden hired hand. But I put it down to the fact that she'd been dragged most of the way across America and over the Atlantic in a box. What lady of

202

refinement wouldn't have had her feathers ruffled by such an unpleasant method of conveyance?

Meanwhile, back at The Bothy, Nick and I scrubbed and cleaned the birds' new quarters. The perches got new AstroTurf and coconut matting, every particle of pea gravel was replaced and everything was disinfected to the level required in an operating theatre. The accommodation for our new friends from Nevada was spotlessly clean, fully reupholstered, wonderfully appointed and welcoming. All we had to do was wait for a month.

It passed surprisingly quickly. All the necessary veterinary checks had been completed, the quarantine period was finished and we got the green light for collection. Nick and I drove up to Evesham with our "Made in Nevada' travelling boxes, loaded them up, I thanked Nick H-M for his generous hospitality and went back to The Bothy.

Once the birds were installed in their spanking new accommodation, I heaved another sigh of relief. And that night we had more than a few drinks to celebrate. It had been a long haul and the pressure had been on, but we'd got there in the end.

I still had reservations about the whole programme but it was what it was and I'd put hope before despair. At least I could forget about them for a while: nothing was going to happen until the next breeding season and that was several months away.

Now the fun could start and I was looking forward to spending some money. The other part of my brief was to put together a game hawking team and I'd already ordered three falcons with excellent game hawking lineage from Martin Jones for the purpose.

Since Christmas was looming, I decided that I needed totally new equipment. Block perches, falconry bags, gloves, even telemetry – I needed new everything. And it was all approved! For the first time in my falconry career, I didn't need to consider whether I could afford to buy a new set of Asborno bells, a supple buckskin falconry glove or a perfectly turned block perch. This time I was like a kid in a sweet shop.

"I'll have one of those, a pair of them and two of the others."

Suddenly, I was able to buy without asking the price. I suppose, by trade, Jim Wiggins was a wheelwright and rather skilled at the art of wood bending, but he also made the most beautiful cadges. Without a moment's thought, I called with my order.

"Jim, what I need is a box cadge to go into the back of the 4x4, but I want a traditional bowed field cadge. Can do?"

"No problem, Mr Cope."

"I'd like it padded with red velvet and secured with brass studs. I'm sure you know what I mean."

"I do. That won't be a problem, but it'll cost mind."

"And that's not's problem either," I replied, grinning like a maniac.

I thought it would look quite good, walking out over the moors with an elegant cadge and beautiful falcons. Then of course, there were the moors themselves to think about. Naturally it was imperative for the Prince's personal falconer to become acquainted with the private grouse hawking moors in Yorkshire. Therefore Lord Ashcombe and I travelled up to Helmsley and stayed at the Black Swan while surveying the newly purchased moor at Leyburn.

We had a couple of days to traipse across the place and were joined by Brigadier Watson for the jaunt. Strange breed, aristocrats. It was bitterly cold, the ground hard as iron and an icy wind cut like a knife but luncheon is de rigeur. Spreading a rug on the heather, they produced a splendid picnic from a wicker basket and munched manfully away despite the harsh conditions. Barking mad, of course.

As for grouse, they seemed to be everywhere. My experience was more of the Scottish moors where you had to yomp for at least six miles to find a covey and even then there would only be a few birds. At Leyburn, the coveys were practically flocks! Since the moor hadn't been shot for over ten years, it was overrun by grouse: running up

204

tracks, exploding like oversized grapeshot from cover and practically tripping you up as you walked.

Lying in my large plush bed at the Black Swan, I stared smiling at the ceiling.

'What a wonderful end to a fabulous year," I thought contentedly.

There been the trips to the States and the gyrfalcons, I had new vehicles, a very nice salary, status and so on; it was quite extraordinarily wonderful and I had to pinch myself to make sure that it wasn't all a dream. Wow! And it wasn't showing any sign of stopping.

But, as with everything in life, there's always something around the corner that'll come up and bite your arse.

Chapter 19 – Otterhills

Dense, water-logged fog blurred the view from the kitchen window; the world outside had become a gloomy land of ghosts and shape-shifters. In the stifled air of the early morning, sounds were muffled and choked into silence but I knew that Nick would be calmly checking that all was well in the aviaries. I'd already seen his dark shade float noiselessly towards the walled garden and seep through the gate. The morning inspection was his first job of the day. In a few minutes, he'd appear in the kitchen, put on the kettle for coffee and greet me with a cheery – "Hiya Copey. How yer doing?" As I waited, I prepared a mental list for the daily discussion.

I had not expected the ashen face that materialised in the doorway from the fog. Lips that were tight with worry had replaced the usual impish grin and he was obviously very upset. I knew immediately that something was wrong.

"Are you OK, Nick? What's up?"

"You'd better come with me, it's Tino."

"What's going on with Tino?"

"She's just sitting on the floor in the corner of the aviary, fluffed out and looking groggy. There's no reaction at all."

"Christ!"

Nick followed hard on my heels as I dashed out, making a beeline for the aviary. Sure enough, when I entered the breeding chamber, I found our very expensive silver gyrfalcon sitting listlessly on the gravel in the corner. That in itself was a bad sign. Eyes that were barely half open looked blankly at the ground and the previous day's titbit of choice fresh quail lay close by but completely untouched. I slowly walked across to her and knelt down on the stones.

"Tuik, tuik, tik, tik, tuik."

I always talk to my falcons, and they talk back; but my usually fluent gyr did not provoke even the slightest of responses. Now I was really worried because there was something seriously wrong with Tino. Rushing back to the house, I rang Neil Forbes and filled him in on the situation.

206

"Get her over immediately," was his response.

Tino barely fluttered a feather as I bundled her into the travelling box that had brought her all the way from Nevada. It took almost an hour to get to the Clockhouse Veterinary Hospital in Stroud, my nerves getting more and more frayed by the minute. But once we'd arrived, not a second was wasted as we were given an immediate slot. I watched anxiously as Neil administered a local anaesthetic and carefully checked Tino's vital functions.

"It's definitely a respiratory infection but it's difficult to determine how far it's gone."

"You think she might have aspergillosis?"

"It could be asper, but I say could. We can't know for certain but yes, that is a possibility. Gyrfalcons are particularly susceptible to aspergillosis, as are other arctic birds. Either way, I need to do some tests and, for the moment, she'll have to stay in the hospital. I'll let you know how we get on."

Nick and I drove back to The Bothy in silence. My mind was a total whirl of worry and fear. I could hear my own prescient words echoing in my ears.

'We're putting all our eggs in one basket. The whole breeding programme is going to be based on two birds. What happens if it all goes pear-shaped?'

Now the female half of the breeding project was languishing in Neil's intensive care unit with what might be a deadly infection. All my fears appeared to coming true and I dreaded to think what the outcome would be. Tino might be a big falcon but gyrs are still quite delicate birds and do get stressed. I'd always worried about bringing an adult all the way from Nevada to a very different climate. I'd even changed her name from Tina to Tino because I refused to have a bird with such a prissy name. Maybe I'd upset her by giving her a male name.

'Don't be so bloody ridiculous,' I told myself.

But there was nothing more that I could do but leave her in Neil's experienced hands. I rang the following morning.

"It's early days, Gary. However, she does have a lung infection but if it is aspergillosis, it's nodular rather than systemic."

"What the hell does that mean?"

"That it attacks the air sacs, the lungs and trachea rather than the liver or the kidneys for example. Not that that minimises the problem. At the moment, we're treating her with anti-virals and she's on an aspirator."

"But has there been any change?"

"As yet, no."

Nor was there any change over the subsequent few days. Basically, they were managing to keep her alive but the big problem was that she wasn't feeding. And without food or nutrients, she would die.

"Do you mind if I come over?"

"To be honest Gary, I don't think that there is any point. We are trying to feed her but at she's simply not responding."

My whole career was hanging by a thread; I had to do something.

"Let me try," I pleaded. "Just let me come over and try to feed her myself. She knows me."

"Fine," Neil sighed. "If you think that you can make a difference, why not?"

Catching up one of the quail that I bred for our birds, I quickly despatched it and cut off the succulent breast meat and a little off the legs. Having chopped it up into small pieces, I stuffed them into my bag and headed for Stroud.

I found Tino lying on a blanket in in intensive care, beautifully housed in an open-fronted cage which was secured with wire mesh. But Tino herself looked little different to when I'd first brought her in to the hospital.

"I've been trying to feed her but she's just not interested," said the nurse.

"Let me have a go. Can you get me some forceps and a metal dish, please? And some Ringer's solution."

"Of course."

"Let's get her out," I said, when the nurse returned with the requested items.

We pulled Tino out on her blanket and I lay down beside her. Picking up a morsel of quail with the forceps, I dipped it into the Ringer's solution; if she fed, at least she would get some nutrition, glucose and vital salts. My heart

208

sank as I looked at the ragged falcon lying there in front of me, her eyes glazed and half open with only the slightest sign of life. Her breathing was so shallow that the rise and fall of the sharp ridge of her breast was almost imperceptible. And then I started talking gyr.

"Tuik-tuik-tuk, tuik-tuik-tuk, tuik-tuik-tuk."

Seeing a slight glimmer of recognition in her eyes, I very carefully picked up a little piece of quail with the forceps, dipped it in the solution and offered it to Tino. Keeping my head turned, I continued my one-sided gyr conversation. Suddenly, she lifted her beak slightly and delicately took the quail from the prongs of the forceps. And once she'd tasted that first titbit, she took another, and then another. They were truly magical moments, enhanced by the sense of victory.

"Whoa! How did you do that?" the nurse asked with amazement.

"It's all about knowing about birds of prey. And being able to talk gyr," I said, grinning.

The strange thing about it is that's it true: people talk about horse whispering but it doesn't matter whether it's a horse, dog or falcon, they all have their own language. All you have to do is learn the language and talk; it's as simple as that. Anyway, in this instance, the important thing was that Tino had got some food inside her which would give her strength.

So the die was cast and for the next five or six days, I travelled over to Stroud to feed Tino and quietly encourage her with a little gyr talk. The powerful combination of ventilator, anti-viral drugs and food began to overcome the infection and Tino gradually flew the road of recovery. After a few more days in hospital, she eventually got her release papers, stamped amber for caution, and was allowed to return to The Bothy.

"There's no evidence of infection now, Gary, but you will have to keep a close eye on her. And that's not just for the next few days. There is a possibility that she could relapse and it'll take around six months before we can sure that she's entirely out of the woods."

Despite Neil's cautionary words, my relief was overwhelming. But I left it another 48 hours before telling Lord Ashcombe.

"It was all very scary but she's back in the breeding chamber now and looks as good as new."

"And thank God for that," his Lordship said fervently.

What I didn't say was that I'd had my doubts about Tino from the very beginning and that feeling hadn't gone away. When we first met in Nevada, I just had a hunch that the silver gyr would be a problem sooner or later. With Magnum, our white gyr semen donor, I knew he was right on the money from the outset. He was never happier than when fornicating with a hat, producing copious amounts of muscular spermatozoa. But when it came to Tino, I was equally sure that she would be the project's nemesis. Not that I had any parallel proof, it was simply an instinct that came from years of experience with birds of prey. But time would tell. At least she'd survived and was safely back in her chamber.

My security warning alert had dropped from the 'severe risk of major disaster' red zone, to the more pacific blue zone that merely indicated a 'general risk of major disaster'. Even without Tino's close encounter with the Grim Reaper, it had been a tough year. As November drifted quietly into December, Joy and I decided to celebrate the festive season in style. It felt time to relax, to eat, drink and be merry. Thus, filled with the spirit of Christmas, we invited a host of friends and family for a feast. Joy sat by the fire, checking the names on the list: my parents, her parents, one or two of her friends, a couple of mine and several ones that we happily shared.

"Um, Gary? Since everyone's said yes, we're going to have about eighteen people turning up for dinner."

"Right."

"We've only got six chairs around one table."

"Ah."

"And we're going to need an enormous turkey to feed them all. Not to mention all the potatoes, sprouts, stuffing, di dah, di dah. Plus, we'll need a lot more wine."

"Fine."

Sudeley Castle's restaurant was, with permission, stripped of several trestle tables and numerous chairs and transported back to The Bothy using a 4x4 shuttle approach. Our plumptious free range turkey weighed in at somewhere around the 30lb mark. Crates of vegetables and other goodies accumulated in the kitchen. And Lord Ashcombe generously sent a case of his best claret from the dusty darkness of the castle cellars to provide the necessary lubrication. Fortunately, there were plenty of mothers, sisters, females in waiting and male wannabe chefs to prepare, assemble and cook. Which, in turn, meant that most people's nerves were moderately tested and patience frequently strained. After all, it was Christmas.

"A few more roast potatoes?"

"I really shouldn't. I'm watching my weight. But since you insist."

"Do have some Brussels sprouts, there are loads."

"Just a couple. Too many of them make me burp awfully."

"Could you pass the cranberry sauce, please?"

"Of course. And more bread sauce?"

"This claret is divine."

"It is, isn't it? His Lordship does have a rather good cellar."

The flickering flames of a battalion of candles lent a warmth to the room and a glow to people's faces. I gazed beneficently down the long table and felt like some medieval king. My revellers ate, drank, chattered and laughed, they read weak jokes from cheap crackers and wore coloured crêpe paper hats that never quite fitted. In contrast, a fine Christmas tree stood proudly silent in the far corner of the room, its dark green needled boughs adorned with bright baubles, glittering tinsel and a profusion of twinkling lights. It was all rather wonderful.

But when one is truly passionate about something, aspects of such are rarely far from one's mind. And since falconry was my overwhelming passion, my thoughts naturally drifted sideways.

'I wonder what you'd fly at wild turkeys?' I mused. 'Gyr peregrine hybrids would probably be the best. There again, why would you bother?'

And then the word 'gyr' turned my thoughts to the New Year and the question marks hanging over the breeding season which would arrive soon enough. Magnum could certainly talk the talk; but would he walk the walk and become a semen factory? Would Tino stay fit and well? And, if so, would she lay eggs? Or would the whole dream be shattered and would I get sacked? Time would tell.

'Every man for himself and the devil take the hindmost. C'est la vie.'

On which profound note, I stopped thinking profound thoughts and proceeded to quaff several more glasses of fine claret. Naturally, I did not forget to toast Lord Ashcombe, Prince Khalid, Joy, both sets of parents, the merry throng, the turkey and the tree, but not necessarily in that order. Nor did I omit to send up a silent prayer, albeit slightly slurred, to Saint Bavo, patron saint of falconers.

Obviously the saintly patron wasn't entirely clear on the detail. As I'd expected, Tino wasn't showing any signs of laying eggs when the breeding season got under way.

"If she doesn't lay eggs, we can't breed and we can't inseminate her. There's no point," I said to Nick. "Maybe it's a knock-on effect from the infection. Maybe she hasn't completely recovered. I don't know."

"So what are we going to do with all the semen from Magnum?"

"Use it, my friend, use it. You never waste good juice."

In the final analysis, Tino wasn't laying anything at all but Magnum was producing semen like a porn star. Clearly we weren't going to be looking gooey-eyed at a clutch of cute little gyr downies while proudly conveying the news to the Prince. Instead we inseminated peregrine falcons and produced exceedingly good white gyr cross peregrine hybrids. Not that Prince Khalid was interested: pure white gyrs were the only birds he wanted, in the belief that they were the best. Ironically, peregrine gyr hybrids were becoming highly regarded in the Middle East but His Royal

Highness was not a follower of fashion and, perhaps, somewhat behind the times.

However, they were fabulous birds which we easily sold on the UK market. In British terms, they had a good commercial value and sold for quite reasonable sums of money. Not that those meagre takings would have impressed the scion of the house of Saud. But for my part, it meant that I was making a financial contribution to the project and the revenues from sales went to Fairlawne.

So as the season came to a close, my focus turned away from thoughts of breeding gyrfalcons and on to the practicalities of grouse hawking. I'd been working with the three falcons I'd acquired from Martin Jones for the purpose and watching them develop. Ling was lean and fiery while sister Siro tended to be so laid back that she'd almost fall off her perch. A short stumpy falcon with oversized feet, De Carnach had little of the elegance of the other two but, overall, he did have a lovely conformation. Never mind that she was a moody little bird, my guess was that she would be the star of the trio. However, they had all progressed admirably.

"They're rather small," observed Lord Ashcombe on one of his 'team' visits. "Are you sure they'll be up to the job, Gary?"

"They'll be fine."

"I hope so. But they're still rather small compared to the sakers His Highness is used to watching fly."

"We're going to be flying at grouse, so peregrines are definitely the best choice. And they'll suit the terrain. Sakers have never proved to be good grouse hawks."

Nevertheless, the conversation left with me with a few niggling doubts. Grouse hawking with peregrines on a small undulating moor in Yorkshire was a far cry from slinging sakers at houbara in the desert. Humping over heathered tussocks and crumbling walls adorned with barbed wire, rather different from racing across a vast expanse of scrubby sand dunes in the comfort of a 4x4. Prince Khalid would certainly see the contrasts between the two styles of falconry but whether he would appreciate and enjoy the Yorkshire version might be debatable. Grouse hawking in Yorkshire was what it was and there was nothing that I could change about the programme. It was my job to ensure that we had the best possible team for the sport and that meant peregrines. Cold comfort perhaps, but reassuring nevertheless.

"Your accommodation's all arranged," Lord Ashcombe said cheerfully. "It's a bit basic but Otterhills Cottage is a delightful little place that Brigadier Watson has up there near Kirkbymoorside. Sykes Cottage isn't available unfortunately because it's let; which is a damned shame because it's nearer to Prince Khalid's moor. Never mind, a bit of a drive won't hurt you and your costs are all covered, naturally."

It was only later, that I took the time to consider the implications of his Lordship's 'bit of a drive'. According to my map, Preston Moor was west of Leyburn and Kirkbymoorside, east of Helmsley. I ran my finger along the little grey lines that represented the small roads that connected the two dots, scribbled a few figures on a scrap of paper and snorted loudly.

"By my reckoning, it's at least 50 miles each way. And that's along country bloody roads which means that it'll take us at least an hour or more to get there!"

"Yeah well, think of the scenic beauty," said Joy, ever the pacifier, "and then think of the money."

"Mmm. It's still a bloody long way," I continued grumpily. "You would have thought they could have found somewhere near Leyburn."

"But they didn't. And anyway, you'll have me for company for at least some of the time."

The Glorious Twelfth being only four days away, Joy and I loaded up the 4x4 for the trek up to Otterhills Cottage. And it wasn't that easy. Three hooded falcons on a cadge, two dogs, a vast array of equipment, a mass of provisions and luggage for two takes up a lot of space! Becky and Bracken nestled down on their blanket, flanked by numerous boxes, with their heads resting on their paws, resigned to the prospect of a long drive.

To say the journey north was harrowing would be an understatement. Every time I had to take a sharp corner or

214

brake hard, I expected to hear the rumble of an avalanche of stuff cascading onto my unsuspecting passengers. The scratch of talons on a hood, the tinkle of bells, a canine sigh – they were all possible causes for concern. But as we headed up on the motorway, the monotonous hum lulled even those sounds to sleep.

It was a different matter after we'd passed through the small market town of Kirkbymoorside. Leaving the metalled tarmac, we turned down Sleightholmedale Road as directed. Road? Little more than a track, negotiating the gaping potholes and fallen rocks exercised all my driving skills and patience. My fears of collapsing luggage and crushed falcons returned with a vengeance. And, as ever on Yorkshire's off-road lanes, ancient sagging gates that refused to work in the way they should frequently barricaded our path. Variously attached to rotting wooden posts by baling twine, rusting chains or barbed wire, they had no love for tender human hands. After almost five miles of this torture, Otterhills Cottage finally appeared.

"It's beautiful," said Joy, taking in the surrounding scenery.

Pockets of wildflowers lent colour to the browns and greens of the steep slopes of the small wooded valley. A riot of rabbits scampered from the banks when we arrived, their scuffling adding to the bubbling sound of the beck whose waters tumbled over ochre rocks. This idyllic, tranquil, pastoral scene might stop a rambler in his (or her) tracks but I didn't feel quite the same.

"It's remote, I'll give you that."

I looked at the herd of heifers in the distance that was peering curiously in our direction. And then at the breaches in the low stone wall which surrounded the cottage.

"As soon as they hear the birds' bells, they'll be over to have a closer look. I'm going to have to rebuild the wall properly before I can put the birds out safely. To be honest, the whole place looks a bit run down."

"I'm sure it'll be fine inside," said Joy, taking a more positive line. "Let's take a look."

Lifting the rock on the ground to the right of the door, as instructed, I found an old iron key that grated in protestation as I turned it in the lock. The door creaked open to reveal a state of dereliction only usually found in an old ruin. But the full horror of the place was only truly apparent when we walked into the dank gloom of the room beyond.

A few sticks of wood in one corner hinted at the possibility that they once been a chair. Otherwise, the only piece of furniture actually standing was an old table in the middle of the room. The bottom of one leg had rotted away, leaving it uselessly hanging an inch above the filthy floor. Another was broken at the halfway point, the lower part bent outwards giving an unhealthy tilt to the whole.

Soot lay in a thick layer around the hearth, lending a black mantle to the detritus of gnarled twigs and greasy black residue that had cascaded down from the choked chimney. We shuffled silently through other rooms, our footsteps echoing dully on floorboards riddled with woodworm.

The rank smell of mildew in the bathroom was testament to the pervasive damp. Lush emerald moss carpeted the bottom of the bathtub, complemented by the more delicate shade of green that coloured its original white ceramic sides. The darkly stained toilet bowl ran down to a stagnant brown puddle and pulling the chain simply produced a dull clunk from the antique iron cistern. It had clearly been a long time since it had experienced the cool freshness of clean water.

In what might have once been a bedroom, black mould crept across the rotting wallpaper like a malignant disease. The paper had fallen away in places to hang down in noxious folds, exposing the damp flaking grey plaster.

The only cheering sight was the magnificent old Rayburn in the kitchen which might provide warmth and a wonderful place to cook – if all the ash and clinker was removed, it was thoroughly cleaned and the blockage in the vent could be penetrated.

Both of us were in a state of shock, staring at each other with wide eyes and disbelief. It was a rare occasion when both of us were stunned into silence but somewhere up in the heavens, a blue moon was assuredly shining.

216

"Jesus!" was the first word I uttered; almost a prayer for help rather than a sacrilegious expletive. "There is absolutely no way that we can stay here for ten weeks. This is a fucking joke!"

Joy bit her lip and nodded. Before she could gather her thoughts to say anything in return, we were both distracted by the rough rasping sound of a Land Rover grinding to a halt outside. A double rap on the front door preceded our visitor's entry. Doffing the flat cap, with one hand, he wiped the other on grubby trousers before speaking.

"You must be Mister 'n Missus Coop. Ah'm Tom, th' handyman at Sleightholmedale Lodge. They said I was to see yer all right. Welcome ter Otter'ills. What d'yer think?"

For a moment, we both stared at him as though he was some kind of strange local breed with an odd sense of humour. Neither of us could see anything remotely funny about the situation, but blurted out our comments with individual style.

"It's a fucking tip! Unbelievable."

"It's not quite what we expected."

"Ah well, it's not exactly a palace but that'd be cuz there hasn't been a body living 'ere for nigh on thirty year."

I looked around me, totally flabbergasted and wondering what on earth to say next.

"No wonder, it's derelict. And what's going on with the windows?"

Tom's eye followed the direction of my accusatory pointing finger.

"That's doon to th' Brigadier an' Lord Ashcombe. His Lordship thought that since they weren't any curtains, a bit of sacking'd do."

As though in mockery, the dirty hessian flapped limply in the sudden breeze through the broken glass of the window behind.

"Sod this!" I exclaimed, absolutely livid with rage. "We're driving back down the motorway and going home."

"Come on, Gary," said Joy, "let's do something about it rather than giving up at the first hurdle. I'm sure something can be sorted out."

Taking advantage of Joy's calming influence, Tom added: "Ah, that's reet, Missus Coop. There's allus something that can be worked out. Come back wi' me to the big house an' we'll see what can be done."

We had to drive the best part of a mile further up the rutted track before we turned up the gravelled drive that led through manicured gardens to Sleightholmedale Lodge. The fine old stone mansion stretched out on either side as we walked into the grand but austere stone entrance. Tom took us into a wonderfully spacious kitchen which was rather more functional and cleaner than Otterhills' sewer.

"Phone's over there, Mister Coop."

His Lordship answered the phone immediately, as though he was waiting for my call. And I let fly, ranting wrathfully in a manner that I had never before adopted with Lord Ashcombe. In short, I was so angry that any grace, politeness or consideration was drowned in a verbal tsunami of invective.

"Be a bit more diplomatic," hissed Joy, trying to calm the troubled waters but with little effect.

"Basically, that's it," I snarled, beginning to run out of steam. "The deal's off, you can forget it. If that's what you think of me, I'm going home."

"I did tell you it was rustic, Gary," said his Lordship plaintively, managing to get a word in for a change.

That merely added fuel to the hot embers which were immediately rekindled.

"It's not bloody fucking rustic, it's a cesspit. Rustic is homely, pleasantly comfortable, simple but welcoming. I like rustic. I don't mind roughing it a bit but this is ridiculous; a bloody tramp wouldn't live here."

"Fine. Let's talk about this sensibly."

"I am talking sensibly. I'm talking realistically and factually, for God's sake."

'Gary, stop. I do understand your feelings so let's tackle the problems. What needs to be done?"

"I-can-not-stay-up-here. You understand! Everything needs to be done."

"In that case, we'll just have to do – everything."

Lord Ashcombe was as good as his word and gave us an open chequebook to renovate the whole place. Amazingly the electrics still worked when the cottage was reconnected but everything else needed a full and total makeover.

"They'll be comin' over from the estate," said Tom mysteriously.

I understood what he meant when most of the staff from Sleightholmedale Lodge turned up at Otterhills, armed with power tools, brushes, scrapers, hammers, screwdrivers and a large part of the stock held by Kirkbymoorside's hardware store. Forget those irritating 'We'll turn your revolting little house into a superior designer dwelling' makeover television shows; this was reality in action. The magnificent ten cleaned, scrubbed, stripped, sanded, polished and painted. Within the space of a week, they'd turned what had been a crap-hole into a wonderfully decorated bijou cottage.

Once the Rayburn was cleaned and refurbished, Tom brought over a pile of seasoned logs and fired up the monster. Now Otterhills Cottage was starting to be warm, inviting and we could cook for ourselves. But it wasn't quite ready for occupancy.

Bracing herself for the job in hand, Joy set off for the second-hand shops in Harrogate. She bought a chintzy deep three piece suite, a rescrubbed pine dining table and chairs, a wooden double bed complete with spring mattress and assortment of other bits of furniture that make a home, a home. And, of course, all purchased with the help of Lord Ashcombe's gracious largesse.

While this was all being done, Joy and I were put up in the Lodge and the falcons housed in one of the barns. Sleightholmedale's staff were wonderful, at the Lodge and Otterhills, and I sincerely hope that they were paid well for their labours. If it had not been for everyone's good offices, Gary Cope the Royal Falconer would have buggered off back to Gloucestershire.

My contribution was to rebuild the wall around the cottage and adapt the spare bedroom to serve as a temporary mews. Falcons, dogs and the Copes happily took possession of Otterhills Cottage. With Prince Khalid due to arrive in one week, I was happy, prepared and excited. It was time to go grouse hawking.

Chapter 20 – The Prince and I

The red grouse season started on 12 August, as it had done for over 150 years. The Glorious Twelfth, engraved on the statute books in the Game Act 1831, was a time-honoured day of note on the shooting calendar.

But Prince Khalid had missed the mark by several days. Since we were flying falcons rather than shooting guns, one might argue that he had simply decided to employ a royal prerogative and be different. In reality, it had much more to do with the fact that Juddmonte Farms sponsored the International Stakes which was the first race at York's Ebor Festival meeting. It just so happened that Juddmonte was Prince Khalid's renowned horse breeding farm and naturally one of his ponies was racing.

So there we were, at Cranehows Bottom on Preston Moor, waiting for the main man to arrive. Richard Coates, the royal keeper of the princely moors was in attendance, accompanied by his young under-keeper, Anthony. John 'Whitty' Whitmore had driven up to join me for the grouse hawking and to serve as my aide-de-camp. And of course, the trio of falcons and brace of dogs. (Understanding the rigours of falconry on windswept moors and having played her part, Joy had returned to the more clement climes of Gloucestershire to ply her own trade.)

I'd chosen the location for the Prince's inaugural grouse hawking flights with great care. When you're flying falcons for VIPs, not only do you have to get the whole spectacle working like magic, you have to ensure that they can see all the wonders you're producing. And I had a funny feeling that neither Prince Khalid or any of his august guests would be amused by a yomp across the heather. Cranehows Bottom was perfect.

Imagine a massive rogue asteroid crashing through the earth's atmosphere several millions of years ago. Superheated by the journey, the molten surface streamed a wake of flame and exploded on impact, leaving a huge smoking crater in Yorkshire's landscape. Now, it was a beautiful natural amphitheatre that allowed fine viewpoints from all points of the compass. Nor would the wind direction matter: there would always be an up-draught somewhere to enable the falcons to wait-on. A thick coating of heather and brush coated the curving sides that led down to a lush green base which disguised the treacherous bogs below. Should an unwary walker step into the thick peat slime, he was likely to find himself deeply and quickly bemired, with a worm's eye view of the ground. But I also knew that Cranehows Bottom was home to a healthy population of grouse.

I glanced at my watch: just gone five thirty. The hawking party was due to arrive at around six o'clock. The waiting was making us all tense and, for the first time in my career, I was feeling distinctly nervous. And it wasn't just me. Richard continually ran his fingers through his thatch of blonde hair and muttered to Anthony in a broad Yorkshire accent. At times, my eyes would catch a glance from his piercing blue eyes, and then both of us would look away. John sat quietly, his head enveloped by rising clouds of white-blue smoke that issued from the side of his mouth as he puffed studiously on his pipe. I rolled another cigarette and looked down the empty track for the fiftieth time.

"What do you call a conservative prince out hawking?"

"Dunno. What do you call a conservative prince out hawking?"

"A right royal cock-up!"

"Where the bloody hell are they?"

After what seemed an age, I finally heard the growl of a Range Rover and the subtler purring undertone of a luxury car. Lord Ashcombe's Rangie bumped into view, followed by the silver Bentley Mulsanne Turbo.

"He's brought the bloody Bentley onto a grouse moor. I don't believe it!"

"Anthony, open tha gate for them. God help us if coachwork's scratched."

The diminutive cavalcade lurched over the rough ground, negotiating the rocks with only the occasional squeal of metal on stone. When they came to a halt, Lord Ashcombe was out first with a guest in tow.

"Hallo Gary, everything all right?"

222

"Absolutely. We're all ready for you, my Lord. How was the racing?"

"Ah, fine. But, um, Prince Khalid's horse didn't win. Lester Piggott came in first on Rodrigo de something. Anyway, I hope we'll get a good show here."

In the meantime, the chauffeur had released the Prince and his guest from the cavernous rear of the Bentley. By the look of the suits, they'd all spent the day at the races. Prince Khalid brushed a fleck of fluff from one lapel of his Saville row attire and strode across. He looked at me over the horn frames of his large glasses, grinned broadly and held out his hand.

"Gary, Gary, how are you?"

"I'm really well, Your Royal Highness. Thank you."

"Good. So, what are we doing?"

"Well, hopefully we'll catch the odd grouse."

"Excellent. It is a beautiful evening for hawking on my English grouse moor."

The sun was slowly sliding down through a clear sky and the moor was bathed in that special golden light. The rolling purple heather, the rocks, barren patches of earth and even the gateposts furred with lichen were all suffused in that warm glow.

And from the depths of Cranehows Bottom we could hear the grouse talking. "Krbek, krbek, krbek, krek-krek-krek-krek." Or were they really saying: "Go back, go back, go back?"

Beautiful. Everything was fitting together nicely and there were lots of nice grouse down there. Inviting everyone to follow, I escorted the party to my pre-planned position and, once they were in place, turned to Lord Ashcombe.

"Shall we start, your Lordship?"

"Why not? Which one are you going to fly first?"

"Ling, I think. She's still a juvenile, so she's learning her trade," I added for the Prince's benefit. "She's probably my favourite of the three falcons we have up here and I think she's got the makings of being an extraordinary grouse hawk."

"You are saying she has potential, I think."

"Yes."

"Is she not a little small?"

"No Sir, she's ideal for grouse."

"And that is an English pointer, I believe."

"That's correct. I know you use salukis for hunting but there's nothing better for grouse than an English pointer."

Picking Ling up from the cadge, I released the dog into the heather and continued the conversation.

"That's Becky, Sir. Watch how she works the cover. Most pointers quarter the ground, zigzagging into the wind. Becky doesn't waste her time with quartering. Look at the way she sniffs the air. When she catches a scent, she changes direction. There, did you see her?"

"Yes. Interesting."

"When she's sure, she'll drop down on her haunches and stalk like a lioness. And then she'll go on point."

Given the numbers of grouse out there, within a matter of minutes Becky went on point, about 50 yards away. Whitty and Richard spread out to the sides, just in case anything went wrong; I struck the braces on Ling's hood and held her up, facing the wind. Of personal choice, I never cast the falcon off the glove, although some believe that gives the bird impetus. It doesn't. I prefer to let the bird rouse and then push off from the glove like a runner off the blocks. Except Ling wasn't doing anything. Her feathers prickled up and then settled, up and down, up and down.

'Rouse, for fuck's sake, rouse.'

My telepathic request eventually got through. Rattling her feathers loudly, she slicked them back down, bobbed her head twice and flew. Unlike most birds, Ling didn't ring up to gain height, she simply went for it in a steep climb that was reminiscent of a Vulcan bomber. She fired up through the sky until she reached her pitch and flattened out. Ling did her part beautifully: spreading her sails, she waited on and started to circle. Becky was set and I went round to head the point. Falcon? Check. Dog? Check. Audience? Check. Time to send in the dog.

"Get 'em up, get 'em up, get 'cm up."

Nothing. To my horror, Becky's bouncing around in the heather like Tigger on springs and I'm as confused as Winnie-the-Pooh. The dog wasn't producing a feather and my heart was pounding with panic.

'You're kidding me! There are birds everywhere and you can't find one?!'

I leaped into the heather with Becky, desperately trying to flush something and got – nothing. Becky had never disappointed before and my guess was that she'd pointed at an old cock grouse. The wily old bird had simply slipped away into the cover of deep heather and pulled his head under the parapet. But it still meant that our first sortie had been a complete and utter failure. It was not the best of debuts and my heart sank a few inches lower. There was little point in chastising the dog: she would simply look hurt, jump in the back of the 4x4 and refuse to work.

Leaving Ling floating in the heavens, I called Becky in and walked back up the slope to give my apologies.

"Sorry about that. It might have been a false point but I think Becky had her nose on a grouse with experience. Damn bird just dug himself him and refused to play. I'll leave Ling up for a bit longer so she can stretch her wings and then bring her down. At least you'll be able to see how she flies."

Prince Khalid nodded in agreement and we stood side by side, staring skywards. After a few more minutes, I could see that Ling was getting tired and threw the lure out on the ground barely a foot away from the Prince's expensive Gucci shoes. I knew what was coming. Ling flipped over, dived in a mighty stoop and cut the lure at tremendous speed. Throwing up, she hit the brakes and dropped lightly down on the lure. The man didn't flinch when a wingtip flicked the knifed crease of one trouser leg but nodded his approval of the flight.

"OK, I'll just put Ling back on the cadge and then we'll give De Carnach a try."

Feeding Ling her reward for her efforts, I switched falcons and returned.

"We'll have to move a bit further down into Cranehows Bottom."

Bringing Becky to heel, I walked off down the narrow track with the others trailed out behind. Reminding myself of the hidden bogs, I picked my way, probing carefully with my stick. Glancing over my shoulder, I saw Richard move very quickly for a big tall man. Grabbing Prince Khalid's suited arm delicately but firmly, he pulled the Prince across the track and away from one I had obviously missed.

'Thank God, and Richard, for that one!' I thought.

I had a vision of my royal employer disappearing up to his thinning pate and asphyxiating on liquid peat while his horn rims bobbed gently on the bubbling disturbed surface of the bog. That would have sounded a death knell in more ways than one.

Disaster averted, I winked at our Yorkshire saviour and moved onwards. Finding a suitable position for the onlookers to stand, I let Becky loose for the second time. Within 15 minutes she was on point and I started praying.

Throughout my life, my primary interest has been in flying falcons rather than killing game birds. However, from what I knew of the Arab mentality and temperament, Prince Khalid would be more impressed by a kill. And since these were his birds, on his moor, it was his wishes that should be met, insha'allah. So on that particular evening, I wanted to catch something.

'Come on Gods, lend a helping hand this time, please.'

Striking De Carnach's hood, I held her up to the wind and she left the glove immediately. Unlike Ling, De Carnach spiralled upwards in a more traditional style but, being a high flyer, she wasn't in a hurry to stop any time soon. She just went up and up and up. Falconers invariably exaggerate when talking of the incredible height attained by their birds. Not that I am one of their number. But when De Carnach finally reached her pitch, the silhouette etched into the sharp evening sky was little more than the size of a sparrow. With De Carnach waiting-on and Becky on a solid point, I sent up another brief prayer to Saint Bavo and Allah as I walked round to head the point.

"Get 'em up, get 'em up."

This time Becky's efforts were rewarded by a four-strong covey of grouse exploding into the air. De Carnach instantaneously flipped over and into a vertical power dive, her wings pumping at seven and a half times per second. The sight of a stooping falcon never fails to evoke awe but De Carnach's flight down an invisible plumbline that evening was beyond description. The old cock bird that headed the covey peeled off in an attempt to lead De Carnach away from the less experienced birds.

'Don't go there,' I begged, 'you're a young falcon.'

But he wasn't the one in De Carnach's hairline sights, which were unwavering. She was a grouse-seeking avian missile and came in hard, taking the tail-end grouse with a smack that resounded around the vast bowl that was Cranehows Bottom. The puff of feathers drifted downwards, slowly following their erstwhile owner who had dropped like a stone into the heather below. The momentum of the flight carried De Carnach past the point of impact, only slowing when she hit the airbrakes and threw up to a stall. And neatly dropped down to despatch the stunned grouse. Most falcons are rubbish at catching things on the ground but De Carnach turned out to be an expert executioner.

I was so delighted with my little falcon's prowess that I wanted to charge over to her immediately but I kept my composure. For approximately five seconds. And then I was off like a startled hare, although I did manage to slow down once I got within a few yards. Kneeling down in the heather, I made in to her carefully. De Carnach tightened her grip on the limp body in her talons, looked at me with a dark glint in her eye and cocked her head to one side.

"Yrch, yrch, yrch, ek-ek, ek-ek."

I swear she was talking to me, saying: "There you go. I bloody well did it for you, didn't I?" Naturally that's an extended broad translation since peregrines have a more limited vocabulary than humans and simpler forms of syntax. I just wanted to reach out and grab her, but paused; this was not a moment to be rushed. Lying down in the heather beside her, I let her break into the head of the grouse and rip out a few choice morsels. A fresh portion of quail on the glove was enough temptation for her to transfer her attention, allowing me to deftly steal the grouse and slip it into my bag.

"Well done, Didi. What a little star!"

There was a big grin on my face as I tramped back up the bank towards the quietly applauding hawking party. It was not with a little pride that I re-joined the group, De Carnach calmly feeding on the glove. I knew that she'd done a superb job; and so did they.

"I've never seen that before."

"That was quite stunning."

"Amazing!"

Lord Ashcombe was clearly delighted and Prince Khalid had a smile that stretched from ear to ear.

"Well done, Gary - very good, very good. And now, what are you going to do with this grouse?"

The obvious answer was – I'm going to eat it – but wondered briefly whether it wouldn't be more courteous to offer the grouse to the Prince. On the other hand, what was a simple grouse to a man worth a fortune? Nothing.

"Normally, I'd eat it but in the circumstances ..."

"Good, Gary, good. It is very important that we eat what we catch. I think I once told you what we do in the desert, when we hunt houbara?"

"Yes, you did talk about cooking houbara when you came to The Bothy."

"Ah yes. So, we dig a pit in the sand and make a fire with the dead wood. Then we boil water in two metal pots, one on top of the other so it is like a pressure cooker. In the top, we put the pieces of houbara with spices: maybe some saffron, cardamom, a little turmeric, thyme and some other. But you do not have those in English, I think. And we cook that for one hour, maybe two."

It was totally surreal. I was standing on the purple heather on a Yorkshire moor in the red-gold glow of the setting sun with a falcon feeding on my glove. Standing next to me was a member of the Saudi royal family, giving me a lesson on the art of cooking game in the desert and detailing his recipe for stewed spiced houbara with fragrant rice.

228

"It sounds excellent."

"Yes, it is very good. Especially since your falcon has caught the houbara after a magnificent chase. And you, Gary, how will you cook your grouse?"

"Um, well usually I just wrap them in bacon and roast them in the oven for a bit. Then I eat them with little roast potatoes, bread sauce, gravy and some steamed vegetables. Oh, and a little redcurrant jelly."

"Maybe now, you will cook your grouse differently?"

"Perhaps. It does sound pretty good."

It was quite bizarre but immediately took me back to the conversation we'd shared some years back when we'd walked through the aviaries at The Bothy. As we had then, the Prince and I chatted, about cooking, falcons and falconry, our shared passions bridging the divides of wealth, culture, religion and politics. We were simply two falconers, enjoying each others company in the rays of the setting sun on Preston Moor. But the shadows were deepening.

"There's just enough light for one more flight. I still need to fly Siro, she's the last falcon on the cadge. Do you want to see another bird fly?"

"No, now we must get back to York. I have to get back to the hotel but thank you, Gary. Thank you very much for all this, your efforts and the successful hawking. It has been very enjoyable, but now I must go. I look forward to our next meeting and we must hope that there will be good successes with the breeding next year."

"I hope so, Sir."

"Gentlemen, it is time that we leave," Prince Khalid announced to the party and walked back towards the Bentley.

"Well done, Gary," said Lord Ashcombe, "that was excellent."

As I watched the line of vehicles jolt back down the track, I was actually quite glad that I hadn't flown Siro. She was a master at waiting-on but her stooping was left wanting and although she had caught a couple of grouse, I doubted that she would really make the grade. De

Carnach's performance had been stellar and a perfect end to the day.

"Do you want to fly Ling again, Gary?"

I grinned. "Oh, bugger off! You know what I want to do Whitty? I want to go home and chill out. On the way back, we're going to pick up a bloody good bottle of wine and cook the grouse – my way. And we'll have that rabbit that Malin caught this morning as well. Tonight we're going to have a veritable feast, put our feet up and relax. We'll pick everything up again tomorrow."

That was Prince Khalid's only day on Preston Moor but we stayed on and, as the season progressed, at least two of the falcons honed their hunting skills. Becky was coming into her own and was proving her worth as a superlative pointer.

And, thanks to the good offices of the staff at Sleightholmedale Lodge and Joy, Otterhills was a very pleasant place to be billeted. Every evening we'd dine on falcon-caught grouse or rabbits nailed by one or another of the Harris hawks. Breakfast, however, usually featured wild brown trout as the centrepiece, baked, grilled or pan-fried - quite delicious.

Being a keen fly fisherman, Whitty's morning rituals invariably included fishing the nearby beck and catching two or three trout for our morning delectation. Once the requisite number was in the keepnet, he would adjourn to the kitchen where he would prepare and cook his slippery catches. Accordingly, we always had wonderful breakfasts.

And one early morning, just after breakfast, there was knock on the door. Slightly surprised, I opened it to find the betweeded figure of Brigadier Watson in the porch.

"Good morning. Can I come in?"

"Good morning, Brigadier. By all means."

Stepping aside to let him pass, I followed behind as he muddled along a hallway that was lined with fishing tackle. Shit! He couldn't help but notice.

"How are you settling in? It all looks very cosy. Good job done by the Lodge chaps, by the looks of it. You've made quite a few improvements to the old place. So, everything's all right?"

230

"Yes, we're fine and they did a marvellous job with the renovations - and amazingly quickly. It was all done in less than a week."

"How did the hawking go with Khalid?"

"Brilliantly, thank you."

"Somebody likes fishing, I suspect," he said, glancing back down the hallway.

"Well, not me, of course." (Which was a total lie, since I loved fishing.) "It's John's. He takes his fishing tackle with him wherever he goes, not that he uses it that much. It's a sort of habit with him, to take his, um, tackle along, part of the ritual."

"Mmm, yes," the Brigadier said, clearly not convinced. "Noticed they were fly rods, you see, and fly tackle."

"Yes, yes, they are, I mean, yes it is, um, fly tackle he uses. Or doesn't."

"You do realise that I've got a lot of brown trout in the beck here?"

"No, I didn't realise that actually, no. Brown trout, really?"

"Yes. Just that I don't like to put it around, prefer to keep it all private. I don't like people catching them because I prefer to keep them for myself. That way, it's not overfished, you see."

"Of course, yes, right."

The aroma of grilled trout is unmistakable to anybody who has had the good fortune to be present at the cooking stage and to have consumed the said fish. John and I, between us, had scoffed three of the Brigadier's personal brown trout only minutes before his arrival. The lingering smell was still drifting through the cottage and there was no question in the man's mind what that, together with the fly tackle, implied. He'd made his point.

"Naturally, we wouldn't dream of fishing the beck for trout. After all, that would be poaching. No, no, rest assured, Brigadier, it hadn't even entered our minds."

"Good, good. Anyway, glad you've settled in and all's fine. Righto, I'll love and leave you now. Things to do and all that."

Thus we had to curtail our delectable breakfasts of wild brown trout. But the wilds of the Yorkshire moors still held plenty of things to be caught and cooked for the table. The mornings were for rabbiting with the Harris hawks while the afternoons were devoted to grouse, the rightful preserve of the falcons. Therefore, Bracken, being a German pointer, was a morning dog and Becky did her English pointing in the afternoon. In summation, it was shortwings before lunch, longwings beyond teatime and full stomachs after feasting on the catches of the day. It really was a rather wonderful way of life.

One particular bright and breezy morning, we were lugging no less than four bunnies back to the car. Preston Moor was alive with rabbits running, jumping, nibbling, humping; the Harris hawks had plenty of choice. Malin and Poacher had been on fine form, each catching two pleasantly plump specimens in fine aggressive style.

Along the way, we crested a low rise and noticed a large lake a few hundred yards to the right of the track. And smack in the middle of the lake floated a raft of ducks.

"Fancy duck for dinner?"

"Definitely. Yours or mine?"

"Let's use Poacher."

Gently easing the hood from her head, I held Poacher into the wind and she was off. It didn't take her long to get her sights aligned and she headed straight for the middle of the group. Of course, the ducks didn't flush because they were all the way out in the middle of the lake. Not that that bothered Poacher. The feathered brown missile smacked into the centre of the raft, scattering ducks like confetti – apart from one. Poacher smashed into his target and bound hard.

"Yeah, she's got one. That's pretty good."

The smile quickly drained from my face as I saw to my horror that the duck was being drowned and sinking quickly with Poacher firmly attached. The whole package was starting to disappear beneath the surface of the lake, some forty yards from the shoreline.

"Bloody hell! What the fuck are we going to do now?"

"WE are not going to do anything, Copey. Nothing for it mate, you're going to have to get in there."

At that time of year, Yorkshire was a very, very cold place. Stripping down to the buff, I plunged into the icy waters and swam out as fast as I possibly could. Fortunately, Poacher's head was still above waterline; underwater, she was still clinging onto a very wet and dead duck. Grabbing her by one wing, I towed Poacher slowly back to shore and to safety. Her talons were still locked on the duck. If I hadn't intervened, Poacher would have gone down like the Titanic and the silly bitch would have drowned herself.

Staggering out of the water with Poacher and duck, I found myself the object of a short natural history documentary on the tenacity of falcons and falconers.

"Excellent. That's a wrap. I've got the whole thing on film," said John, lowering the video camera. "It would be worth screening apart from the fact that it would probably get an 'X' rating for the full frontal shots of a man bollock-naked, rising from the lake. There again, there isn't really much to see, is there?"

Freezing waters and biting winds are cruel mistresses to the male body. I glared fiercely at the amateur videographer who insisted on filming everything from grouse hawking to idiot bird rescues from lakes.

"Fuck off, Whitty you bastard, and give me a hand."

At least Poacher was none the worse for wear for the ordeal and the duck went rather well with orange sauce.

And so the remaining days drifted on with more rabbiting and grouse hawking. Sometimes we went out alone, on others we took out hawking parties of VIPs, invited by Prince Khalid - but the man himself never reappeared.

Back in Gloucestershire once more, I ruminated over the preceding weeks, considering the ups and downs of it all. Becky had been brilliant, two out of the three falcons had turned out to be spot on the money and we'd caught plenty of grouse. Which, after all, had been the object of the exercise. I hadn't been entirely surprised at Prince Khalid's once-only appearance, which only corroborated what I'd thought about the combination of Arabs and grouse hawking. Nevertheless, I was pleased that he'd been pleased.

In the final analysis, I'd done my job: I'd pulled together a solid team, caught grouse in style and entertained the Prince and his friends. Once out on the moor, you had to play the ringmaster and coordinate everything under pressure. To do the job properly, I'd had to be compere, narrator, manager and leader, as well as flying the falcons and directing the dogs.

"Yeah, I ticked all the boxes," I said to the flames flickering in fireplace.

It was all done and dusted for now. But there were still two big worries, gnawing relentlessly on my mental bones. Prince Khalid bin Abdullah al Saud wasn't interested in watching falcons fly at the grouse on his bloody Yorkshire moor and where would that leave me when the Glorious Twelfth hit the calendar next? And then there was the whole business of breeding gyrfalcons. To lay or not to lay? That was the question. I wasn't sure that Tino would have an answer.

Chapter 21 – The great fire of Walden

Depending on your interpretation of the name, either Magnum was shooting bullets as fast as Dirty Harry or should have been renamed Methuselah, given the amount of sparkling semen he contained. With the breeding season well underway, Nick and I were busily inseminating peregrines with his copious offerings. But we were still waiting for Tino to demonstrate even the slightest inclination of broodiness. Everything rested on that single bird laying eggs.

"Gary, she's making a scrape on her nesting ledge," called Nick breathlessly through the kitchen door.

"Who?"

"Tino!"

"Well, she's not going to a make a great big nest like a stork, is she? Come to think of it, maybe we'd be better off if she was a stork!"

"Ha, ha, ha. Seriously, she really is making a scrape. So she might lay eggs."

"Maybe. Let's hope so."

I followed Nick into the walled garden and across to Tino's breeding enclosure. Sure enough, she was scratching away at the gravel in a half-hearted manner. Any aviculturist worth his or her salt knows when a bird is switched on or not and Tino's libido didn't look like it was on anywhere near full power. Not that there was anything that I could do to make the damn bird lay eggs.

"It's not very convincing, is it?"

"I suppose not," said Nick, sounding somewhat deflated.

To lay or not to lay? By the end of the season, Tino had given her answer to the question: no! So another year went by without one pure white gyrfalcon being produced but, once again, Magnum fathered some excellent hybrids.

Before I knew it, late summer was fast approaching and Yorkshire's grouse were calling. Accordingly, Lord Ashcombe's visits to The Bothy became a little more regular and he brought welcome news to our discussions.

"After last year's somewhat fraught visit to Otterhills, you'll be pleased to know that we've managed to get you a place in Redmire. It's a lot closer to Preston Moor, so there'll be a lot less travelling to and fro."

"Where's Redmire?"

"It's about five miles west of Leyburn. Then the moor itself is just a couple of miles further on. This time, you've got a whole farmhouse to yourself and it's in a much better state of repair than Otterhills."

"That's brilliant. The travelling last year was ridiculous. It took me over an hour to get from Helmsley to Preston Moor; a hundred miles round trip. Thank God for Redmire!"

"Yes, well - that was last year, as you say. History, Gary."

"And it's liveable?"

"Absolutely, don't worry."

I had a strong feeling that his Lordship was telling the truth this time rather than omitting the odd detail as before.

"There's one other thing."

'Here come the details,' I thought.

"Prince Khalid's people have bought another moor. Walden, a few miles south of Redmire and, apparently, it's the highest point in Wensleydale. The idea is that it will only be used for hawking."

"They've already bought it? But I haven't even seen it."

"I realise that. Bit of a knee-jerk purchase by the sounds of it but I'm sure they've done their research. And anyway, there's no shortage of grouse in Yorkshire."

"True, but is Walden Moor any good for grouse hawking? Still, what's done is done."

Early August arrived softly that year, bringing warm sunny days and mellow evenings. But the thrill of anticipation that normally sparked in the days before the start of the grouse hawking season was dulled and damped down. Joy and I had been drifting away from each other for some time; the ties of our relationship had grown fragile and thin. Time had corroded the anchors and our disparate work commitments had only served to increase the emotional distance between us. I turned 21 on the day that we were married and Joy was a lissom nineteen. Youthful idealism and young love seemed a long way back down the

236

road we had travelled. Now, she was a dedicated businesswoman running her own company in the city environment of Gloucester. As Prince Khalid's falconer, my life was inextricably bound to birds of prey and my al fresco offices were in green fields and on open moorland.

"What time are you leaving in the morning?" Joy asked, the night before my departure north.

"Early as usual, my love - about five-forty five, six o'clock-ish, so I won't wake you. The truck's all packed, so I just need to throw in the dogs and birds tomorrow."

"I probably will be asleep when you leave, so I'll say goodbye now." She kissed me once, gently. "Hope it all goes well and I'll see you when you get back."

"Yeah. I'll give you a ring from Yorkshire to let you know I've arrived safely."

"'Kay."

Joy snuggled down into her pillow and closed her eyes. I kissed the hair on the back of her head and stared into the darkness.

"Love you," I said.

"Mmm."

I felt confused and unsure. It just didn't feel right.

'What's happened to us?' I thought. 'And why is it happening now?'

The questions lingered in my mind, falling slowly like autumn leaves warning of the winter to come. The night finally turned my waking images into dreams that were forgotten by the morning. As the rays of sunlight banished the darkness, all those questions blossomed in my head once more but I left Joy sleeping and left the room.

Drinking a last cup of coffee, I stared through the kitchen window at the rural idyll beyond. As though Turner had painted The Bothy with light, the view was that of an oasis of tall trees silhouetted against the broad canvas of the sky. Apples glowed warmly in the early morning sun and the lush green grass was alive with wild rabbits. Black, white and brown, they nibbled away contentedly without fear, as though they knew that I would never hunt them. I smiled at the thought: a falconer surrounded by untouchable rabbits. Almost tame, I regarded them more as friends than prey.

The cadge was loaded up with the three falcons and installed in its appointed place. Then the dogs climbed into the back of the truck, intertwining and overlapping in the tiny space walled by boxes and equipment. Shutting them safely inside, I rolled a cigarette and leaned against the side of the Mitsubishi Shogun Turbo. Lighting up, I took a long pull, blew a stream of smoke into the air and looked at the bedroom window above.

'You're not going to be here when I get back, are you?' I murmured.

I'll see you when you get back, she'd said. But the words had sounded mechanical and hollow.

'Why? It's not as though we've been arguing. I don't understand.'

'So go and sort it out,' said a strident little voice in my head. 'Go back inside, wake her up and talk. It's called having an adult discussion. Tell her that whatever is going wrong needs sorting and that you want to put it right. Together.'

'Leave it to fate,' said another. 'If that's what she wants, let her go. Give her the freedom to decide, to stay or fly.'

'What throw it all away? Turn your back on her? If you don't talk, she'll walk. Get in there.'

'You can't force it. What would you do if she was a falcon? Keep her on the leash, tied to the block, never fly her?'

That gave me pause for thought. I've always treated relationships and women in the same way that I have with falconry and falcons. One of the things that I've always loved about falconry is that your relationship with the bird is based on trust. Every time one flies a falcon loose, she has a choice: either she'll fly, hunt and return to you or she'll disappear over the horizon to find her own destiny. I treat my relationships with people, whoever they are, in the same vein. I'll always do the best I can but if you choose to leave and not return, then I won't put obstacles in your path. I have no right to chain and cage you every hour of every day.

"If it's not good enough for you, then you must leave," I said quietly, looking up at the empty window. "It would be wrong to try to keep you if you don't want to stay."

Grinding the butt of my cigarette under my heel, I turned back to the truck, hauled myself in and turned the key. I glanced at the window one more time before wrenching the Shogun round in a tight circle and lurching down the bumpy track from The Bothy. About half way down, I hit the brakes and ground to a halt. Lighting another cigarette, I listened to the idling growl of the engine and felt my heart pounding.

'Go back, go back now,' said Strident. 'There's still time. Tell her that you want her to stay, that it'll be all right.'

'Just because you want something doesn't mean you have the right to force them,' retorted Little Karma. 'Joy's either with you or she's not. If she wants to go, she's got her reasons. You might not agree with those reasons but you have to accept them.'

"Joy's part of my life," I said aloud. "She's always been there, in the good times and the bad. I don't want to lose her."

'You've lost falcons before. They've flown out of your life and you didn't know why. But you accepted their right to leave and their decisions. If Joy wants to leave, let her fly.'

I stared sightlessly through the windscreen, torn in both directions at once. Joy had been so instrumental in everything I had done, supporting me every step of the way. She was my emotional rock, my invaluable practical helpmate, lover, friend and advisor. The *sine qua non* of my life, Joy was indispensable to every facet of my being.

"Maybe if I went back I could make a difference."

'Let the falcon fly,' said Karma.

Shakespeare's lines from Othello came to mind and seemed to encapsulate everything that I was feeling.

'If I do prove her haggard,

Though that her jesses were my dear heartstrings,

I'd whistle her off and let her down the wind
To prey at fortune.'

Othello's words to Iago reflected his conflicting emotions about Desdemona: on the one hand, his love and devotion and on the other, his loathing for her infidelity. Not that I thought that Joy had been unfaithful, but that that little piece of dialogue had resonance by interpretation. There were jesses on my dear heart strings and I should cut them off, let Joy fly downwind and let her prey at fortune. If I loved her, I should sever the ties and give her the freedom to choose a new life. So be it: I'd cut the jesses and let her fly free.

"Either she'll come back or she won't."

Releasing the handbrake, I headed out onto the road and north to Yorkshire. As the miles rolled by, I tried to push the nagging fears from my mind and focus on things of more immediate concern. I had a grouse hawking season to manage and there were more than a few things to consider. Would Walden Moor give value for money on the purchase price of around two million quid? How good would it be for flying falcons and would it provide lift? How big was it and how were the grouse distributed? And what would the farmhouse at Redmire be like?

When I arrived, a little later in the morning than I'd intended, I found Whitty sitting on a bench outside, his head wreathed in the billows of smoke from his pipe. After expelling one final enormous cumulous of smoke, he knocked the dottle from the bowl, pushed the pipe into the pocket of his checked shirt and ambled across to the Shogun.

"All right, Copey?"

"Yeah, I'm all right, everything's fine. You've not been inside?"

"Nope. That would be because you didn't tell me where the key is hidden."

"Ah, sorry about that."

"No matter," he said, rubbing a spec of tobacco off one leg of his plus fours. "Outside's been done up proud. They've put up a brand new mews and weathering shelters."

240

"These are brilliant," I said later, as we installed the birds in the mews.

In fact, everything about the farmhouse was wonderful and far better than I'd hoped. Compared to Otterhills, this was a palace. It didn't take long before we were settled in and chattering the day away.

But as night fell, Bracken made it very clear that he needed to pee. Forgetting for a moment what a complete rogue he was – a common trait in German pointers – I let him bound through the doorway and into the dark. And, as ever, he did his disappearing act, vanishing into the ebony shadows in which stealth mode took over. Holding himself as still as a statue, he suddenly melted into the night without warning. After a few moments, I began to whistle and call but to no avail.

"Shit. The old bugger's gone down to check out Redmire. Brackeeeern. Brackeeeern."

Nothing. And then, in the distance, I heard them calling on the night air.

"Ow-hooo, ow-hooo, yow-yow-yer, yap-yap-yap."

Every dog in Redmire was baying at the moon and I was fairly certain of the cause.

"Hear that?" I said to John.

"Yeah. It's Bracken, isn't it?"

"Yup. He's raising a right ruckus in Redmire. But what can we do about it?"

"Not a lot. We'll just have to wait until the bloody dog comes back."

About two thirty in the morning, one slobbering mud-covered German pointer turned up at the door looking rather sheepish. He looked mournfully up at my scowling face and stretched his neck out in an apologetic manner. For all the world it looked as though he was telepathically sending a message that said: "I'm very sorry and I really didn't mean to be naughty but I couldn't resist investigating the area and I really won't do it again".

He almost made me smile but I maintained the scowl. Not that I gave him a bollocking; it wouldn't have made any difference, as I knew from the numerous times he slunk off from The Bothy.

"You little git, get in!"

Bracken immediately scooted past me and curled up in his bed. Not the best way to endear ourselves to the good burghers of Redmire!

The next few days were taken up with getting the falcons flying and honing their hunting skills. Ling was flying brilliantly, De Carnach was flying well and Siro was flying like a pregnant puffin.

In between the hawking sessions, Prince Khalid's gamekeeper, Richard Coates volunteered to give me the guided tour of Walden Moor. After half an hour of lurching and grinding up a bumpy winding track, we reached the summit.

"Wow, what a view! This really is the place that time forgot."

"Yeah, it is beautiful."

"Stunning, but a bit high for my liking."

"What do you mean?"

"It's not the best place to fly falcons. This is basically a hilltop plateau. It reminds me a bit of Table Top Mountain near Cape Town. It isn't as high but the shape's similar. The thing is, it always worries me if I'm flying falcons at grouse from high points. If the grouse flips off down the side, you've got a big problem."

"I think you'll probably have to at least give it a go," said Richard, "after all, that's what the Prince bought it for. And you've still got Preston Moor as your main grouse hawking location."

"Yeah, I guess you're right. But I'll give it a few more days on Preston first."

Some forty-eight hours later, in the afternoon, I was out on the weathering grounds having a quiet cigarette and considering the various aspects of flying Walden Moor. Looking up at the Table Top lookalike in the distance, I still wasn't terribly keen on the prospect. Then a plume of brown and white smoke rose upwards from the plateau. The plume quickly became a column that expanded and grew as the smoke roiled in the air.

"That can't be right. Whitty, get over here," I yelled. "What d'you think" I said as he arrived.

242

"I think that's a bloody fire, is what I think. But I don't know what it's all about. It's way too early to be burning off the heather and anyway that would be Richard's territory up there. Either way, it's not bloody right. Better give him a call now."

Richard was over in a trice, ripping down the lane to the farmhouse as though practising his rallying skills. Leaping out of his Landy, it didn't take him long to assess the situation.

"Bloody hell. The frigging moor's on fire!"

Grabbing his phone, Richard dialled 999 without hesitation.

"Fire service, please … Walden Moor's on fire … I'm about six miles away … yes, there's a bloody great mass of smoke spewing into the sky and I think I can see flames … Thank you." He cut the call and ran back towards the Shogun. "Let's go," he shouted over his shoulder.

Richard drove up the narrow lane as fast as he could; not that we were expecting any traffic coming from the opposite direction. Until a white van came rattling round a corner, forcing us onto the grass verge.

"Bloody idiots," snarled Richard.

"You know them?" I asked.

"No. I just hate people who don't how to drive on the moors. Fuck 'em."

It took another 20 minutes to reach the top of the moor but even as we drove, we could hear the thunder of the flames and taste the acrid smoke drifting through the air. But it wasn't until we saw the scale of the inferno that we realised the true horror and power of the fire. This was truly Milton's burning furnace and hell made manifest. Dense, choking smoke billowed up from a rippling wall of fire that sent up flames whose tongues must have reached some fifty feet. The heat was intense, reaching out with invisible fingers to burn and scorch. Heather crackled and spat as it burned, lending top notes to the baseline of the fire's roars.

Moorland fires are always a big problem, especially those that get out of control. And this one was totally, monstrously and dangerously out of control. Such dire circumstances draw people together and this was no exception. There were people from all the surrounding villages, keepers and under-keepers from other moors, all determined to fight the fire. The word beating took on a whole new meaning as we attacked the fringes of the fire with rubber flails. But as fast as we beat out our small individual patches of fire, others quickly appeared and we'd be driven back by the heat. It was clear that we had as much hope of calming the conflagration with flails as King Canute had in holding back the tide.

Meanwhile firemen sent out from stations across the county were struggling to drive their large tenders and engines up the lane. We'd had difficulty driving up the track in the Shogun, so it was no mean feat for the fire fighters to get as far as they did. Setting up a base camp on the flank of the moor, their only source of water was the stream flowing through Deepdale Gill. With speed and efficiency born of experience, the firemen connected long sections of pipe together, running the jointed snake up the hillside and pumped water frantically. The installation of sleeping quarters, a canteen and stores was a clear indication that they knew they were playing the long game.

What makes a moorland fire so difficult to contain is that it burns its way down into the dense root systems of peat moss deep below the surface. It wasn't enough to quell the flames of burning heather; smouldering pockets erupted without warning, creating new blazes that were fanned by the wind. And the only way to counteract those was to dig deep into the peat below. Fires such as this might keep burning for weeks, destroying flora and fauna, causing damage that could take decades to repair. Not only was an environmental and commercial disaster, it would put paid to any hopes of grouse hawking on Walden Moor. Not that that aspect bothered me too much, since I hadn't thought it was much good for falconry purposes anyway.

After three, perhaps four hours of battling the hot forces of nature, John and I were filthy, covered in sweat mixed with soot, earth and gritty smoke detritus. My chest was heaving with the effort of breathing the thick, poisoned air, the physical exertion and the emotional stress. A huge feeling of sadness washed over me as I watched that wonderful piece of untamed England blacken and wither in the fire's cruel embrace.

"Whitty, I've got to get out of here. We're pissing in the wind and I'm done."

"Yeah, I agree. We're going to have to leave it to those poor sods," he said, nodding towards the professional firefighters. "They know what they're doing. And they've got the kit."

In the absence of taxis, or even passing white vans, we staggered back to the farmhouse on foot. Hot baths washed away the filth and smell, hot food in our bellies brought back a little strength, but nothing could erase the sheer horror. Switching on the television, the breaking news was already being broadcast from the base camp. The camera angle was such that the reporter was speaking under a grey-brown sky, shot with orange flames and golden sparks.

"Chief Fire Officer of the North Yorkshire Fire and Rescue Service, Eric Clark, talked to me only a few minutes ago. In his opinion, the massive fire on Walden Moor is probably the worst he has seen since 1976 when an estimated 2,000 acres of moorland in the county were destroyed. One of the worst spots then was on the Earl of Swinton's grouse moor at Colsterdale, west of Masham; a direct parallel to Walden, which is privately owned but would also be used to hunt grouse.

"The fear is that the fire could travel to adjacent moors, as it did in '76, and firefighters are being hampered by the poor access to adequate water supplies, made more difficult by the terrain. In addition, the recent weeks of dry weather has resulted in tinder dry conditions and there is no indication on imminent rains. Mr Clark fears that while the main fires may be contained in the short term, fires deep in the peat may continue to burn for months with the potential to reignite top fires.

"Mr Clark said that at this stage it was too early to say who or what had caused the fire. However, he did say that previous incidents had been attributed to discarded cigarettes, abandoned lighted BBQs and similar incendiary devices, but was not ruling out arson. That may be discovered in the future, but tonight, firemen from all over the county and beyond are fighting a desperate battle on the tragedy that Walden Moor has become."

Pictures of hell beamed into the room for a few more seconds before the director cut back to the anchor in the studio. I switched off the set and phoned Lord Ashcombe to give him the news. Although he wasn't due to arrive for at least another week, this was an emergency and he arrived the following day. We took him up immediately to see the sad and fearful sight. The blaze seemed to have abated little since we'd left even though the firefighters had been battling through the night. And Richard had been there through all those dark and glaring hours. Apparently, he'd only left in the morning, perhaps feeling that since the moor was essentially his responsibility, it had been his duty to stay.

Thinking back, I remembered the two guys in the white van that had pushed us off the road. Had they been responsible for causing the fire? Some time later I heard that two poachers had been questioned but released without charge, and they might have been the same men. I suspected they were and that one of them had dropped a lighted cigarette in the heather. Nothing was ever proved and nobody prosecuted. But the fires burned for over three weeks, destroying a large tract of moorland.

Thus our grouse hawking was confined to Preston Moor but was very much on track. Of the three falcons, Ling was the star and fast becoming one of the most amazing grouse hawks that I'd ever worked with. On one occasion, having missed one grouse, she was standing on a post in the middle of the moor looking somewhere between grouchy and despondent. I was just about to pull out the lure and call her back in when a cock broke cover. Obviously not the most observant of grouse, his flightline took him straight towards her and then about three feet above her head. Deciding suddenly to play goshawk, Ling shot vertically upwards, clamped on and pulled the bird out of the sky, "Got ya!" I could hear her saying.

On another occasion, Dashing Ling (as we finally called her) chased a grouse down the side of the moor after a fine

246

stoop. When I got to where I thought she should be, there was no sign of either bird. Telemetry was called for and, when turned on, obediently found a faint signal.

'Peep, peep, peep, peep.'

But there was no sign of an actual falcon. The track ran across the moor, parallel to a beck which at one point ran through a concrete culvert. It seemed an unlikely place to find Ling: the big tube was buried half underground and designed to let the water through, especially when it was swollen in the winter. Nevertheless, I leaned over and directed the yagi towards the opening.

'Peep-peep-peep-peep-peep.'

Peering into the grey light of the culvert, I found Ling paddling in the water with the grouse held tightly in her talons. Obviously the wily grouse had thought that the culvert would provide sanctuary but Ling had simply followed him in and nailed him. She was truly amazing and went on to catch 49 grouse in succession without missing a single bird.

On one particular day in the season, Lord Ashcombe brought one Mr Wills as a guest who, I suspected, was connected to the family of cigarette fame. Naturally he was keen to see some sport and a little excitement. Once on the moor, I released Becky into the heather and then turned my attention to attaching the telemetry transmitter to De Carnach.

"Copey, your bloody dog's on point!" said Whitty.

Turning round, I saw Becky some 40 yards to the right, solid as a rock.

"Shit," I said, finishing off as quickly as I could.

De Carnach knew exactly what a pointing dog meant and she'd been working with Becky for a while. In fact, when dog and falcon start to work well together, they tend to leave the falconer out of the game. They think they know it all, so one has to be a bit careful.

Once on the wing, De Carnach mounted up over the dog and I headed up the point some fifty yards away from my 4x4 and Lord Ashcombe's Range Rover. Messrs Ashcombe and Wills were standing nearby with bated breath while John had moved out to the left flank. As soon as I sent Becky in, she flushed a covey of grouse and De Carnach dropped in a vertical stoop. One bird headed straight for the vehicles and that was the one that she targeted. Smacking it down, De Carnach flipped over and nailed it, barely 15 yards from our guests.

'That'll do,' I thought, as I picked her up and gave her her reward.

We'd only been out for around ten minutes. Mr Wills looked delighted and Lord Ashcombe was positively preening.

"Well done, Gary, absolutely marvellous. Damn good flight."

"Thank you, your Lordship. We'll have another flight then. This time it'll be Ling."

Becky was still playing around in the heather while I was in the process of putting De Carnach on the cadge in exchange for Ling.

"Er, Copey?"

"What?"

"Becky's on point again. In exactly the same place as last time, so it could just be hot scent."

The question was, was it simply a hot scent, an olfactory memory of recent grouse? Or it could be a real point. Stephen Frank had told me a long time ago to always trust your dog, and Stephen was a man whose judgement I respected.

"Maybe it is and maybe not, but we have to trust the dog."

When all the players were in place, I sent Becky in, who promptly shuffled around in the heather as though she wasn't quite sure herself.

'Go on, please," I thought as my eyes followed the wandering dog's nose.

Suddenly an old cock bird got up, obviously left behind from the first covey. He too headed for the pair of vehicles and down came Ling right behind him, closing, closing – but not closing enough! And the grouse flew straight between Lord Ashcombe and Wills Jnr (as I thought of him), to take refuge under the Range Rover. Accordingly, the falcon sailed past overhead, flipped over and climbed.

248

"That grouse deserves to escape," I said as I walked across to the two gentlemen.

"You're not going to re-flush?" asked Wills Jnr.

"No, Sir. It's always been one of my principles: if something reaches cover and outwits the falcon, then that's it. I just don't think re-flushing's fair."

"Of course," said Wills Jnr, turning a delicate shade of pink.

The grouse, however, was clearly not of the same mind and must have had a death wish. He suddenly exploded from beneath the exhaust pipe, flipped up and over the Rangie and flew back between the two onlookers. Ling spotted him immediately and, although not at a great pitch, barrelled down and bound to the grouse within a yard of Lord Ashcombe and Wills Jnr. Simultaneously, their jaws dropped and their eyes popped.

"That was extraordinary, Gary, Absolutely wonderful. If I'd read it in a book I'd have said – not a chance, could never happen."

"It never happened," I said drily, with a big grin splitting my face from ear to ear.

"It bloody did," retorted his Lordship, "amazing!"

"I don't think I've ever seen anything quite like that," added Wills Jnr. "That was fantastic."

A Red Letter day, without question: within ten minutes we'd caught a brace of grouse, one of them in great style and the other at close quarters, and the guests were delighted. It was absolutely perfect. The funny thing is, that the best flights I've had with falcons have always been those when the quarry got away. The shooting fraternity, on the other hand, tend to get upset if they don't kill lots of things. And that's one of the main differences between a sporting gun and a falconer.

So, despite the fire on Walden Moor, it was a good season for grouse hawking.

But a few days before I was due to return to Gloucestershire, I received a phone call from my dear sister-in-law, Ali. One of my closest friends, Ali hadn't called me in Yorkshire to talk about grouse.

"I'm really sorry, Gary, Joy's packed up and left. She's left you, I'm afraid. I am so, so sorry."

The long drive back home in the dark seemed very solitary and lonely. During those four and a half hours, my mind spun round and round, filled with myriad thoughts. Images from the fire belched across my mind's eye. I thought about how well the falcons had done, how delighted Lord Ashcombe had been. And then the bigger things brought in the shadows of fear and sadness. What was I going back to and what would there be? Whatever the answer to those and all the other questions that bubbled up through the mental mire of despondency, I knew that life would be very different from the one I'd known.

When I finally got back to The Bothy, Ali was there with her husband Dave and so were my parents. They tried to fill the gap and make things easier but it changed nothing. Ali had re-arranged the furniture but Joy had taken those pieces that were hers and I could see the gaps. There were empty rectangles on the wall that had once held pictures, books that were absent from the shelves. But the biggest hole was the one that had been left by Joy herself and it wasn't quite home anymore.

Dad had lit a fire because he knew that it usually cheered me up but the cold that I felt was inside my bones. We chewed the fat over dinner and they asked politely how everything in Yorkshire had gone; I answered politely and recounted various anecdotes to please. But inevitably, the talk turned to Joy.

"I'm sure it will all work out in the end."

"She just needs a break to think, but I'm sure she'll come round."

"Take your time and then talk to her. Look at both sides, listen and you'll both see that you're better off together. It'll be all right."

People always try to say the right thing but sometimes the best thing to say is nothing. Coming back to an empty house would have been horrible and I did appreciate them being there. But there came a point when I just wanted to be alone. When they all eventually left it was something of a relief. I needed to be alone, to come to terms with the

250

realisation that the status quo had changed and to face the fact that I was moving onto a new chapter in my life.

Stoking up the fire, I smiled fondly at the two dogs lying in front of the hearth, melting their brains as usual. I poured myself a large Scotch, sat down in the armchair pre-warmed by the flames and considered reality.

'It's happened. Woah! Times have changed,' I thought, taking a large sip. 'I suppose I'll have to move on.'

Chapter 22 – Lady in white

Moving on is not so easy when your whole life has fallen apart. Totally distraught and emotionally in pieces, there was little else to but throw myself into my career. I think that's what people do when their personal life is shot through with holes: they fill them in with work during the day. But when dusk falls, the holes reappear. So to insulate yourself from the pain, you add a few layers with even more work and longer hours.

Ironically, that side of life was going rather well and business continued as usual. Grouse hawking in Yorkshire was flourishing, providing fine sporting spectacles for a steady stream of VIPs supplied by Lord Ashcombe. Rabbit hawking gave a more yeoman-like form of entertainment, as well as filling the pot. The falcons and dogs had honed their skills, working perfectly in teams and displaying their individual skills with brilliance. Magnum maintained his ejaculatory performances, 'fathering' a multitude of stunning gyr peregrine hybrids but not the magic pure white gyr of our dreams. Naturally, Tino remained virginally aloof and not one egg appeared in her scrapes to give us hope.

Somehow, winter turned to spring, then summer and autumn until we reached the full circle. So the seasons rolled by, each with its individual tasks, challenges, highs and lows. Quite a few solstices passed before the pattern changed; in fact, just after I arrived back from a grouse hawking trip.

"Gary! You're back."

"Clearly," I said drily.

"It's Joanna. How were the northern wilds?"

"Joanna! Sorry, my love, I'm just a bit tired and didn't recognise your voice. I've only just got back. But yes, Yorkshire was fine."

"How can you not recognise your almost best friend's voice?" she said in mock horror. "Anyway, it's wonderful that you're back as it D's birthday party on Saturday and we both expect you to be here."

"Right. Um, great. Time?"

As I often do at these charades, I found myself sitting on the sidelines, nursing a glass of beer and feeling rather lost. Apart from the host and hostess, I didn't know a soul and wondered why on earth I'd come.

"You on your own then?"

I turned sideways to find a guy sitting a few feet away on the wall where I'd perched. Clearly, he too was alone and, from the flat tone of voice, I sensed that our stories might share a few similarities.

"Yeah."

"It's not good, being at a party on your own - especially when you're used to being with someone."

"No."

"Kay and I always went to parties together. Kay's my wife, I mean, ex-wife. She left me and then filed for divorce. Parties with her were good fun but even that disappeared in the end. I thought we were fine and never saw it coming, the big 'I'm leaving you' speech. Lovely girl, though. How about you?"

'Shit.' The last thing I wanted to do was talk about Joy to a complete stranger.

"Divorced."

"Tough, isn't it?"

And I found myself being forced to swap ex-wife tales, annotated with sad, lonely comments in the margin. Fortunately, he terminated our ex-husband bonding after a few minutes and went off in search of another drink. Heaving an audible sigh of relief, I realised that I was verging on being mind-numbingly bored.

"That's it, time to go," I said to the vacant spaces crowding in on me. "I have made my appearance, taken drink and have now had enough."

I was about to take the penultimate gulp of beer but froze as glass met lip. My gaze was arrested by the sight of an apparition floating across the lawn. The gauze of her white summer dress shimmered in the soft light seeping from the house as the young woman walked slowly across my near horizon. Her dark hair rippled in the cool night breeze, contrasting with almost iridescent fabric. She was carrying a youngster, braced on her hip, and was followed by an extremely well-dressed man.

"Wow!"

Putting my glass back on the wall, my eyes followed the vision and I could feel my blood pounding.

'She's going to be part of my life, she is going to be part of my life …'

The mantra repeated itself in my head, as though repetition would give life to the words.

"Don't be stupid," I said aloud.

But that didn't banish the thoughts from my mind. It was another half an hour before I finished my beer and headed to the house to bid my farewells.

"Joanna, thank you so much for inviting me. Great party."

"I take it you're on your way?"

"Yeah, I've got to get back to the birds."

"Uh-huh. Anyway, good to see you and glad that you enjoyed it."

"Just before I go, who's the dark haired girl in the white dress?"

Joanna scanned the room before turning back.

"That's Helena. Why do you ask?"

"I was just wondering. She's, she caught my eye, that's all."

"Forget it, you've got no chance. Helena's married, extremely happy and, she's a princess." One eyebrow rose a little disdainfully as she added: "She's way out of your league!"

"Right. I'll be off then." And was.

Shortly afterwards, I left for South Africa with my mother to spend Christmas with my brother Brian in Johannesburg. Memories of the party and Helena faded in the mellow African sunshine. By the time that the New Year was under way, I was back in Gloucestershire with the birds and Nick for company.

But, at the end of February an old buddy of mine turned up on the doorstep and drinking was proposed accordingly. The 'vivacious atmosphere' and the 'place to be seen socialising' were phrases that pointed towards sampling the

254

delights of the Montpellier Wine Bar, in the 'village'. At least, they did to a lad who had come down from the backwoods of Cheshire. So willy-nilly, we headed for Cheltenham.

Unfortunately, it lived up to all my expectations. The clamour assailed my ears and the crush at the bar was hot and perspiring. It smelled of beer, sweat and a heavy mix of perfume that jarred every olfactory nerve. The mass of bodies had a life of its own, sucking me agonisingly slowly towards the front until I was only two people way from ordering our drinks.

"This is bloody ridiculous," I muttered, weighing up the desire for alcohol against the amount of time required to obtain said alcohol. "Ow!"

The pressure applied by the average descending heel, worn by even the most delicate of creatures, has been estimated to be at least 30 pounds per square inch. That might not sound much, but trust me, when a heel lands on your foot, it bloody hurts. And the lady in front of me had just stepped back and crushed my boot.

"Oh, I'm terribly sorry. Are you all right?"

"Fine," I said, wincing with pain.

"Oh, here, get into the bar, get in."

Squeezing past her, I grabbed at the bar for support and lifted the injured foot off the ground.

"Really, I'm so sorry. Are you sure you're all right?"

"Honestly, I'm fine," I said, shaking my head in negation. "I know you."

"I don't think so. We've never met before."

"No, we haven't actually met, but I definitely recognise you."

"Really?"

As she started to back away, the crowd threatened to close the gap.

"You were at D's party last August. You were wearing a white dress and had a little boy on your hip."

"Absolutely right, I didn't see you there," she said, relaxing a little. "Wait a minute, you're The Falconer, aren't you? Let me buy you a drink. Call it compensation for pain incurred."

Helena managed to organise the drinks far faster than I could have done. A few minutes later, we were having a polite conversation in a small space between a wall and two crowded tables of revellers. It was all rather weird, in a nice sort of way. After comparing party notes for a while, my focus turned to the moment.

"I assume you're here with someone," I asked.

"Mm-mmm," she said, taking a sip of wine, "a girlfriend who lives round the corner."

"Not with your husband?"

"No, we separated. My husband and I have parted company," she said in quasi-regal tones. "I'm living alone. Listen, I'd better catch up with my friend. We should be going."

"What's your name? Can I give you a call?"

There was only a brief pause before she said: "Sure. And it's Helena."

"Helena. I'd like to see you again, Helena. Oh, and I'm Gary."

While I started to check my pockets for pen and paper, she calmly produced both from her handbag. [What doesn't a woman have in those dark cavernous recesses, disguised by the compact façade?] We swapped phone numbers.

"I'll call you."

She nodded once, before being absorbed by the crowds and disappearing from view. And I stood there thinking that she was one of the most extraordinary women I'd ever met. Conflicting emotions and thoughts danced through my head over the next few days.

I suppose that many people in my situation find themselves in a similar predicament. When you've been through the highs of a marriage and the lows of divorce, you don't feel that you can, or want to, go through the whole thing again. You don't think that you'll find another soul-mate and you sure as hell don't want to re-tread the hellish paths of betrayal. Little voices in my head.

'There's something special about Helena, you know there is.'

'Admit it, you're just frightened of being hurt again!'

'Oh, yeah? Why don't you also admit that you're intrigued? You're attracted to her, you want to see her again; so take the chance.'

'It's not worth the gamble. Pull up the drawbridge and stay in the comfort zone.'

'And always wonder what might have been? Correct me if I'm wrong, but haven't you been using words like *extraordinary* and that you *feel this is right, deep down in your heart.*'

'Be realistic. You're seriously going to throw yourself into a relationship with a woman you barely know because you fancy her and, for some bizarre reason, believe that she's fated to be *part of your life.* Please!'

'Listen to yourself. You've always trusted your feelings, so why doubt them now? Call her.'

Who knows what the little voices in <u>her</u> head had been saying but when I plucked up the courage to ring, I invited her out to The Bothy to see the birds. After she'd agreed, I thought it was quite brave of her to drive from the well-lit thoroughfares of Cheltenham, through darkened lanes to a house in the middle of nowhere to meet a man she'd only met briefly in a bar.

"Come in, come in," I said, ushering Helena into the warmth. "It's wonderful to see you again."

"It's lovely," she said, glancing around the room and then sitting down in the middle of the sofa.

She perched on the very edge, her arms wrapped around her as though she were cold, even though I had the fire blazing. There was a certain vulnerability about Helena that made me want to put my arms protectively around her. Instead, I asked her whether she'd like anything to drink.

"Tea, please."

Of course, she got the guided tour of the aviaries and I'm sure I talked about falconry and falcons, breeding and artificial insemination. I probably regaled her with anecdotes of displays and hawking grouse in Yorkshire. And I suspect that I explained the ins and outs of training birds of prey and dogs. Helena sat, listened and actually seemed to find it all interesting. Unfortunately, I'm better at talking than listening and so babbled on, hoping she wasn't wondering whether I was totally imbalanced or just unbelievably boring. And although I have absolutely no recollection of anything that she said that night (other than a few little details), I put it down to the fact that she was rather shy. Which was perfectly understandable.

"'Scuse me, I need to go for a pee."

Getting up from the armchair, I walked past her on the sofa, en route to the loo. Without breaking my stride, I opened my mouth to release one of my worst ever lines. Not that I have that many.

"Would you mind awfully if I kissed you?"

And without waiting for an answer, scuttled off thinking: 'That was terrible. What in God's name was I thinking?'

I freely admit that I'm a lot better with falcons than I am with women. But even though I wasn't very good at that sort of thing, I cursed myself for saying something quite so crass. Feeling more than a little embarrassed, when I got back to the room, I aimed for the armchair.

"No. Why don't you?"

"Why don't I what?"

"Kiss me."

I practically bounded across the room to stand quivering in front of her, and then gently planted a kiss on her lips. And that was it – the first kiss. Beyond that, it was all very innocent.

"More tea?"

"Please. But go back to the story of ..."

So the conversation continued and, as the evening progressed, the wariness decreased. It was a warm, comfortable and magical time that I certainly won't forget. But all good things come to an end.

"I have to go now."

"Of course. But I'd love to see you again."

"I'd love to see you too," she replied softly.

As Helena drove down the lane from The Bothy, I watched the car's lights until they disappeared in the night. Meeting Helena was a bolt out of the blue - neither engineered or expected, it just came out of the ether and I was totally bowled over.

258

That evening was just the beginning: after that we started dating and, as we dated, we fell in love. But that didn't make me lose sight of the fact that the falcons still needed to be flown and that gyrs had to be bred.

Chapter 23 – The mechanics of reproduction

It would be nice to think that breeding falcons was akin to running an avian dating agency. Imagine the adverts that might feature in the Personal Columns.

'Stunning athletic male gyrfalcon looking for sexy mate for fun and games. Preference for same breed but will happily consider peregrine, saker, barbary falcon or similar. Fertile females only, please.'

'Looking for energetic, good-looking male falcon for company and reproduction. I'm a stunning peregrine chick with a twinkle in her eye and a proven breeder. Love being dominated.'

Just put the two of them together in an aviary and before you can say 'voyeurism', they are off like rockets. The next thing you know, they're producing wonderful birds that turn into spectacular flyers.

Of course, putting two birds together for natural insemination and crossing your fingers can work, but it's not always quite so simple when it comes to commercial breeding. Thus forced insemination tends to be the normal course of action. Or, should I say, abnormal course of action. And perhaps the strangest aspect of the process is that of collecting semen by what one might call – hat shagging. A vulgar turn of phrase, but distinctly apt.

Suffice it to say that one needs a specially prepared hat. Therefore, here are a few simple instructions for you to follow.

You will need one Biggle's style hat, similar to the leather helmets worn by aviators in the First and Second World wars, with earflaps. (These can be found on eBay in a multitude of fetching designs.) Take a piece of foam pipe lagging, cut it to the required length and glue it around the lower part of the hat to make a rim. The crown of the hat should then be waterproofed with, I would suggest, liquid paraffin. And voila, your semen-collecting headpiece is complete. However, I should offer a word of caution at this point: every falcon relates to only one hat. It's a bit like a baby with its comfort blanket.

The idea is that you put the ghastly thing on and then encourage the bird to jump onto the hat. Once conditioned, said bird will hop on board when the appropriate rituals are performed and shag the hell out of the hat which, please remember, you are wearing.

Magnum was no exception and would immediately recognise his personal 'comfort' hat when it appeared. Naturally, Dave Jamieson had included Magnum's hat in the package since it was a vital accessory to our gyr stud. And it was time to dig out the hat.

"You know you look a total prat?" Nick said, bending double with laughter.

"Wait till you have to wear the hideous thing," I warned. "Just give me the stepladder."

Slipping into Magnum's aviary, I set up the stepladder below his nest ledge which was around seven feet off the ground. Climbing up until we were more or less eyeball-to-eyeball, I then started my best gyr chat-up lines accompanied by much chuffing and bowing.

"Tuik, tuik, tik, tik, tuik, tuik."

After a few moments of this shameless come-on talk added to the sight of his favourite sex toy, Magnum decided to declare his intentions.

"Tik, tuik, tik, tik, tuik, tuik."

Once I'd got him reacting, it was time to change to coy slut mode. I climbed back down the ladder, walked across to the middle of the aviary and turned my back on him.

"Bwae-eay, bwae-eay, beay-wae," I wailed.

That roughly translates as: 'chase me, chase me, come and get me'.

As I hoped for, and expected, I heard the flapping wings of one randy falcon. Magnum landed with a thud on my head and began to furiously copulate with the hat. I held my breath and kept perfectly still; even Nick had stifled his laughter. Four seconds later, I felt Magnum shudder and knew he'd ejaculated. The niceties of foreplay, I'm afraid, don't really have a place in falconidae fornication. Nor are there any post-coital pleasantries; having sated his lust, Magnum pushed off from the hat and returned to his ledge.

Carefully removing the hat, I handed it quickly to Nick before playing the dutiful and thankful female. Climbing back up the ladder, it was my bounden duty to thank Magnum for his bounty and praise his virility.

"Tuik, tuik, tik, te-ik, tuik."

Magnum preened, looked disgustingly pleased with himself and graciously grabbed the quail I flopped down on the ledge. When it comes courtship among falcons, the male always gets the chocolates.

With the ladder under one arm, I scooted back to the kitchen where Nick was waiting patiently with the hat.

"I thought, since it's sunny, I'd better bring it inside quickly. And I kept the hat shaded."

"Good thinking."

I was pleased that Nick had remembered: UV rays destroy semen. Taking the capillary tube from Nick's outstretched hand, I carefully sucked up the tiny teardrop of falcon essence from the hat. Reversing the process, I then expelled it into a little Eppendorf storage container, snapped on the lid and put in the fridge. I've always found that the best place in the fridge for semen is just above the salad tray.

"That should be good for 48 hours. Have we got any likely recipients?"

"I'll check," said Nick. "Just make sure you don't use it in the salad dressing."

"Ha, ha."

"You never know, this might be Tino's finest hour."

"I wish."

But the thought lingered. Nick and I had both noticed that, for the first time ever, Tino was looking definitely broody and all the signs were that she was ready to breed. She'd already made a magnificent scrape on her nest ledge and gone into egg lethargy. To the uninitiated, it can look quite frightening: the bird looks horribly ill and about to die. At the same time, they manage to look seriously pissed off. It's a nasty combination. Accordingly, we were both getting rather excited.

Unless the falcon is with another bird, the first egg will always be infertile. Once that egg has been laid, you need

262

to inseminate her within two hours while the muscles are still distended. Basically put, that's the window of opportunity when she's gagging for it, using the unscientific phrase. Insemination during that period will usually result in a fertile egg being produced within about 36 hours.

And then there are two different ways of artificial insemination.

On the one hand, there's the natural voluntary version where you have an agreeable consenting adult on your hands, who's prepared to stand and deliver. Sweet talk her nicely, add a few dirty words in falcon-speak and she'll swing her tail to one side and say 'take me, take me'. In professional terms, that means that she will allow you to inseminate her using the appropriate tool. In other words, you have a compliant female on your hands; which is what I thought we had in Tino.

The other way requires a little more artifice and persuasion which, in scientific terms, is referred to as forced insemination.

Whatever the level of libido, I'd found that falcons tended to lay their eggs in the middle of the night. But there were always exceptions to that rule, which meant that they needed to be monitored 24 hours every day. Accordingly, we'd installed cameras with night vision capabilities in all the aviaries. And, of course that meant someone being on duty every minute, all the time.

I'd gone to bed at about two-thirty in the morning, having handed over to Nick. I was warm, cosy and enjoying cuddling up to Helena's back. It had been a long day and I was looking forward to drifting off to never-never land. But as the languorous fingers of sleep started to creep over me, rapping knuckles on the bedroom door snatched them quickly away.

"Gaz, Gaz, get up quick. She's laid!"

"Tino?"

"Yeah."

"Bloody hell! I had a feeling this might be her night."

Bounding out of bed with unusual alacrity, I pulled on a pair of jeans and a pullover at the speed of light.

The monitor was downstairs in the incubator room. Switching to the channel covering Tino's aviary, we could clearly see her sitting motionless on her ledge. I pushed the button to give us two-way audio and began to vocalise.

"Tuik, tuik, tuik, tuik."

Although she was in pitch blackness and didn't have a clue what was going on, she could obviously hear another gyrfalcon calling. Shifting her position very slightly, she revealed – an egg. She'd laid one marvellous, magical egg.

"Yes!" I said, punching the air.

Nick and I grinned at each other maniacally.

"Don't panic, Captain Mainwaring. Panic stations! Nick, get the coffee on. I'll get the semen out of the fridge to bring it up to room temperature. I think we've got three shots of Magnum's in there. We've got two hours. Towels, we need towels and the insemination tools."

A yawning Helena appeared at the door in her pyjamas.

"What time is it? And what's the panic?"

"Tino's laid an egg so we need to forcibly inseminate her and the sooner the better."

"Can I help?"

"Um, sure. Yeah. Helena, can you get some coffee on. So Nick, forget that. Give me a hand with the kit."

Preparation and awareness are the keys to successful artificial insemination. Everything has to be in place and everyone involved has to know their job. It follows the same principle as a Formula One pit crew changing a car's wheel in the middle of the race. As soon as the car comes into the box, precision and speed are perfectly choreographed. Nick and I had carried out forced inseminations on numerous occasions and we knew what we were doing. Peregrines, sakers, lanners et al – we inseminated all of those but we hadn't been faced with Tino. And we hadn't done it with white gyrs. There's no difference, I told myself.

"OK team, I think we're there. Let's have a cup of coffee. Nick, you know the ropes. You good to go?"

"Yes, Captain."

"Helena, this is the insemination tool. Basically it's a hypodermic syringe with a fired glass tube in place of a

264

needle. I've sucked up the semen into it already. What we're going to do is to get Tino to prolapse."

"Isn't that dangerous?"

"It is if you don't know what you're doing. Don't worry, once she's been inseminated with the syringe and that's withdrawn, the prolapse should retract back naturally. If it doesn't, you're in deep shit." Seeing her alarm, I added: "Don't worry, I've done this hundreds of times and I've never had that happen. And never will, touch wood. OK, here's what I want you to do: when she's prolapsed, I want you to hand me the syringe. Rest it on the palm of your hand like this," I said, demonstrating the required position. "You OK with that?"

"Yes, Sir," she said slightly nervously.

But she grinned and snapped off a half-arsed salute. I looked at my hand holding the syringe; it was shaking like a leaf. It reminded of a scene from one of my favourite movies, Zulu, starring Michael Caine. Stanley Baker played Lieutenant Chard and there was that bit when he was trying to load his pistol but his hand was shaking badly. I felt just like that, loading bullets before the battle of Rorke's Drift.

"You ready to go, Gary?" said Nick in the distance.

"No, I'm not ready to go. Just give me a minute will you?"

I went out onto the porch and looked up at the stars. I might have done the job several times before but this was the big one because the pressure was on to breed white gyrs. I breathed in the cool night air and exhaled slowly, again and again until I felt myself calmed. Walking back inside, I picked up the syringe and looked at my hand. Rock steady, just like Chard.

"Let's do it."

Nick and I slipped into the aviary as quietly as we could but we knew that Tino had heard us. There was just enough light in the aviary to see her shifting on the ledge and we could hear the scratch of talons. Draping the towel across my upturned palms, I managed to position myself so her back was towards me while she had Nick in her focus. Moving swiftly, I dropped the towel over her shoulders, pinned her wings to her sides and grabbed her off the ledge. At which point she screamed abuse at me and continued to do so as I wrapped the loose ends of the towel around her.

"Gary, here," said Nick, holding out Tino's hood.

In one deft motion, I slipped the hood over her head and tightened the braces. That shut off the foul language but didn't stop her struggling.

"OK, I've got her. Back to the kitchen."

Once inside, I sat down on a chair and flipped her on her back in my lap. Knowing the drill, Nick grabbed hold of her legs, carefully avoiding the flexing talons. We both knew that we had one very pissed off, three-pound gyrfalcon and there'd be no margin for error if we didn't stay in control. Let's face it, who wouldn't be pissed off if they were abducted in the middle of the night and then spread-eagled in a strange position? Apart from the unexpectedness of it all, it was so undignified.

Very carefully but firmly, I started to massage her lower abdomen, gently forcing the muscles down. After a few moments, I could feel that she'd prolapsed.

"Helena, insemination tool please."

Her hand was out in an instant with the syringe lying on her palm exactly as I'd requested. I slowly inserted the tube into Tino's cloaca and began to depress the plunger even more slowly, simultaneously easing the pressure of my fingers on her muscles. My concentration was totally focused, as it's not the easiest of operations. Each hand is going through completely different motions and one seems contrary to the other. It's not dissimilar to the old game of tapping your head and rubbing your stomach at the same time.

"That's it," I said as I eased the syringe's tube out. "Helena, can you take it? Touch wood, that's her inseminated."

We sat there for a moment to allow Tino's musculature to realign and then I gently ran my fingers down her abdomen.

"Good, that feels fine. Looks like the prolapse has retracted." A gentle sigh of relief came from Helena's direction. "Let's get her back in the aviary."

266

With Tino fully re-bundled in the towel, Nick and I returned her to the aviary. Once inside, we simply plopped her on the ground, slipped off the hood, removed the towel and left her alone.

Dashing back to the house, we both headed straight for the monitor. What we were hoping to see was one gyrfalcon named Tino, calmly sitting on her ledge. But there was always the worry that we'd see her crashing around the aviary like a demented dervish. Nick flipped on the monitor and there she was, cool as a cucumber and sitting squarely on her egg.

"Excellent."

"Is that her?" Helena asked, looking over my shoulder.

"Yup."

"Isn't she traumatised? It's all a bit brutal."

"No, she's not traumatised and it really isn't brutal. If you think about it, the actual insemination process only lasted two or three minutes. It's all about action, action, action. As long as it's done professionally and properly, they're back in the aviary before they know what's happened."

"She does look comfortable."

"And she is, she's fine. Now all we need is that second, fertile egg."

"Gary, if you two want to keep peering at that monitor in the hope that Tino lays another egg, feel free. Personally, I'm going back to bed."

To our complete delight and within the allotted time span, Tino laid a second egg. With inseminations in between, she laid a total of four eggs. To say that we were excited would be something of an understatement.

After Tino had kept them warm for ten days, the eggs were transferred into the incubators. Practising the arcane art of candling, I held each egg up in front of the powerful beam of the torch that Nick was holding.

"This one's fertile. No, this one's a dud. But this one's fertile. And this one might be. Bloody hell, Nick, two are definitely fertile and we could have a third."

"Fantastic."

We both punched the air with elation and practically danced around the room. As the incubation progressed, we continued to candle the eggs and monitor every avicultural aspect known to man - but we noticed that something was definitely wrong. They were just not developing in the way that they should have been and, sadly, when it came to the point of hatching, they failed. We were devastated. But we also needed some answers. I sent the eggs to Neil Forbes for laboratory tests.

In the meantime, Tino had laid a second clutch. Nick, Helena and I had carried out the same procedures in terms of inseminations and done everything we could to ensure success. We could only hope that the second clutch would prove to be more fruitful than the first. And while we waited, I heard from Neil.

"The tests are back from the lab Gary, but I'm afraid it's not looking good. In broad terms, it appears that your gyr's carrying a virus which she's passing on to the embryos. That's weakening the embryos because they haven't got the antibodies to fight it and the result is that they don't hatch. Unfortunately, the chances of producing healthy young falcons from Tino are, to be blunt, remote."

"Isn't there anything that we can do?"

"To be honest, you're doing everything you can do. I'm sorry."

Nevertheless, we went through all the procedures with the second clutch of eggs in the hope a miracle would happen. We weighed, sprayed and monitored them and then we prayed over them. But the result was just the same – nothing. We'd drawn a blank. Gutted, devastated, angry, depressed, worried: this was a toxic mixture of dark emotions. After all the effort and hard work, the time and money, we'd got nothing back.

Of course, the bad news had to be reported to our royal master, and who knew what the outcome of that might be? Once I'd received the findings of the lab tests and Neil's report, I compiled my own report to add to the pile and sent it to Prince Khalid's people.

Naturally, I also sent a summary of the dire situation to Lord Ashcombe. Eventually, his Lordship turned up at The Bothy one bright Saturday morning.

"Bloody shame about the gyrs. Pity, would have nice to produce some white ones."

"Tino's the ringer, as you saw in the report. Magnum's proved to be a serious stud and we've produced some superb hybrids. But, I agree, white gyrs would have been the jewels in the proverbial."

"Anyway, Prince Khalid's got the results and read the report. Said he'd like to come up and visit."

"What was his reaction? Did he make any comments?"

"No, not really. Obviously he's disappointed but no, nothing really. Just said he'd like to come to The Bothy."

"Did he say when?"

"Sorry, of course he did. This weekend."

'This weekend' was three days away! As usual before a visit from His Royal Highness, Nick and I went into overdrive to get the place looking pristine. We strimmed, trimmed, pruned, scrubbed and cleaned until everything was beautiful, and we were knackered. Everything was ready for Prince Khalid except our mind-sets. We had no idea what to expect and if Lord Ashcombe had any idea, he wasn't sharing. We didn't even know the purpose of the visit. What would the Prince's 'school report' conclude about us?

'Failed. Could do better. All operations to be aborted and personnel fired.'

'Failed. Waste of time and money. Remove personnel and consider legal action."

'Failed. Remove personnel permanently.'

Nick was worried, Helena was worried and I was seriously worried. All we could do was wait for Sunday; we'd find out what our fate would be when Prince Khalid gave judgement.

Chapter 24 – End of the day

For some unknown reason, when Prince Khalid visited The Bothy, the weather was invariably wonderful and this time was no exception. But despite the fact that it was gloriously sunny, I felt a certain chill as I watched the now familiar Bentley bump up the lane, followed by the ever-present black Range Rover. Were there thunderheads gathering on the horizon or would we bask in the warmth of his presence?

Standing on the lawn in front of the house, I watched him descend from the car and walk towards me. The broad smile was reassuring.

"Good morning, Your Royal Highness."

"Gary, good morning. It has been too long since I visited The Bothy. I'm looking forward to seeing how things are here, so let us start with the room of incubators."

"Of course, Sir."

It was always his first port of call on arrival, as though he wanted an electronic preview of reality. The room was silent and the monitors blank; everything had been switched off. His brief reverse nod towards them was a clear command. I flipped the switches and the monitors hummed into life, distant eyes beaming images back to the screens.

"Ah, I see a white gyrfalcon. Very good."

"Yes, your Royal Highness. That's Magnum, our semen donor." Touching a button, I changed the view to another aviary. "And this bird was produced from his semen. A gyr peregrine hybrid."

"You can look into the aviaries at night, I think?"

"Absolutely, all of the cameras have night vision. That's vital during the breeding season."

Leaning past me, he pressed the button himself, bringing up an image of Tino.

"Perhaps you would like to go outside and see the birds," I suggested quickly.

It was enough to take his focus away from the monitor.

"Yes, yes, we should do this."

270

Several birds had been put on Arab wakars in the walled garden for inspection. As we walked outside and passed by the gate, the security detail fell in step behind as though pulled by an invisible line. But the Prince seemed oblivious to their presence. He walked along the line of birds, nodding appreciatively. It was a truly beautiful group of birds that included more than a few gyr hybrids.

"These are very good, Gary, very good. I would like to walk with you through the aviary block, come."

Turning at the hip as he walked, the Prince held up his hand with the palm facing outwards. The movement was fleeting but it was as though his security people had found a brick wall in their path. The precedent of our aviary walks was well established but obviously Prince Khalid thought the minders needed reminding. Brawn and brains are not necessarily found in the same package.

We walked slowly down the corridor, pausing now and then to allow him to look at the occupants of the aviaries. When we got to Magnum's enclosure, I stopped.

"Instead of looking through from the outside, would you like to go in?"

"Yes, indeed."

Squeezing through the little door required bowing a little, but once inside we could stand upright once more. It still meant that we were looking up at Magnum while the handsome white gyr looked imperiously down. When I handed the Prince a falconry glove, he slipped it onto his hand with practised familiarity. Given a quail leg, he held it firmly in his fist, between thumb and forefinger and raised the glove. Even though Magnum had finished his sex-and-the-hat antics, he was still remarkably tame, dropped down on the glove and pulled at the leg with gusto. It didn't take more than a few bites before he'd snaffled the lot and then proceeded to unequivocally thank the Prince.

"Tuik, tik-tik, tuik, tik."

Prince Khalid's face positively beamed with joy and fell in love with Magnum, just as I had done.

'Good move on your part, young Gary,' I thought to myself.

Having played his part, Magnum pushed off from the glove and flew back to his ledge. We stayed there for a good couple of minutes, watching him clean his beak on the edge and preen.

Leaving him to his own devices, we continued our walk down the corridor with me providing a running commentary on the remaining population in the aviary. Tino merited few words from me, save to mention that she was our dud from Nevada; the Prince didn't say a word. In fact, during the course of our walk he said relatively little apart from asking a few questions. But when we reached the end of the aviary block, he stopped, turned towards me and smiled.

"It is good that I have seen all this and it is clear that we need more birds for you to work with. So this is what we are going to do, we will get more birds. You still have your contacts in America, yes?"

"Yes, um, yes absolutely."

"Can you get more contacts?"

"I'm sure, yes."

"Good. Then you must go back to America."

Inside the head of Gary Cope, there was a little character jumping up and down, punching the air and shouting hallelujah. Outwardly, I was wide-eyed, grinning from ear to ear and looking vaguely insane. Not that his Royal Highness commented on my appearance or even observed it since he was now looking at the far side of the walled garden.

"Along that wall, over there, we will build new aviaries for the birds that you will bring back from America. This is what I have decided, because I see that you must have more birds to work with. Next year, Gary, next year you will go to America and buy more birds, we build these new aviaries and take this project on for great things."

"Wow, that's wonderful!"

Striding back onto the weathering, he gestured to his small entourage.

"Now, I must leave. It was a good meeting, Gary."

With that, he walked through the gateway to the walled garden and on to the Bentley.

272

"I'll be back on 45 minutes," said Lord Ashcombe. And then hurried after the fast disappearing group of visitors.

I went back into the kitchen to find Nick sitting at the table, staring blankly at a magazine. A cigarette was smouldering away in an ashtray that was already overflowing with butts and Nick generally didn't smoke that much. At the sound of footsteps, his head snapped up and the look on his face was full of fear and apprehension.

"It's all right, mate, we're still in a job."

"You're kidding?"

"Nope, he didn't even mention the problem with Tino or the fact that we hadn't managed to produce any white gyrs. In fact, he wants us to buy more birds."

"Un-fucking-believable! All right."

By the time I'd filled Nick in with all the details, his eyes were blazing and he was laughing hysterically with relief. Then Helena rang from work, eager for news and ever hopeful.

"He wants to expand the project."

"Expand it? Why?"

"Because he thinks that we need more birds to really make it work. I've got to go back to the States to buy more falcons, he's going to build more aviaries and that way the project stands a far better chance of being successful."

"Gary, that's wonderful."

She came over to The Bothy that night to celebrate; a very good end to a very good day. Helena was also there a couple of months later. We were having a nice lazy morning, drinking coffee in front of the fire when I switched on Sky News on the television.

"Very sketchy news at the moment. We believe that a plane has crashed into the World Trade Centre in New York. Um, that's happened within the last few moments. There are no details at this stage as to what sort of plane it is, but it could well be a, er, large plane. We're hearing reports of a 737, not yet confirmed, although it is a jet."

When Kay Burley passed over to CBS, the picture on the screen was not of a coiffed or slick anchor but a view of the top of the twin towers. Thick brown smoke poured across the blue sky from the crippled tower and a large black ragged hole was a blot on its side. We watched in horror as the situation unfolded in graphic detail, birds and chores were momentarily forgotten. Like millions of others around the world, we were transfixed by the images beamed into the room, each one worse than the last as the tragedy deepened.

Another jet, another tower and then both collapsed, brought down by terrible acts of terrorism that killed almost 3,000 people. Even though we were sitting in the comfort of The Bothy, several thousand miles from New York, it was clearly evident that this was going to have a huge impact on the United States as a whole but I didn't realise how much it was to affect the global stage. Nor did it occur to me that even our own futures might be affected and that the shock waves would somehow touch me personally.

However, life went on much the same as normal at The Bothy and although I expected to hear something from either Prince Khalid or Fairlawne, there was nothing. Lord Ashcombe came over on frequent weekend visits; I always asked the same question and he always replied with the same answer.

"Is there any news from the Prince?" I'd ask.

"No nothing, nothing."

Everything was quiet and the lines of communication were dead. Christmas came and went without any word, the silence echoing through January.

And then, in early February, Becky, my English pointer took a turn for the worse. She was old now, her legs had gone and I'd putting off the inevitable decision to have her put to sleep. Anybody who has loved a dog, or any animal, will know that its one of the most difficult decisions to take.

One cold February evening, I looked at her lying on the kitchen floor. It had been a while since she'd been in the kennels outside. Even though it was warm, she seemed to shivering and I realised that I'd had enough – had enough for her. I phoned the vet and explained the situation.

"Can you come out?"

"Of course, Mr Cope. I'm on my way."

He arrived some fifteen minutes later, a young guy armed with his medical bag. Ushering him into the kitchen, I pointed to Becky, lying in her bed by the radiator.

"Have a look at her and see what you think."

I watched him check her heart and lungs, lift her eyelids and stretch her legs, touching all the parts that I knew so well. I could feel the lump in my throat and the tears mist my eyes. Becky had been so instrumental in making the grouse hawking such a resounding success. She really was a wonderful dog, the best game dog I'd ever had, and my friend.

"I'm sorry, but it is time for her to go."

"Yeah, I knew that really, it's just …"

"I know. Do you want me to come back tomorrow?"

"No. No, let's do it now."

I'd had to have Bracken put down a few years earlier and had him in my arms when the deed was done. Rather than just having a dog put to sleep where he or she lay, I always felt that I should have the dog in my arms and this time was no different. Gathering Becky up from her bed, I wrapped my arms around her as the vet shaved her leg in preparation for the injection.

"Are you ready? Shall we do it?"

"Hold on for a moment. I want her to go with something positive, something she'll relate to – sorry, you'll think I'm silly but …"

"Take your time, don't worry."

So I started to give her the commands that she loved on the grouse moor.

"Steady, steady Becky. Don't you put them up yet. Hang on Baba, no, no. Go on then, get 'em up, get 'em up!" And then the sound of grouse calling: "Krbek, krbek, krbek, krek-krek-krek."

Her little ears pricked up; perhaps she was there, feeling the breeze on her face and the excitement of the chase. And that's when I wanted her to go. I nodded to the vet. Putting the needle into her leg, he depressed the syringe's plunger. I could feel her heart beating – but nothing happened. We waited for a full minute but she was still there.

"Sorry, that should have taken her; Pentobarbital usually works in about 30 seconds. She's obviously a strong dog with a strong spirit. Her legs may have gone but her spirit's strong. I'll have to give her another shot."

Taking another vial from his bag, he reloaded the syringe and looked at me, waiting. I raised my fingers slightly and he nodded, understanding immediately.

"Come on Becky, come on. Steady, steady, don't you flush the bloody grouse yet. Steady, OK, get 'em up, get 'em up!"

As soon as Becky pricked up her ears, the vet put the needle into her leg and injected a second dose of the chemical. But once again there was no effect and the vet's hand was noticeably shaking. A sheen of sweat shone on his forehead.

"I, I've never seen anything like it before. The dog's body is buggered but she's got the heart of a lion."

"For Christ's sake, let's get this done."

"Yes, of course," he said, bending to the task once again.

'Third time's the charm' runs the saying. Within seconds of Becky getting that third shot, I felt her go limp, saw her eyes close and she'd gone.

"There'll be no charge," the vet said.

Tears poured down my cheeks, two little streams that found their confluence underneath my chin and dripped onto my arms.

"Do you want me to take her?"

I shook my head, unable to speak.

"I'll leave you then, Mr Cope." All I could do was nod. "I'm so sorry," he added before he let himself out.

Becky had always loved eating the fallen apples in the orchard. We had so many apple trees at The Bothy and when the autumn winds brought the fruit down, she would stuff herself full of them. Bloated and heavy with windfalls, she'd waddle slowly across the paddock, for all the world like a mobile barrel of fermenting cider.

'That's the place,' I thought, 'under the apple trees.'

It was getting late and too dark to see outside. I wrapped Becky's cold body in a blanket, deciding that I'd bury her

276

the following morning, in the shade of the apple trees. It just seemed appropriate.

Snowflakes were drifting softly down onto the gently undulating white landscape that had appeared overnight. Under its coverlet of snow, the ground felt like iron as I dug her grave beneath the branches of Becky's favourite apple tree. I gently laid her in that dark hole in the ground, covered her over and placed a large piece of Cotswold stone on the grave. I thanked her for everything she'd done.

"I'll see you later, Becky."

It was the end of an era. She'd put me on the grouse hawking map and had been key to my success. Your grouse or game hawk is only as good as your dog, because the dog is everything. Without a good dog, you'll fail, no matter how good a falcon you're flying. The dog has to be spot on – and Becky was the best I'd ever had.

Like Becky, her understudy Demi came from the Embercombe line and therefore had an impeccable pedigree. Not that I thought that she could reach the dizzy heights attained by Becky, but Demi was only six, coming on well and as fit as a flea.

Nick was getting married soon; that meant he had thoughts to think and things to do.

"Do you mind if I leave early," he asked.

"No, no. You go as soon as you need."

"Great, thanks Boss. I'll feed Demi before I leave."

"Yeah, carry on."

He'd only been gone a few minutes before he reappeared at the kitchen door with an ashen face.

"Nick? What's up?"

"It's Demi. She's …"

"Shit. We didn't leave the gate open, did we? Has she got out?"

"No, Gary, she's dead."

"What do you mean, she's dead? She was bounding around as fit as a fiddle earlier. How can she be dead?"

"I don't know." He paused, his eyes staring. "I went into the mews and she was lying in her bed. I thought she was just dozing at first and then I realised she wasn't moving at

all. When I got closer, she wasn't breathing, she was just
… dead."

"I can't believe it."

I dashed outside, across the garden to the rear paddock
where we had built a large mews. The dogs' beds had been
put at the far end among some bales of straw. And it was
there that I found Demi, lying stone dead in her bed with
her tongue hanging down from her mouth. Kneeling down
beside her, I put my hand on her cold head and cried for the
second time in a month.

"I can't believe it," I whispered. "Why? Why?"

It was only later that we were told that she'd had a heart
attack.

It snowed on the day after she died. The wind whipped
up spinning snow-devils on the soft white carpet, set
against an almost opaque backdrop of drifting snowflakes.
I dug another grave in the hard ground, next to Becky's
grave below the branches of the same apple tree and there
laid Demi to rest.

Did I believe in omens and portents? I didn't know. In
the spring of 1066, the sight of Halley's Comet in the skies
was regarded as an evil omen, a portent of the doom to
come. The autumn brought death to King Harold and
several thousand Anglo-Saxons at the Battle of Hastings.
Looking up at the drifting grey skies after I'd buried Demi,
I thought of that comet.

"What's going on?" I asked, blinking away the delicate
crystals of snow. "It's all going so horribly wrong."

While I mourned the loss of two precious friends, my
mind also turned to more pragmatic concerns. I wondered
what on earth I was going to do in the oncoming grouse
season without dogs. However, the breeding season was
imminent and a more immediate concern. Once out of the
hawking season, I always put the game hawks into aviaries;
the same principle as putting a horse out to grass, in
reverse.

Without question, Ling was my best grouse hawk and
had a sterling record. The previous season had seen her
catch 49 grouse in succession without missing one. With

that level of performance in mind, I naturally hoped she would breed and accordingly moved her into an aviary.

I'd noticed her making a decent scrape on her ledge and, when I was passing her aviary, thought I stop off to see if she'd laid any eggs. Stepping inside, I made sure that the safety catch was on before making my approach. There she was, fat as a goose before Christmas, glaring down at me before flying off the ledge and past my shoulder. Hitting the aviary door, the impact broke the catch and suddenly she was out in the safety corridor.

"Bloody bird," I muttered.

It wasn't that much of a concern since the corridor that ran the length of the aviary block was quite secure. Constructed of wood and chicken wire with a closed door at the end, there was nowhere for her to go and collecting her up would simply be a minor nuisance. Looking out past the open door, I spotted Ling sitting on the gravel floor at the end of the corridor. She wasn't going anywhere.

'I wonder if there are any eggs,' I thought. 'Nothing. Pity.'

Stepping out through the doorway, I walked slowly towards her. Since I didn't have a glove with me, the plan was to simply grab her and put her back in the aviary. I made a mental note to repair the safety catch as soon as possible. Ling was only around five yards away when she started to waddle towards me with that silly falcon's gait, reminiscent of a drunken sailor. I thought it was rather endearing until she hung a hard right and headed towards – a hole.

"Where did that bloody hole come from?"

To my absolute horror, Ling squeezed herself through the grapefruit-sized hole in the wire. It was academic whether the wire had been breeched by a fox or a dog - I hadn't noticed the damn hole. But Ling had and she was out, in the open air without jesses, telemetry or bells. Fat as a goose, she hadn't been handled for four or five months and she was in no hurry to get back. She flew up and onto the eight feet high red brick wall that surrounded the garden where she roused, tucked one leg up and just sat there.

Memory took me back to a field in Newent where a young boy was chasing a kestrel. And I heard Martin Jones shouting at me: "Don't run!"

"Do not panic," I told myself, feeling my heart pounding as though it wanted to burst from my chest. "Do not run, do not panic, do not run, do not panic."

My footsteps matched the metronomic sounds of the words as I walked to the gateway with measured paces. Once beyond the containment of the walled garden, I looked up and saw Ling was facing in the opposite direction. With only sound absorbing grass between me and The Bothy, I ran like the proverbial wind.

"Nick, Ling's out."

"What do you mean, Ling's out? How? What happened?"

"I'll explain later, now's not the time. Grab a quail and I'll get a glove and the lure. We need to get out there now."

Fortunately, Ling was still sitting calmly on the wall, watching the world go by.

"Frankly, if we get this bird back, it'll be a bleeding miracle," I said to Nick.

As soon as I threw out the lure, Ling bobbed her head, spread her wings and dived downwards.

"Yay."

But instead of binding to the lure as expected, she cut it, flying straight past and over the walled garden towards the Scudamores' farm. Without exchanging a word, Nick and I dashed to the 4x4, leaped in and gunned the engine. Panic levels were rising as we rattled down the lane to the farm. And there she was, sunning herself on the roof of a worker's cottage. On another occasion, I might have commented on how beautiful Ling looked in the sunlight - but this wasn't one of those occasions. This was more of a 'that's-my-best-game-hawk-sitting-up-there-without-bells-or-telemetry-shit' moment.

As we carefully made our way towards her, a cock pheasant suddenly appeared and trundled down the farmyard. Ling may have been flown mainly at grouse but she knew a fine pheasant when she saw one and had nailed quite a few in her time. When she started to bob her head, I
280

knew that we were in with a chance. If she hit the bird, we'd be able to go in and grab her.

"Please, please Ling, plough into that bloody pheasant. Go, baby go!"

It all looked very promising until a tractor came lurching and belching down the yard. The pheasant took one look at the rusting machinery and darted off to the right. Ling assessed the situation: pheasant takes evasive action, ridiculous unsightly machine making too much noise and pheasant unlikely to reappear.

"Bollocks to that. I'm off!" one could almost hear her saying.

And with that, Ling flitted over the back of the house and into the distance. Searching for a falcon without bells or telemetry is a futile exercise and almost certainly doomed to failure. Nevertheless, I searched the highways and byways for ten days before I resigned myself to the fact that looking for a needle in a haystack was a total waste of time. I never saw her again.

The only solace to be had was that least she was fat and could survive for a while before needing to hunt. And if there was ever a trained falcon on God's earth that could earn a living, it was Ling. I knew that she was perfectly capable of taking care of herself and killing her own meals. Heaven alone knows where she went. Perhaps she headed for the south coast or met an attractive tiercel and reared a brood or two in the crags of Cornwall. I hoped and prayed that there'd be a happy ending to her tale. But losing Ling was another rip in the fabric of life and I feared what might come next.

One Saturday morning, shortly afterwards, Lord Ashcombe turned up at The Bothy and I could tell immediately that something was wrong. There was no cheery greeting or smile.

"Can I come in?"

"Sure. Would you like a cup of coffee?"

"Yes please, I'd love one."

"Grab a seat and I'll bring the coffee through."

He slumped onto the sofa at one end. When I returned from the kitchen, I found him pushing an ashtray around in slow circles on the small table next to the arm. Lifting his eyes from the rotating ashtray, he raised his head and gave me a look that just seemed rather glum.

"You're still keeping off the cigarettes, I see."

"Yes, it's probably a good thing."

"D'you mind if I do?" I lit up a Marlboro without waiting for his permission. "So, what's the news? Anything from Prince Khalid?"

"Yes. But I'm afraid that its bad news. He's closing your breeding project down."

The words hit me like a hammer blow to the solar plexus and I could physically feel the pain.

"Why? It doesn't make sense. I mean, when he came here, you know, all that business about me going to America to get more birds, building new aviaries and making the project bigger. That's what he wanted. It's what he promised. Now you say he wants to shut it down, throw it all away. Why?"

"I haven't got all the answers, Gary. All I can tell you is that since 9/11, that awful business with the World Trade Centre, Prince Khalid's more or less gone to ground. He's not even travelling anywhere. Apparently he was meant to be making a visit to his stables in Kentucky recently and cancelled without giving a specific reason. From what I've heard, all of his non-essential operations are either being mothballed or closed down. And, I'm afraid, your breeding project falls into the second category."

It was a far cry from our usual jovial meetings, and it was far shorter. He felt awkward, I felt desolate. A cold numbness spread through my body, freezing thought and movement.

"How long have we got?"

I could hear the leaden tone in my voice, the dull acceptance of the sentence given.

"About a year."

"What happens now?"

"You need to find new homes for all the birds and then dismantle the whole project."

Without saying another word, Lord Ashcombe stood up and left. I just sat there, staring into the middle distance
282

feeling more alone and devastated than I'd ever felt before. I didn't understand why Prince Khalid was doing this, after all the things that he'd said. What in hell was I going to do? How could everything suddenly go so badly wrong? And why me, why me?

Except it wasn't just me, there was Nick to consider as well. I didn't have the heart to coldly phone him up over the weekend and say 'That's it mate'. It would hit him hard; just about to get married, perhaps thinking of starting a family – and now this.

I dreaded Monday. Black thoughts whirled around my head, stinging, biting, gnawing away at my life's core.

"Hi Gary. How you doing?" he said cheerfully as he came into the kitchen.

"Um, not so good. Sit down Nick, I've got some bad news."

"What's up? It's not one of the birds, is it?" He searched my face for clues. "Shit, is it Magnum?"

"No Nick, Magnum's fine. It's nothing like that. Lord Ashcombe came round on Saturday. Prince Khalid's closing the project down."

"You're joking?"

I gave him a summary of my conversation with Lord Ashcombe.

"And that's as much as we know. The bottom line is that everything goes within the next twelve months. Nick, I am so sorry. Don't worry about hanging on with me, you need to get another job, so you need to start looking. Obviously, I'll sort everything out and make sure that you get your redundancy money."

"Bloody hell!"

He looked stunned. Pale faced and wide eyed, all the stuffing had been pulled out of him and scattered on the floor.

"But what about you? What will you do?" Nick asked.

"I'll survive."

My voice sounded like an old cracked record as I repeated the ridiculous words. At the end of the day the ship was sinking, The Bothy was sinking, and since I was the captain of the ship, I'd have to stay at the helm until the last. Get the crew off and hang on to the tiller - a fine philosophy for a landlubber.

"What are you going to do?" Helena asked.

"You're the second person to ask that question today. I don't know Helena, I really do not know."

"All right, where are you going to live?"

"They offered me the chance of staying at The Bothy but I'd have to pay the going rate. Unfortunately, since I'll be an unemployed forty-five year old falconer, that's not a particularly realistic proposition. Anyway, I don't know, there's something inside of me that's gone. The dream's died, Helena, it's died and I need to get away."

And that fantastic lady said: "Why don't you came and live with me in Cheltenham?"

"That would be great, if it's OK with you."

"If it wasn't, I wouldn't have suggested the idea."

Had it not been for her benevolence, the only prospects on the housing horizon would have been hedgerows and doorways. But before I left country for town, all that I'd worked for had to be torn down. The few months took on agonising definition as we slowly dismantled the project.

Prince Khalid's number crunchers agreed to my conditions in respect of the birds: they were not to be sold on the open market. The birds were my friends and I loved them all. Each one would be found a suitable home where I knew they would be happy. One by one, the falcons and hawks disappeared from The Bothy; then there were few birds and no dogs. It was all getting quieter and quieter.

And in the middle of it all, I received a phone call from a representative of the Fairlawne team. He didn't even give his name.

"Mr Cope, we'd like to finalise the details concerning the Prince's breeding project at The Bothy in Gloucestershire. As you are the principal employee and the leader of the stated project, it behoves us to discuss arrangements as to your entitlements and rights. And, of course, make some proposals in respect of any future employment with Prince Khalid through Fairlawne's management team. Accordingly, we have arranged a time for you to meet us at Cadogan Square. As per our diary,

284

that will be at 11.30 next Tuesday. May I assume that you will be able to attend?"

"Yes, that'd be OK. Do I have a choice?"

"No, Mr Cope. However, please be assured that we are doing our best to minimise the disruption and plan for the future."

Whose future, I wondered, theirs or mine? I travelled down to London by train on the appointed day but this time there was no seat arranged in first class. The building in Cadogan Square was just as imposing as it had been before, but this time there was no excitement and it was not as inviting. I felt as though I was attending a court hearing rather than an office meeting. The sound of the bell had barely died before a young man in a suit opened the door.

"Mr Cope?"

"Yes, I'm here for a meeting."

"They're expecting you. Please follow me."

He led me along the same oak panelled corridor that I'd walked along before, but this time we did not climb the grand staircase that led to the Prince's office. Instead, we walked past, following yet another corridor and stopped at the double doors at the end.

"Please, go in," said the young man, opening one of the doors.

A handful of be-suited men were sitting round a long polished table that stretched the length of the room. His Royal Highness was not present and I was confronted by a group of people who I had never met. As I stood in the doorway, I could feel their eyes assessing me in a way that seemed cold and analytical. Here were accountants and lawyers, considering cuts in expenditure, limiting financial and employment liabilities, with little thought for humanity.

"Mr Cope, thank you for coming down to London at such relatively short notice. Please, take a seat," the self-appointed chairperson said, indicating the chair at the end of the table, furthest away from the door.

"As you are aware, His Royal Highness has decided to close down the project in Gloucestershire. We appreciate that this must be a blow to you but I am sure that you in turn will appreciate that his portfolio of business interests is diverse and widespread. Rationalisation is unfortunately a necessary tool to maintain the fiscal and actual efficiency of such a portfolio. So, where are we now?"

Apart from that brief appeal for me to understand the invidious situation that the penurious Prince had found himself in and the token nod to this minor disruption in my life, it was all business. What progress had I made with disposing of the birds? When did I expect the process to be completed? What measures had I taken to dispose of removable items? Could I account for expenditure incurred and revenues received? Collectively and independently, the gentlemen of Fairlawne went through their lists of checks and balances. And when that part of the meeting was concluded, the chairman turned to the subject of my future.

"On His Royal Highness' behalf, I would like to thank you for your efforts in running the project and your work in dismantling it. I'm sure that it is not a pleasant task and the prospect of potential unemployment might be a concern. Naturally, that has been considered and we would like to offer you employment on the Fairlawne estate as an estate worker. The position would include accommodation in the grounds, subject to availability, but that can discussed at a later date. In consideration of the nature of the work, the salary ..."

As he droned on, I tuned out. I thought about it for a while as his voice became little more than an irritating buzz. No. The answer had to be no.

"Thank you very much for your offer and I am very grateful. However, I'm not an estate worker, I'm a professional falconer. On that basis, I'll reject your offer but thank you all the same."

The train journey back to Cheltenham was a pale shadow of the last. The previous time it had been filled with anticipation, challenging thoughts and wide-eyed dreams. The end of this journey was devoid of hope, empty of plans and a career in tatters.

Back at The Bothy, we moved everything out, bit by bit. Finally, there were only four birds left and those were mine; including my old Harris hawk Poacher who had been with me on so many trips and shared myriad memories. They were all were all moving with me to Helena's gracious four-bedroom Regency house on Carlton Street in Cheltenham.

"How do feel about moving into town?" she'd asked on one occasion. "You've never lived in a town before."

"It's OK. Really, it'll be fine. It'll be a new experience and we should always embrace new experiences. So it'll be fine."

Inwardly, I was petrified but at least I would have a home.

The Bothy was emptied of furniture and it was all moved down to Carlton Street, together with anything of value. The remainder was put on a bonfire and burned. Nothing was left but there was one final task to carry out.

One Friday evening, when Helena was about to prepare dinner, I asked her to pause for a while.

"I've got to back up there and drop off the keys."

"Do you want me to come with you?"

"Thank you, but no. This is something that I have to do on my own."

She gave me a sad smile of support. Helena understood, as she always did.

The drive to The Bothy took less than half an hour but seemed much longer. Bumping up the drive, as I had so many times before, I parked the car by the darkened house. Walking slowly over the grass to the apple trees, I sat down by the two graves.

"Hi Becky, hi Demi. I miss you guys. You were wonderful friends and you still are. We had some great times together and I wouldn't have got anywhere without you. Thanks, for all your hard work, your help and your friendship. Thanks for everything. I've got to go now but I'll see you later."

I looked at the silly headstones I'd put up and trashed them both. I didn't want anyone to know the graves were there, least of all anyone who came to live at The Bothy.

Turning away, I headed over to the silent aviary block. Opening the door, I stepped into the safety corridor and closed the door behind me as I'd always done.

"What'd you do that for? There aren't birds here."

My voice sounded hollowly in the silence. The chatter of imprinted falcons was only a memory but I could still hear them in my head.

"Tuik, tuik, tik, tik, tuik."

They knew I was there, could hear my boots on the gravel, my breathing. Now, that read: they'd known I was there. There was nothing but the sound of the wind; that and the sound of my footsteps as I walked along the block. The aviaries were empty of the birds that brought them to life and there was nothing left.

"Maybe they'll see my ghost in a hundred years time, drifting through the block carrying a bowl of quail."

My whimsical thought was mocked by silence. Leaving the aviaries behind me, I walked across to The Bothy, opened the door, walked in and switched on the light. That too was an empty shell, heavy with silence. But every movement and footfall shattered the quiet, bouncing strident echoes between the walls; those echoes that only sound so loud in rooms that have been stripped bare.

It reminded of when my father died three or four years earlier. I made the mistake of going to see the body after he had died and found an empty shell. There was nothing there.

'That's not my Dad,' I'd thought. 'Who is that? It's just an empty container.'

And The Bothy felt just the same. All the life had been drained away, leaving another empty shell. I decided to walk through all the rooms, in part to ensure that nothing had been inadvertently left behind, but also to say goodbye. And as I walked into each room, something magical occurred and in my mind's eye, they came alive:

Joy and I were celebrating Christmas in the lounge with our parents. I could see the cheerfully decorated Christmas tree and a roaring fire blazing in the wood-burner. We called it the Furnace because of the amount of heat it generated. And there was Dad, loading in more logs and stoking the flames.

I could see the incubators in the dining room and the monitors by the wall. Suddenly it seemed that it was

288

midnight and there I was, feeding little baby birds by hand. I was there in kitchen with a falcon in my lap and Nick was holding the bird by its legs. Helena was standing nearby with a syringe loaded and ready for insemination. And then there was the bedroom with all the secrets that it held.

For those moments, The Bothy was alive and its spirit murmured in my ear as I walked down the stairs. Going out onto the porch, I closed that most wonderful oak door for the last time. I walked over to the paddock, breathed in its very special air that was so delicately perfumed by the scent of fruit trees and wildflowers. At the far end, I could see the rabbits poking their heads above the sea of waving grass. I could almost hear them talking.

"Ooh look, he's back."

"Think he's staying?"

"Dunno. I hope so."

I locked the doors for the last time and left the keys in their allotted place. As I walked away from The Bothy, I heard a familiar soft cooing call. I looked up at the wood pigeon sitting plumply on the roof and smiled. And suddenly I was twelve years old again, looking up at that tower in the churchyard. Squinting through the sunlight, I heard the kestrels calling, saw their flight and fell in love for the first time.

It all seemed so sad and I felt shocked by the finality of the moment. I looked at my watch; Helena was waiting for me at home.

And I could hear my Dad's voice saying, "Come on son, come on. It's time to fly."

That was it, the adventure was over and my career as a falconer had ended. Or had it?

END

GLOSSARY

Bate, to: to beat the air with the wings

Bind to, to: to grab and hold the quarry or lure

Block: a perch for falcons

Blood feathers: [feathers] in blood, that are still growing

Bow perch: a perch for hawks, buzzards and eagles

Braces: straps on a hood, used for opening and closing

Cadge: a portable perch on which several falcons are transported to the field

Carry, to: to fly away carrying the lure or quarry

Cast off: to let the bird fly from the fist

Cloaca: single external opening for the urinary, intestinal and genital tracts

Creance: a long line on which the bird is flown during training

Crop: an expanded area along the oesophagus where food is initially stored before being transferred to the bird's stomach

Enter: to introduce the bird to quarry

Eyass: a young bird, not yet able to fly

Hack: to allow a bird the freedom to come and go as she pleases

Haggard [falcon]: a bird taken from the wild with mature plumage

Hard penned: referring to feathers that have finished growing; the blood has drained from the quill and the base, turned white

Hood: a covering placed over the bird's head to prevent reactions to visual stimuli and to keep her calm

Intermewed: a bird that has been moulted out in the mews

Jesses: straps that pass through eyelets on the anklets around the bird's legs

Lanneret: a male lanner falcon

Leash: usually made of leather or braided material, used to tie the bird to its perch

Lure: a simulated quarry swung on a line to tempt the falcon to return to the falconer

Make in, to: to approach the falcon when she is on the lure or quarry

Mews: housing; a secure place where hawks and falcons are kept

Mutes: droppings of a bird of prey

Passage hawk: a bird taken from the wild but still in immature plumage

Pitch: the height at which a falcon waits on (varies from bird to bird)

Quarry: any kind of game at which a hawk or falcon is flown

Ring up, to: when a falcon climbs into the sky

Screen perch: comprised of a fabric screen or wall with a horizontal bar at the top on which the bird stands

Serve, to: to flush the quarry from cover for the falcon

Stoop, to: when a falcon power dives from height

Telemetry: electronic device for locating birds comprising a radio transmitter attached to the falcon's leg and a receiver (see yagi)

Throw up, to: when a falcon flies vertically up after a stoop

Tiercel: a male Peregrine falcon,

Wait on, to: when the falcon circles at a good height awaiting the quarry to be flushed

Weathering: an area where the birds are placed on perches out of the mews in the open air

Yagi: receiving antenna element of telemetry equipment

Mini Bios
Gary Michael Cope
In a career spanning 36 years, Gary has dedicated himself to the ancient art of falconry and breeding birds of prey. Following his boyhood passion, he embarked on an adventure that took Gary from flying a 'kestrel for a knave' to flying falcons for a Prince, making all his dreams come true as a professional falconer. More recently, he gives presentations on birds of prey and wildlife conservation as a public speaker. In addition, Gary is currently working on a sequel to 'Time to Fly' at his Gloucestershire home deep in the Cotswolds that he shares with his hounds and hawks.

Rob Flemming
Journalist, writer and photographer, Rob has spent the majority of his career as a freelance, generally preferring the greater freedom. However he occasionally has a minor aberration: in recent years Rob worked as a Senior Reporter for the Khaleej Times in Dubai and regional UK newspaper, the Express & Echo, based in Exeter. Rob has written features and news stories for a wide variety of magazines and journals, ghosted, rewritten or edited several books for private clients, not to mention having numerous photographs published. And currently he's also working on a satirical novel based against the backdrop of Dubai.

Anne Barclay
Anne is a former journalist who now edits and ghost-writes, taking stories from raw material to publisher-ready manuscripts. *Profession of Pleasure*, the memoirs of a 50-year old working girl, was ghosted by Anne and published by Robert Hale of London. She also worked with celebrity chef Keith Floyd on several books, and a TV series. Anne is currently working on an anthology of short stories to be followed by a novel revolving round the world of gliding.

7488037R00165

Printed in Great Britain
by Amazon.co.uk, Ltd.,
Marston Gate.